THE GENESIS AND EXODUS CITATIONS
OF
APHRAHAT THE PERSIAN SAGE

MONOGRAPHS
OF THE PESHIṬṬA INSTITUTE
LEIDEN

VOLUME III

LEIDEN
E. J. BRILL
1983

THE GENESIS AND EXODUS CITATIONS
OF
APHRAHAT THE PERSIAN SAGE

BY

ROBERT J. OWENS, JR.

LEIDEN
E. J. BRILL
1983

ISBN   90 04 06969 0

To my parents,

Robert and Betty Owens,

who taught us to love learning

and sacrificed so that we could pursue it

TABLE OF CONTENTS

x

ABSTRACT

This study investigates the quotations of the biblical
books of Genesis and Exodus that occur in the Demonstrations of
Aphrahat the Persian Sage, a collection of twenty-three theological essays written in Syriac between A.D. 337   and 345. It
defines itself primarily as a contribution to knowledge of the
history of the ancient Syriac version of the Old Testament.
Because the oldest extant manuscripts of the Syriac Old Testament
(Peshitta) date from the fifth and sixth centuries--a period that
is probably at least three centuries later than the first Syriac
bible translation, the bible quotations in the Syriac patristic
writings of the preceding centuries are at present the only primary source of information concerning the nature of the Syriac
bible in its earliest stages of development.

In this work, those features of the Demonstrations are
discussed which especially invite and justify study of the bible
quotations: their relatively early date, their obvious genuine-
ness and literary integrity, the quality of the extant Syriac
manuscripts, and the very large number of quotations. Past
assessments of the general value and significance of Aphrahat's
quotations are surveyed and their inadequacies identified.
Notice is taken of the scholarly consensus that most of the

quotations were made from memory and reflect basically the Peshitta text, handled freely. Detailed analysis is presented of past study of the Pentateuch citations specifically and of the conflicting theories of John Pinkerton, who saw in Aphrahat's citations a Syriac Pentateuch that was a more literal translation of the Hebrew original, and of Anton Baumstark and Arthur Vööbus, who claimed to find a Pentateuch text that was much less literal than the later Peshitta text and that was essentially a translation of an Aramaic Jewish targum.

The main body of the study identifies and reproduces the text of all the citations and allusions in the Demonstrations (a total of 221) that may provide evidence of the text of Genesis and Exodus known to Aphrahat. This is based on a fresh collation of the Syriac manuscripts of the Demonstrations. Each citation is analyzed and its value as a textual witness discussed. For each biblical verse that is attested, its affinities with and differences from the principal ancient bible versions are shown.

The conclusion of the study is that, while Aphrahat's citations of Genesis and Exodus are not worthless as textual witnesses, nevertheless great caution must be exercised in using them, because Aphrahat often seems to quote inexactly. The evidence suggests a general habit of memoriter rather than transcriptional quotation. The most drastic departures from the Peshitta appear almost always to result from casualness, intentional paraphrase, or error on Aphrahat's part rather than from a deviant scripture text. In those citations that invite confidence in their literalness, a somewhat ambiguous body of textual evidence is found. The vast majority of the citations agree with most or all of the Peshitta manuscripts and demonstrate that already in the fourth century Aphrahat knew a text of Genesis and Exodus that was essentially a Peshitta text. A small number of the citations, however, show affinities with one or more of the targums, the Septuagint, or the Vulgate. While these do not substantiate the theory of a wildly deviant, primitive Syriac text, they also fail to validate the view that Aphrahat knew a text that was much more literal to the Hebrew than the later Peshitta.

ACKNOWLEDGEMENTS

The successful completion of this work, which was originally undertaken in 1978 as my Ph.D. dissertation at the Johns
Hopkins University, is due in large measure to the guidance and
encouragement of Delbert R. Hillers, W. W. Spence Professor of
Semitic Languages at the Hopkins, who served as the dissertation
adviser. I was first taught Syriac and introduced to the trea-
sures of Syriac literature by him, and he first alerted me to
Aphrahat's use of scripture as a potentially important subject
for investigation. His suggestions and criticisms have been
invaluable throughout the preparation of this study; I gratefully
acknowledge his help.

Professor Alexander A. Di Lella, O.F.M., of the Catholic
University of America, served as reader for the dissertation and
gave very generously of his time to make a number of helpful and
important suggestions. Professors Robert Murray, S.J., of the
University of London, and P. A. H. de Boer, of the University of
Leiden, each gave useful advice at the very beginning of the project, and Professor de Boer graciously commended the completed
work to his associates at the Peshitta Institute and at E. J.
Brill. Access to several indispensable books was made possible
by the special help of Norman Desmarias, Librarian of St. Mary's
Seminary and University, Baltimore. Thomas Stokes, Librarian

and colleague at Emmanuel School of Religion in Johnson City, Tennessee, provided assistance in preparing the manuscript for publication. The cost of the research and publication was underwritten by Dr. and Mrs. Willard Amoss of Fallston, Maryland, and by Dr. and Mrs. John Platt of Johnson City, Tennessee. I am pleased to acknowledge my debt to these individuals also.

Special thanks is due my wife, Mary Ann. Not only did she support this project materially with her own labor, her confidence in me and her willingness to shield me from many of the normal duties of family life were decisive in bringing this book into existence. Throughout many months she resisted the temptation--surely strong at times--to decree the banishment of Aphrahat from our lives. I am deeply grateful for her help.

ABBREVIATIONS

The abbreviations used in this work are those set forth in "Instructions for Contributors," Journal of Biblical Literature 95 (1976) 331-346 and employed in Scholars Press publications. Designations for Peshitta manuscripts are those used in The Old Testament in Syriac According to the Peshiṭta Version (Leiden: Brill). Designations for Septuagint manuscripts and witnesses are those used in Septuaginta, vetus testamentum graecum (Göttingen: Vandenhoeck & Ruprecht). Exceptions and additional abbreviations are as follows:

Aphr	Aphrahat
Baarda	Tjitze Baarda, The Gospel Quotations of Aphrahat the Persian Sage, 1: Aphrahat's Text of the Fourth Gospel (Amsterdam: Vrije Universitet, 1975).
Bert	Georg Bert, Aphrahat's des persischen Weisen Homilien, aus dem Syrischen übersetzt und erläutert (TU 3/3-4; Leipzig: Heinrichs, 1888).
ch(s)	chapter(s)
cn	correction
Dem(s)	Demonstration(s)
Ephraem (Comm)	R.-M. Tonneau, ed., Sancti Ephraem syri in Genesim et in Exodum commentarii (CSCO 152, scriptores syri 71; Louvain: Durbecq, 1955).
LXX	Septuagint. For Genesis, = text printed

in John W. Wevers, ed., <u>Septuaginta,</u>
<u>vetus testamentum graecum</u>, 1: <u>Genesis</u>
(Göttingen: Vandenhoeck & Ruprecht,
1974). For Exodus, = text printed in
A. E. Brooke et al., eds., <u>The Old Tes-</u>
<u>tament in Greek</u>, 1/2: <u>Exodus and Levit-</u>
<u>icus</u> (Cambridge: Cambridge University,
1909).

mg   marginal gloss

ms(s)   manuscript(s)

MT   Massoretic Text, = text printed in K.
Elliger and W. Rudolph, eds., <u>Biblia</u>
<u>hebraica stuttgartensia</u> (Stuttgart:
Deutsche Bibelstiftung, 1977).

P   Peshitta. OT references outside Gen
and Exod are to ms 7a1. NT references
are to text printed in <u>The New Testament</u>
<u>in Syriac</u> (London: British and Foreign
Bible Society, n.d.).

Parisot   Ioannes Parisot, "Aphraatis sapientis
persae, Demonstrationes," <u>Patrologia</u>
<u>syriaca</u> (ed. R. Graffin; Paris: Firmin-
Didot, 1894-1907). References are to
volume 1 unless preceded by "II."

pr   praemittit/unt

Sam   Samaritan Pentateuch, = text printed
in A. F. von Gall, ed., <u>Der hebräische</u>
<u>Pentateuch der Samaritaner</u> (5 vols.;
Giessen: Topelmann, 1914-1918).

TF   Fragment Targum, = text printed in Moses
Ginsberger, ed., <u>Das Fragmententhargum</u>
<u>(Thargum Jeruschalmi zum Pentateuch)</u>
(Berlin: Calvary, 1899).

TG^{A-G} Targum fragments printed in Paul Kahle,
<u>Masoreten des Westens</u>, II (BWAT 14;
Stuttgart: Kohlhammer, 1930).

Tgs   TO, TJ^1, and TN^1

TJ^1 Targum Jerushalmi 1 (Pseudo-Jonathan),
= text printed in David Rieder, ed.,

Pseudo-Jonathan: Targum Jonathan ben
Uziel on the Pentateuch, Copied from
the London MS. (British Museum Add.
27031) (Jerusalem: Salomon, 1974).

TN[1]   Targum Neofiti 1, = text printed in
Alejandro Díez Macho, ed., Neophyti I.
Targum palestinense MS de la bibliotheca
vaticana (6 vols.; Madrid/Barcelona:
Consejo Superior de Investigaciones
Científicas, 1968-1979).

TO   Targum Onkelos, = text printed in
Alexander Sperber, ed., The Bible in
Aramaic, 1: The Pentateuch According to
Targum Onkelos (Leiden: Brill, 1959).

TSam   Samaritan Targum, = text printed in
Adolph Brüll, ed., Das samaritanische
Targum zum Pentateuch (7 parts; Frankfurt
am Main, 1873-1876 [reprinted Hildesheim:
Olms, 1971]).

Vg   Latin Vulgate, = text printed in Robert
Weber et al., eds., Biblia sacra iuxta
vulgatum versionem (2 vols.; Stuttgart:
Württembergische Bibelanstalt, 1975).

vs(s)   verse(s)

Wright   William Wright, The Homilies of Aphraates,
the Persian Sage edited from Syriac Manuscripts of the Fifth and Sixth Centuries
in the British Museum with an English
Translation, 1: The Syriac Text (London:
Williams & Norgate, 1869).

//   parallels

CHAPTER I

INTRODUCTION

The collation and analysis of Syriac biblical mss which
is being carried out by The Peshitta Institute at Leiden in the
process of publishing a critical editio minor of the Peshitta
constitutes a major step forward for biblical text-critical
scholarship. When completed, The Old Testament in Syriac
According to the Peshitta Version will make available in reliable form the readings of all Syriac bible mss through the
twelfth century, including lectionaries but not the so-called
"massoretic" mss. Nevertheless, even this significant accom-
plishment will leave gaps in our understanding of the nature
and history of the Peshitta OT. In the General Preface, published separately along with the first definitive section
(Part IV/3) of The Old Testament in Syriac in 1972, the editors
wrote:

> In our opinion the time has not yet come to reconstruct the
> "original" Peshitta Old Testament. Perhaps the evidence
> collected here will give new impetus to research into this
> complicated subject. A prerequisite for such a large-scale
> reconstruction would be much better knowledge of the Old
> Testament quotations preserved in the patristic literature
> of the Syriac Churches.[1]

Again more recently, in 1977, in the "Preface" to Part I/1,
the general editor repeated the need for evaluation of Syriac

patristic bible quotations: " . . . and as soon as reliable editions of the patristic literature of the Syrian Churches are available account has to be taken of quotations from the Old Testament. . . ."[2] M. H. Goshen-Gottstein had already called for study of the patristic citations several years earlier in his "Prolegomena to a Critical Edition of the Peshitta."[3]

A. The Demonstrations of Aphrahat the Persian Sage

As one contribution toward supplying this expressed need, the study presented here undertakes an analysis of the quotations from Gen and Exod found within that anonymous collection of Syriac writings commonly referred to as the "Demonstrations" of Aphrahat the Persian Sage. These writings will be already familiar to most readers of this study, who will also have access to the several full treatments of the introductory matters, most notably the exhaustive discussion by Parisot[4] and the recent study (conveniently in English) by Tjitze Baarda.[5] Therefore, it is necessary here to discuss only the four characteristics of the Dems which pertain directly to an investigation of their biblical citations.

1. Date of Composition

First, their date of composition in the middle of the fourth century A.D. places them among the earliest surviving pieces of Syriac literature.[6] Specific statements by the author himself show that the Dems were composed within an eight-year period in three stages: Dems I-X (commonly called

3

"Book I"), which stand together as a presentation of basic
aspects of Christian faith and life; Dems XI-XXII ("Book II"),
most of which treat questions and difficulties posed for Christianity by Judaism; and Dem XXIII, which is occupied largely
with chronological calculations of biblical history and which
stands by itself outside the acrostic framework that includes
I-XXII.

The most comprehensive statement made by Aphr[7] concerning the time of his writing is found toward the end of Dem XXII
(1044:11-20),[8] where, after listing in order the titles of the
first twenty-one Dems, he explains:

> I wrote the first ten in the year 648 of the reign of
> Alexander son of Philip the Macedonian, as I wrote at their
> conclusion. These other twelve I have written in the year
> 655 of the reign of the Greeks and of the Romans, which is
> the reign of Alexander, and in the year 35 of the Persian
> king.

Taking the customary date 312/311 B.C. for the accession of
Seleucus I and A.D. 309 for that of Shapur II ("the Persian
king"), one arrives at a date of A.D. 336/337 for the composition of Book I and A.D. 343/344 for Book II.

In this reference to a chronological note at the end of
Dem X in his earlier book, Aphr's memory apparently fails him.
He does write a colophon at the end of Dem X, but it contains
no mention of the date. The chronological note in Book I occurs
instead within Dem V, where A.D. 336/337 is confirmed as the
time of writing.[9] Corroboration of the date given for Book II
is found in a colophon at the end of Dem XIV.[10] A reference at

the end of Dem XXIII shows its date to be A.D. 345 (II 149:1-6):
"I have written to you this letter, my beloved, in the month Ab
of the year 656 of the reign of Alexander son of Philip the
Macedonian in the year 36 of Shapur, the Persian king, who
inflicted the persecution."

Thus written between A.D. 337 and 345, the Dems are
over a century older than our oldest extant Syriac bible ms,
ms 5b1 (in which the text of Gen-Exod is dated by colophon "in
the year 775" [= A.D. 463/464][11]), and perhaps as much as three
centuries older than ms 7a1, whose text is printed as the basic
text in the Leiden edition of the Peshitta. While Kahle's
widely followed proposal of a first-century date for the first
translation of the OT into Syriac may be too early,[12] it is
nonetheless certain that the first Syriac translation was far
earlier than the oldest extant Syriac mss. Therefore, whatever fourth-century Syriac bible texts may be found preserved
in the Dems are welcome light in a period totally devoid of
continuous-text sources.

2. Genuineness and Literary Integrity

Unlike some Syriac patristic works (several of the hymns
attributed to Ephraem, for example) whose authorship and literary
connections are in doubt, there is virtually no question that the
twenty-three Dems are from one writer.[13] Not only are the first
twenty-two arranged in an alphabetic acrostic according to the
initial letter of the initial word in each, the author himself

directly indicates the unity of the collection by statements in the colophon in Dem X[14] and especially in the passage quoted above from Dem XXII (1044:11-20). Nor can Dem XXIII, not part of the acrostic, be easily called into question since the author himself explicitly links it with Book II (II 149:8-10): "I have written this letter to you . . . after I wrote those earlier twelve treatises, which are arranged one after the other according to their letters."

This apparent integrity of the Dems as a collection has been uniformly accepted in the modern period since the discovery of the Syriac mss among the possessions of the monastery of Sancta Maria Deipara in the Nitrian desert and their first publication by Wright in 1869. Previously, only an imperfect version of the collection had been available in Armenian translation, which, though ancient,[15] does not include the entire series of treatises. It omits Dems XX-XXIII entirely, and the Syriac order is lost in Book II, where the various Dems occur as follows: XI, XIII, XV, XII, XVI, XVII, XVIII, XIX, XIV. The editor of the Armenian text, Antonelli, considered Dem XIV to be spurious on internal grounds, though he was encouraged in this view by its omission from the list of the titles of the Dems by Gennadius of Marseilles about A.D. 495.[16]

Only J. M. Fiey, among modern scholars, has chosen to discount the evidence of the Syriac mss themselves and to challenge the integrity of the collection.[17] He questions the authenticity of the Syriac order of the Dems within Book II,

proposing to remove Dem XIV from that series and set it by
itself and to insert Dem XXIII within Book II instead (but not
necessarily in the fourth position). He does not go so far as
to assert definitely that Dem XIV is not written by the author
of the other twenty-two Dems, but he implies that further study
of its style and vocabulary might lead to that conclusion.[18]

Fiey hearkens back to the arguments advanced by Antonelli:
Gennadius did not mention Dem XIV in his list; the Armenian
translator set Dem XIV apart as the last in the series; the style
of Dem XIV is different from the other Dems; the synodical nature
of Dem XIV is unique within Book II, which otherwise consists of
essays treating Judaism; and the author himself in Dem XXII
describes the Dem following "On the Sabbath" (Dem XIII) as "cette
exhortation Des rixes et des dissensions." In addition, Fiey
points out that Dem XIV carries its own colophon, a feature that
elsewhere occurs only in concluding (X and XXII) or independent
(XXIII) Dems. He argues further that the most suitable historical setting for Dem XIV is the period prior to the death of Papa
(A.D. 329), catholicos of Seleucia-Ctesiphon, a date earlier than
Book I of the Dems.

The observations of Antonelli and Fiey are not invalid.
No one can deny the exceptional nature of Dem XIV within Book II;
as a lengthy ecclesiastical communique, it fits uneasily into the
series of shorter treatises on Judaism. (The question of style
and vocabulary, however, as Fiey himself admits, cannot be con-
clusively answered.) And the presence of the colophon indeed

suggests an independently circulated document. On the other
hand, these internal considerations are not compelling, and
they stand contradicted by the Syriac text itself. Fiey fails
to account for the acrostic arrangement in the Syriac, confirmed
by both mss (see below, "3. Quality of the Manuscripts"), whose
testimony is identical at this point. "In the Syriac original
the fact is beyond question that <u>Demonstr.</u> XIV is an integral
part of the series. . . ."[19]

Why indeed would a Syriac redactor have chosen at some
point to remove Dem XXIII from Book II and replace it with Dem
XIV, when the latter does not have close thematic connections
with Dems XI-XIII and XV-XXII? And after having thus removed
it, why would he have been further motivated to alter the first
sentence of the newly independent Dem (XXIII) so as to remove
the original word (which would have had to have begun with a
letter between <u>kaph</u> and <u>taw</u>) and replace it with one beginning
with <u>alaph</u> (ܐܪܘܒܚ)? Or if, as Fiey may assume,[20] the
entire acrostic arrangement of the Dems is secondary, why would
such a device have been chosen for a collection of treatises too
large to be entirely included within it? Is it not altogether
improbable that a later compiler would have reworked the opening
sentences of the various Dems in order to produce the (only
partially successful) acrostic pattern, leaving no trace of his
manipulations in the process?

Fiey's failure effectively to answer, even to acknowledge these questions is fatal to his own theory. The correctness

8

of some of Antonelli's observations notwithstanding, the
Armenian version and Gennadius's list hardly qualify as superior
evidence, to be preferred over the Syriac mss themselves.
Gennadius probably never actually saw a text of the Dems but
drew up his list of their titles from second-hand sources.[21]
As a result, his list is unreliable, its most telling defect
being the duplicate listing of some Dems under different titles
(e.g., De resurrectione [= Dem VIII] and De vita post mortem [=
Dem VIII]).[22] The inferior state of the Armenian version has
already been described. There is simply no justification for
considering such a version to be the more accurate testimony to
the original order of the Dems when it is so defective as to
lack four undisputably genuine Dems. All the more so when it
is remembered that the Armenian language of the version will by
itself have obscured the acrostic pattern of the Syriac[23] and
that the absence of Dem XXII will have deprived the Armenian
translator (and his readers) of the Syriac writer's own list of
the first twenty-one Dems.

Nor can Fiey's placement of Dem XIV in the lifetime of
Papa command acceptance as an important argument. This "synodical
letter" lacks specific references to any known historical events.
Therefore, no proposed historical setting for it can be more
than conjecture. The one piece of primary historical information
contained in Dem XIV, the chronological note in its colophon
(see above), is discarded by Fiey as secondary (He refers to "le
colophon du scribe, si différent de la souscription de l'auteur

lui-même").[24]   Internal evidence for this judgment is not apparent, however. The various colophons and chronological notes
within the Dems are not rigidly uniform. Fiey's excision of
this chronological notice seems arbitrary.

Fiey's proposal can be confidently rejected. Although
Dem XIV stands in some tension with the other writings in Book
II and although its colophon heightens the possibility of independent circulation, there are no convincing reasons for taking
the acrostic arrangement of the Syriac mss as anything but the
author's own device. Perhaps the author himself circulated Dem
XIV independently or at least wrote it separately, before deciding to include it in Book II of his Dems. This remains speculation, of course, but it more reasonably accounts both for the
acrostic order and for the individuality of Dem XIV than does
Fiey's theory. In studying the OT quotations in the Dems, one
can be confident that he is examining a series of writings that
come from one author within the relatively short period of
eight years.

3. Quality of the Manuscripts

A third characteristic of the Dems that makes their OT
quotations an especially inviting subject for analysis is the
quality of their mss. Four different Syriac mss survive, providing two separate witnesses for almost all parts of the Dems
and three witnesses for a portion of Dem XXIII.

The most complete ms, commonly designated "A,"[25]

(British Museum Additional MS 14619) contains all twenty-three Dems and the initial letter from Aphr's enquirer. Only a few folios are missing or damaged; overall the ms (vellum) is in good condition. Although the scribe has not dated it explicitly, paleographical assessment of its fine, regular Estrangela script leaves no doubt that it was made in the sixth century.[26]

The second and third mss were originally registered as one (B.M. Add. MS 17182), but they are in fact two different texts. The first, commonly designated "B," consists of folios 1-99 and includes only Book I of the Dems (and the prefixed Letter). A colophon recognizes the incompleteness of the text, referring to its contents as "the earlier letters of the Persian sage." A second colophon explains that the book was purchased by a certain ܡܳܪܝ, ܡܳܠܟܐ, priest in a village near Damascus, in the year 785 (= A.D. 473/474) and was copied in Edessa. Wright describes its script as a "good, regular, though by no means elegant Estrangela."[27] This ms, also vellum, is in good condition, with only a few damaged or missing folios. Folios 100-175 of the same catalogue number constitute an originally separate work, commonly designated "B."[28] It contains Book II and Dem XXIII, although as a result of missing and damaged leaves Dems XI, XII, and part of XIII (to 552:12) are lost. A colophon dates the ms in "the year 823 of the Greeks" (= A.D. 511/512). Apparently the colophon originally also named the owner of the ms and his convent as well, but these have been erased. The script is "a fine, regular Estrangela."[29]

The fourth, and least important, is found in folios
159a-170a of B.M. Oriental MS 1017. This ms, which contains
selections by Barhebraeus and assorted other short compositions,
reproduces sections 1-47 of Dem XXIII at the beginning of an
anonymous chronographical work, following a superscription which
describes it as "the Demonstration of the Grape" and attributes
it to "the sage Aphraḥaṭ who is St. Jacob." This ms, commonly
designated "C," is written in Serṭa script and carries the date
"the year of the Greeks 1675" (= A.D. 1364).

The most important Syriac mss thus come from within
about 150 years of the actual writing of the Dems, not as short
an interval as might be desired, but not so great a period as
to lead one to expect extensive corruption or alteration. Can
these mss be taken as substantially reliable witnesses to the
text that Aphr wrote? With only two mss to compare for most
parts of the Dems, one cannot construct a textual genealogy by
which to determine the historical relationship of the individual
mss. Except in the case of clear mechanical error, one is left
with the uncomfortable necessity of making ad hoc decisions
between variants solely on the subjective basis of what seems
most suitable to the context. Nevertheless, as Baarda has emphasized, "Two manuscripts are more than one."[30] Mss A and B-B
present a sufficiently large number of non-orthographic variants
to make it fairly certain that one is not simply a copy of the
other. Such a judgment must be tentative, but it appears wholly
probable that for any given passage, one has two different

textual witnesses which have been transmitted separately. At
the same time, in no passage of the Dems are there extensive,
wildly divergent variants; the same essential text emerges from
all the Syriac mss.

For these reasons virtually all students of Aphr's text
have placed a high degree of confidence in the reliability of
the Syriac mss. Only Jacob Neusner is critical:

> . . . even the most obvious lower-criticism of the text has
> been neglected. As a result, sentences are sometimes
> repeated, misplaced, and confused, but neither the transla-
> tors nor the editors have paid much attention to improving
> the text in even simple, obvious ways.[31]

This is a puzzling statement, especially since Neusner himself
appears not to have found it necessary to make significant
changes in the readings of the Syriac mss when preparing his
English translations from Book II. Nor does he provide lists
of specific examples of such corruptions. In close study of
more than two hundred passages in the Dems I have encountered
none of the problems Neusner describes; neither has Baarda in
his work with the Gospel citations.[32] Consequently, I cannot
accept Neusner's assessment.

An additional question must be asked about the mss, however, in the light of the use to which they are put in this
study. It is not enough to be confident that the mss preserve
the essential text of the Dems; one must also ask, In the
150-year interval between Aphr's writing and the production of
the extant mss did the biblical quotations within the Dems
escape accidental or intentional correction to later biblical

text-forms known to the scribes? F. J. A. Hort makes plain

the pertinence of this question:

> Wherever a transcriber of a patristic treatise was copying
> a quotation differing from the text to which he was accus-
> tomed, he had virtually two originals before him, one pre-
> sent to his eyes, the other to his mind; and, if the differ-
> ence struck him, he was not unlikely to treat the written
> exemplar as having blundered.[33]

There is in fact good reason to believe that one can recover

from the Syriac mss a text-form for each biblical quotation that

is free from accommodation to later textual tradition. This is

Baarda's verdict, although his reasons are not of equal merit.[34]

Baarda's weakest argument is that the small number of

extant Syriac mss of the Dems may indicate that Aphr's work was

not ever in great demand: " . . . the type of theology which

the author betrays in his work presumably may have been felt as

somewhat unorthodox in the time after Ephraem. . . ."[35] If the

work were unpopular, it would naturally have been re-copied only

infrequently, "and in such a case transcriptional errors are cor-

respondingly few. . . ."[36] Certainly Baarda's reasoning is logi-

cal, if one can grant his basic assumption that few surviving mss

evidence lack of popularity. But this premise is a deduction

e silentio, and the picture could change completely with a single

discovery of additional Syriac mss of the Dems. Vööbus's recent

discoveries are fresh reminders that our current corpus of known

Syriac works represents at best a small sampling of the Syriac

literature once current in the ancient East.[37] There is simply

not sufficient historical data to be certain that Aphr's works

were only rarely reproduced. Nor can one be at all sure that
his theology would have predisposed his writings to censure.
While Aphr's identity as "the Persian sage" might possibly have
invoked against his work that prejudice in the West that came to
associate all Persian writings with Nestorianism,[38] there is no
evidence of Nestorian doctrine in his work. On the contrary,
"it would be difficult . . . to point out anything in it to
which exception could be so seriously taken as to be a bar to
its acceptance."[39]

    Two other reasons that Baarda cites for assuming the
authenticity of the text of the biblical quotations are much
more substantial. As already mentioned, the 150-year interval
between author and scribes is relatively short, short enough
that not many "generations" of copies will have had time to
reproduce themselves. It is impossible, of course, to prove that
a given scribe in this interval could not have known an OT text
somewhat different from Aphr's; in fact, the opposite is indicated by the list of variants given below. However, "the transmission of the texts was accomplished in a period when the Syriac
Vulgate was not yet considered the textus receptus of Syria,
which it gradually became afterwards."[40] This means that even
if Aphr's bible text were different at some point from that
known to the scribe, such a scribe will probably have lacked the
concept of an "official" scripture text as a motivation for consciously emending the quotations in the Dems.

    On the other hand, my study exposes a number of places

in the Gen and Exod quotations where the Syriac mss differ
(other than orthographically) and where one of the variants
exactly coincides with P (or a well-attested reading within the
P tradition) or very closely approaches it. In such instances,
barring evident corruption or mechanical error, the best methodology is to assume that the reading most different from P represents Aphr's original text and that the variant is a later
scribal correction, whether intentional or not.[41] (Obviously I
proceed here from the prior assumption that there is not chaos
in the transmission of Aphr's text in the first 150 years and
that in the case of ms variation at least one of the mss preserves Aphr's text.[42]) The clarity with which accommodation to
P stands out in these passages when the criterion of dissimi-
larity is applied justifies confidence that the available Syriac
mss provide adequate basis for recovering the original text-form
of Aphr's quotations. The ability to make comparison between
two mss (rarely between three, in Dem XXIII) is decisive.[43]

The passages containing these variations are: 011, 017,
064, 072, 084, 092, 101, 115, 117, 134, 139, 140, 149, 158, 169,
171, 186, 190, 193, 196, 199, 212, 215. Eight of these (011,
084, 092, 115, 139, 171, 196, 212) contain ms variations in
which it is impossible to be certain which ms contains the original reading. But there is almost no doubt in the other fifteen.
Furthermore, an interesting picture emerges from their variation.
In twelve of the fifteen, the reading of ms A betrays accommodation to P, and mss B-B reproduce a deviant text that appears to

be Aphr's original. While this pattern is not entirely consistent, it is sufficiently so to confirm one's confidence in the
independence of ms A from mss B–B. The scribe in ms A has a
greater tendency to conform the biblical quotations to P than
the scribes in mss B–B. This confirms the validity of basing
textual decisions on a comparison of the mss.

A word is in order at this point about the editions of
the Dems by Wright and Parisot. Neither constitutes a diplo-
matic reproduction of any one of the mss; both are eclectic,
basing their text sometimes on ms A, more often on mss B–B.
For Dem XXIII Parisot alone makes use of ms C, although he fails
to indicate the many times when this ms represents numerals by
means of Syriac consonants in passages where mss A and B–B
write out the numerals; Wright includes no readings from ms C.
Both present a complete critical apparatus of variant readings,
so that in either edition the reader has access to all the
Syriac ms evidence (except ms C). The Dems, therefore, are a
fortunate exception amid the general dearth of critical editions
of Syriac patristic works. Despite the quality of these editions,
I have based my own work with the quotations directly on the
Syriac mss themselves (A, B–B, and C), using photocopies and
microfilms purchased from the British Library. I have sought
thereby the highest degree of accuracy and reliability;[44] the
editions of Wright and Parisot, though generally accurate, are
not entirely free of errors.

4. Number of Citations

Another characteristic of the Dems that makes them especially suitable for this study is their exceptionally large number of biblical quotations and allusions. Although assessment of the textual value of these citations is a difficult and often uncertain task, Aphr's frequent quotation of biblical material makes the Dems a storehouse of potentially important Syriac textual evidence. He calls himself a "student of the holy scriptures," (1049:3-4) and, accordingly, it is the biblical text which forms the basis for his teaching throughout the Dems. "Das hervorstechendste Merkmal der Afrahatschen Homilien ist das Bibelzitat," according to Leo Haefeli. "Das alt- und neutestamentliche Bibelzitat bedeutet für unseren Autor den Stab, auf den er sich fortwährend stützt."[45]

Frank Gavin found approximately 1056 explicit quotations from the OT in Aphr and 564 from the NT.[46] Wright's index of biblical quotations lists 794 from the OT and 446 from the NT. Parisot's index, which explicitly includes close allusions as well as quotations, contains 987 from the OT and 753 from the NT, an average of about four citations per column of Syriac text. Since it is known that both indexes fall somewhat short of being complete, the actual number of quotations and close allusions is larger yet than these figures indicate.[47] Students of the Syriac bible text simply cannot ignore such a large collection of citations.

B. Purposes and Goals

This study seeks to accomplish five objectives:

1. To identify all the citations and allusions in the Dems that may provide evidence of the text of Gen and Exod known to Aphr. As already mentioned, the indexes of biblical quotations in Wright and Parisot (and Bert) are not entirely adequate for text-critical purposes. Not only do they omit some important citations, but each one also includes some allusions that are too distant to be of value for textual study. It has been necessary to carry out an independent search through all twenty-three Dems, as a result of which the collection was made of all biblical references which merit study as possible witnesses to Aphr's scripture text. All of those references are discussed below in chapters II and III.

Because no comprehensive collection of such references has been prepared before, because very little knowledge exists yet of Syriac patristic bible quotations generally, and because the view has been advanced that Aphr quotes a primitive Syriac Pentateuch text that is considerably more paraphrastic than P, I have chosen to be somewhat more inclusive in establishing the collection of citations than might seem necessary. It is possible that seemingly paraphrastic citations might prove to be more literal reproductions of a deviant source-text; sound empirical methodology dictates that one not exclude such citations from analysis, a priori. All passages have been included which take the form of a scripture citation—that is, which are

presented by an introductory formula--or which clearly evoke a
specific reference within Gen or Exod.

Of the 221 passages thus identified, only about 120 are
introduced by a formula of citation. The various formulae used,
in order of frequency are: "(As) N said/preached/commanded/tes-
tified";[48] "Thus N said/testified/commanded"; "As it is written";
"Thus it is written"; "Again it is written." A few times a
quotation is marked by ܡܠ , either by itself or in addition to
a formula. More elaborate introductions are used infrequently:
"There was said to Abraham this word"; "And the matter of the
sojourning was recorded"; "This word is written"; "The word that
God said to Abraham"; "The word was promised to Abraham." Only
six times does Aphr make reference to the place from which the
citation is taken, and these are usually not specific enough to
be very helpful: "According to what is written in the book of
the generations"; "We hear again from Beriytha [= Genesis]";
"At the beginning of the whole Law thus it is written"; "For
the Holy One commanded in the Law"; ". . . three commandments
of the Ten"; "For it is written in the Holy Law."

I have not confined myself to those references that are
introduced by a formula of citation, nor have I relied uncritically upon the formulae themselves in defining the citations,
for two main reasons. For one thing, it is not always easy to
be certain that a direct quotation follows the formula, because,
except in the case of vocative or imperative clauses, the formula usually is immediately followed by dalath prefixed to the

subsequent word. This <u>dalath</u> may be a pleonasm on a formal quotation, but it may also function actively as a conjunction introducing an indirect quotation, paraphrase, or quite distant allusion.[49] So, for example, in #191 below ܝܢ ܙܒܗ

. . . ܟܬܒܐܠ ܟܐܠܟ ܢܫܟܕ ܟܝܪܕ ܟܘܒܬܟܒ

may be rendered either: "For it is written in the Holy Law: 'God said to Moses. . . .'" or "For it is written in the Holy Law that God said to Moses. . . ." And in fact Aphr sometimes follows a formula of citation with a summary of or deduction from a biblical text instead of the words of the text itself. Nor is it always clear where the quotation introduced by a formula is intended to end. This problem is not frequent, but there are occasions where the end of the formal quotation is not evident from the syntax itself.

Secondly, close reading of the Dems shows that Aphr often falls into the language of a scripture text without formally introducing his statement as a citation. My judgment, elaborated below, is that Aphr probably never cites Gen or Exod except from memory; he knows his bible so well that he can cite its text with little conscious effort. Only at times does he feel the need to emphasize that a given statement is from holy scripture. To consider only Aphr's formal citations would be to miss many reflections of his bible text.

It will be clear from these comments that the student of Aphr's citations finds himself in the difficult situation of having to confirm his identification of the citations by means

of comparison with known bible texts. Final identification of
a passage as a reproduction of Aphr's bible text and determination of its limits rest at least partly upon being able to find
strong similarity between it and a specific bible text. As long
as one refrains from premature negative judgments about paraphrastic quotations and allusions, the circularity and subjec-
tivity of this process need not be serious weaknesses. The group
of passages assembled in this study may be confidently regarded
as including all those in the Dems that have potential as witnesses to Aphr's text of Gen-Exod. Only in one respect may the
group prove to be defective. My analysis has revealed many citations that conflate a portion of a vs from Gen or Exod with one
from another biblical book. Often this has become clear, however, only after close study. It is not impossible that close
study of what appear to be citations from other biblical books
may turn up some conflations involving portions of vss from Gen-
Exod. If such additional fragments are identified, however, they
will probably be very few in number and of little or no value
textually.

The decision to study Aphr's citations of Gen-Exod rather
than of the entire Pentateuch has been based entirely on practi-
cal considerations. The amount of quotational material from the
entire Pentateuch is very large. Parisot's index lists almost
350 citations from Gen-Deut, a figure that would surely be considerably expanded by further examination. To provide the Syriac
text and thorough discussion of all those passages would require

a work of unwieldy size. More important, a critical edition of
P is so far available only for Gen and Exod of the Pentateuchal
books;[50] elsewhere one has to rely on Ceriani's facsimile edition
of ms 7a1,[51] the unsatisfactory edition by Samuel Lee,[52] or the
uncritical text in the polyglots and in the Urmia and Mosul editions.[53] To try to assess the textual significance of Aphr's
citations without being able to compare them to the full corpus
of the extant P mss would be to operate with a considerable
handicap. The wisest course is to postpone study of citations
from the other books until a critical edition of their Syriac
text is produced.

Also, an exhaustive study of the history of the P text
of Exod has been recently completed by M. Koster,[54] whose conclusions apply to a large extent to the text of Gen as well.[55]
Koster's reconstruction of the course of development of the P
text of these two books provides a valuable framework within
which Aphr's citations can be interpreted. No such reconstruction has yet been established for the other Pentateuchal books,
however, which do not share with Exod as many significant mss
(most notably the first part of ms 5b1) as does Gen. This too
encourages the deferment of a study of the citations of Lev-Deut,
which I hope to undertake at a later time.

The body of citations gathered from Gen-Exod is itself
sufficiently large to provide a reliable exposure of Aphr's text
of the Pentateuch. If Parisot's index can be taken as a guide,
in the Gen-Exod citations one may well have half or more of all

the Pentateuch citations in the Dems. Not only may the type of
bible text known to Aphr be adequately identified from these
citations, the general reliability of Aphr's citations as textual witnesses may be sufficiently tested.

2. To supply the text of Aphr's Gen-Exod citations based
on a fresh collation of the Syriac mss. Because it is absolutely
necessary to subject each citation to critical evaluation before
attempting to use it as a textual witness, scholarship is better
served in a study such as this if the various sentences containing the citations are reproduced directly from the mss, rather
than if one supplies only reconstructions of the bible texts
that are thought to be reflected in the citations.[56] Therefore,
in chapters II and III below I have provided the actual Syriac
text of each passage from the Dems in which a citation occurs
that seems worthy of study. This will enable the reader more
readily to understand and to evaluate my assessments of the textual significance of the various citations. If further knowledge of Syriac patristic citations and early P materials should
modify my analysis of some of the citations in the Dems, it is
hoped that the study will continue to have value as a reliable
compendium of the Gen-Exod quotations.

Although the Armenian version of the Dems may have some
small role to play in shedding additional light on the subject of
Aphr's quotations, that version cannot simply be laid alongside
the Syriac mss as a fifth witness to the text of the Dems. A
comprehensive study of its overall relationship to the Syriac mss

must be undertaken before its text of the citations can be utilized safely. Even more important, a specialist in the textual
history of the Armenian bible must sift the bible quotations in
the Armenian version of the Dems in order to identify those
that have suffered secondary accommodation to the Armenian OT.
Parisot warns about this aspect of the Armenian text of the
Dems: "Tandem Scripturae loca ad armeniacam seu graecam Bib-
liorum versionem sunt accommodata. . . ."[57] Until these tasks,
which are beyond my ability, are completed, the Armenian readings of the citations cannot be safely used.

     3. To analyze each citation to assess its value as a
witness to Aphr's bible text. Past study of patristic bible
citations in other languages, especially Greek and Latin, has
shown that no citation should be accepted prima facie as an
exact reproduction of the author's bible text; only after critical analysis can the textual witness of a citation be determined.

> Therefore the critic must assess cautiously the probability
> that the citation represents accurately the witness of the
> ancient Bible whose form he seeks. Every possibility must
> be weighed carefully, and the reading must be criticized in
> terms of principles which are constructed to bring possible
> readings within the range of possibility. . . .[58]

Even when, as in the case of the Dems, one feels confident that
the original quotations are relatively free of secondary scribal
corrections, still one must come to terms with the many factors
that might have caused the author himself not to quote his text
literally.

One of the first questions to ask is whether the citation is made from memory or from actually consulting a bible ms. Naturally, memoriter citations will be more vulnerable to error than transcriptional citations. This is not to say that one must disregard memory citations altogether; the prodigious memorizing of scripture by early ecclesiastics is well-known,[59] and their extensive use of the bible text will in many cases have implanted its words firmly in the memory. Baarda's verdict about Aphr's capability in this respect is that his familiarity with the bible text "is so impressive that we may safely assume that even in cases where he cited from memory he remained faithful to the text which he knew from ecclesiastical use or from private studies."[60] One suspects that usage, rather than formal exercises in memorization, will have been primarily responsible for most of the recall of scripture of which a writer like Aphr is capable.

From such circumstances one can expect that the writer's memory will be most accurate for biblical vss that are unique and distinctive. Vss that recur in similar form in more than one biblical passage, or which include clauses or phrases which are used repeatedly in only slightly different form, will be those most liable to contamination and accidental conflation when quoted from memory. The possibility of such error will also increase when a series of thematically related quotations are presented in close succession, as happens frequently in the Dems.

There are, of course, no infallible criteria by which
to determine whether a particular citation is from memory. The
two most often relied upon, length and formulaic introduction,
are of little use in Aphr's citations from Gen-Exod. None of
these citations is so lengthy as to make overwhelmingly probable
that it was not made from memory, and, as already discussed,
there are a number of cases in which an obviously loose citation
(i.e., one that is unmistakeably paraphrastic) is introduced by
a formula.[61] One is forced into the circular process of judging
the citations from the standard of known biblical texts; if a
general pattern of paraphrase or erroneous citation is evident,
then one can reasonably deduce that Aphr cites from memory, frequently if not always. In characterizing a loose citation as
memoriter, one does not, of course, exclude the possibility that
Aphr might be quoting casually, without attempting to cite his
text exactly. Some inexact references are obviously mere allusions, and even formal quotations may not in every case be
intended to be literal.

Therefore, it is also important to try to ascertain
Aphr's seriousness of intention in making a given citation. A
vs that is given emphasis as it is cited and which is then
referred back to or which has key importance in the following
discussion will obviously have a greater likelihood of having
been quoted carefully than one which is hastily mentioned in
passing. Consideration of the context is therefore indispen-
able. Generally, allusion to a single biblical term or short

phrase cannot be taken as a textual witness, unless a numeral
or very distinctive phrase (e.g., the description of Joseph's
coat in #145) is involved.

One must determine for every citation "that it has not
been adjusted to fit either the argument or the grammar and
rhythm of the context in which it occurs."[62]   Rearrangement of
the word-order of a text may be made, consciously or not, for
stylistic reasons or to lend emphasis to a particular part of
the vs. Inconsequential changes in grammatical forms (such as
the use of the participle plus ܟܘ instead of the imperfect,
or the shift from second-person imperfect to the imperative)
may also occur out of purely personal stylistic preference.
Most suspect are citations of biblical clauses or phrases that
are not set off by themselves but rather are included within
larger sentences of Aphr's own composition. In such cases, one
may look for adjustments in grammar and syntax that make the
quoted passage more compatible with the surrounding sentence.

In this connection too, one must be alert to Aphr's
understandable tendency to quote only as much of a biblical vs
or passage as is relevant to his interest at a particular point.
Because he does not quote his bible texts as separated lemmata
at the head of a unit of discussion, commentary fashion, but
intersperses them wherever appropriate within the body of his
essays, it is obvious that he will have had no reason in many
cases to cite the entire biblical sentence, nor indeed the entire
unit of material (sometimes larger than a sentence) which in

later tradition has become delineated and numbered as a vs. In analyzing the citations which present only a portion of what is now considered to be a vs, I have been guided by the principle recommended by Metzger for Greek Gospel citations:

> . . . surely it is easier to explain the existence of vari-
> ous shorter forms of the verse in the writings of the
> Fathers as arising from the circumstance of their alluding
> to only as much of the substance of the passage as suited
> their purpose, than to assume that an expansion of the pas-
> sage . . . happened to be incorporated in an early ancestor
> of all extant . . . manuscripts . . . as well as versions.[63]

Usually I have not felt justified in basing textual conclusions on the absence of a vs-portion from a citation.

It is usually helpful, occasionally troublesome, when Aphr cites the same passage of scripture more than once, because he often does not cite the passage precisely the same way each time. Comparing such citations often makes it easier to iden-tify accommodations to context, stylistic alterations, and other departures from his bible text which may be present. While theoretically one must acknowledge the possibility that Aphr knows more than one text-form for a given vs, the actual likeli-hood of competing versions being in his memory is less than that confusion of parallel passages from within one text or simple freedom in quotation will be responsible for differences in cita-tions of the same vs. This opinion is shared by Wevers concern-ing the LXX citations in the Greek patristic sources:

> Der Gebrauch von Bibelstellen bei Kirchenvätern ist häufig
> nicht sehr genau; das hat zur Folge, dass ein einziger
> Kirchenschriftsteller oft Zeuge für drei oder vier Text-
> formen einer einzigen Stelle sein soll. Das aber ist offen-
> sichtlich absurd.[64]

When both Syriac mss of the Dems have Aphr at one point citing
a vs in agreement with P and at another point diverging from P,
it is generally a safe assumption that his bible text = P in
that vs and that the second citation is not exact.

Inescapably, in assessing the value of the citations one
has to compare the text-form with that of known bible mss. In a
quotation that appears to be important within its context and
carefully made and that is generally free of obvious paraphrastic tendencies, a reading that is entirely unattested elsewhere
must be accorded serious consideration as a feature of Aphr's
text. But when a deviant reading occurs within a citation that
appears to be less careful or which contains other obvious marks
of paraphrase, or when an explanation for such a reading can be
found in the context or in accidental confusion of similar vss,
then the citation cannot safely be considered a reliable witness
to Aphr's text; one must assume departure from his bible text
in the process of quotation.

4. To set forth, where possible, the text that is
attested by each citation or group of citations, along with a
critical apparatus showing its agreements with and differences
from the other principal ancient texts of the OT. With a number
of the citations, no certain witness to Aphr's bible text is
provided, either because the citation shows itself clearly to
be inexact or because major questions about the nature and literalness of the citation cannot be answered with confidence.
In such cases it suffices to present the citation itself and to

discuss its difficulties and possibilities. In the other cases,
when one can be reasonably certain of the textual value of a
citation, it has seemed best for the sake of clarity and convenience, following the discussion of the citation or cluster of
citations, to set forth by itself the bible text that is attested,
along with a listing of the readings of the P mss and the other
important ancient witnesses.

My choice of ancient witnesses to compare with Aphr's
citations calls for little explanation. In addition to the
Syriac mss presented in Part I/1 of The Old Testament in Syriac
According to the Peshiṭta Version, those versions whose text
might reasonably be related to Aphr's fourth-century exemplar
have been included: the Massoretic Hebrew text (checked against
the Dead Sea Scroll texts, the Nash papyrus, and the quotations
in the Mishna),[65] the Samaritan Pentateuch, Targum Onkelos, Targum Jerushalmi I, Targum Neophyti I, the so-called Fragment Targum, the targum fragments published by Kahle (see Abbreviations
above), the Samaritan Targum,[66] the Septuagint, and the Latin
Vulgate. Later non-Peshitta Syriac versions and versions primarily based on the Septuagint have not been compared.

In an effort to gain additional help in recognizing any
authentic wildly deviant readings that might be present in Aphr's
quotations, I have also compared the biblical citations in
Ephraem's commentary on Gen and Exod. This has been done on the
assumption that, if Baumstark and Vööbus are correct (see below)
that the early Syriac Pentateuch text was far more paraphrastic

and expansionistic than later extant bible mss, the bible text
known to Ephraem and Aphr would both show some signs of this,
though they need not be identical at every point.[67] The additional witness of Ephraem might prevent one from mistaking a
wildly deviant reading in Aphr for a mere loose quotation. It
must be stressed that no pretense is made here of studying all
the Gen-Exod quotations in Ephraem's large corpus of writings;
the commentary was selected simply because it offers the read-
iest access to a sizeable group of Ephraem's Gen –Exod citations.
Nor have intensive analyses been carried out of the citations
in the commentary. Some of them, as in the Dems, appear to be
partial, paraphrastic, or contaminated by parallel (especially
NT) passages. Hidal, who has studied the commentary carefully,
explains:

> Sehr oft sind in den Bibeltext erklärende Worter eingefügt,
> zuweilen nur verdeutlichende oder paraphrasierende, zuweilen
> auch solche, die eine gewisse Auslegung bieten. Da das
> Problem von Ephräms Bibeltext noch nicht befriedigend
> behandelt worden ist, kann es manchmal schwerfallen zu ent-
> scheiden, was zum eigentlichen Text gehört und was kommen-
> tierender Zusatz ist.[68]

Where the textual witness of the commentary seems at all doubtful, I have simply avoided using it.

     5. To arrive at an overall description of the Syriac
text of Gen-Exod known to Aphr. After assessing the reliability
of the individual citations, and after surveying the agreements
and disagreements of the individual attested texts with other
Syriac mss and ancient versions, I propose, in the Conclusion,
a summarizing description of Aphr's exemplar of Gen and Exod.

C. Past Study of Aphr's Pentateuch Citations

When Wright published the Syriac mss of the Dems in 1869,

the introduction included his preliminary assessment of the tex-

tual significance of the biblical citations:

> . . . like most of the other ancient Fathers, Aphraates
> seems to me to quote the Peshiṭta merely from memory, some-
> times mistaking the book in which the passage occurs, and at
> other times, mixing up the words of two or more passages of
> Scripture.[69]

Almost immediately, Theodor Nöldeke, in a review of The Homilies

of Aphraates, the Persian Sage, expressed his general agreement

with Wright's assessment:

> Soweit ich die Sache geprüft habe . . . ist im Allgemeinen
> unser gedruckter Text der Peschita [sic] weit besser als der
> im Aphraates gebotne, und das ist . . . ganz natürlich, da
> jener durchweg aus dem Gedächtniss citiert und ihm daher
> leicht kleine Veränderungen im Wortlaut, Auslassungen oder
> Vermischung zweier Stellen begegnen.[70]

A few years later, in 1876, Nöldeke published an only slightly less

negative view of the importance of the citations, an opinion that

probably was now based on extensive work with the Dems inasmuch as

only four years later the first edition of his Kurzgefasste

Syrische Grammatik appeared, in which were cited over 500 passages

from the Dems:

> Deutliche Spuren eines älteren Zustandes finden wir noch in
> Menge bei Aphraates und bei Ephraïm. Freilich dürfen wir auf
> die Abweichungen jenes, der aus dem Gedächtnisse citierte
> und daher auch wohl dieselbe Stelle in verschiedener Gestalt
> anführt, nur dann Gewicht legen, wenn sie von anderer Seite
> her eine Stütze finden.[71]

Subsequent studies by P. F. Frankl on the Syriac text of

Chronicles and by F. Baethgen on the text of Psalms[72] took

account of some readings in Aphr's citations but emphasized the memoriter and often unreliable nature of the citations as textual

witnesses, a caution voiced also by Eberhard Baumann in his study

of the Job text:

> Schon Ephrem ist daher mit grosser Vorsicht zu benutzen, noch
> mehr aber Aphraates. Da er nur ganz gelegentlich in seinen
> Homilien auch Ijob citiert, zweifellos nach dem Gedächtnis,
> sind Ungenauigkeiten von vornherein zu erwarten. Er kom-
> biniert Sätze, die im Gedanken ähnlich sind, aber im Texte
> weit entfernt stehen, ändert in der Reihenfolge und flicht
> Eignes ein.[73]

Sasse, who apparently looked at Aphr's citations in some detail

(He cites twenty-one OT and fourteen NT citations specifically),

commented similarly: "Attamen magnopere dolendum est, quod aeque

ac plurimi veterum patrum etiam Aphraates negligenter egit in

citandis utriusque testamenti locis atque e memoria, non secundum

textum Peshitthae locos saepissime attulit."[74]

Parisot was aware of the divergence from P in some of

Aphr's citations and did not stress inaccuracy in quotation as

the explanation:

> Vetus Testamentum citat e Versione Peshita [sic]; plures
> tamen auctorem inter et Bibliorum textum deprehenduntur
> varietates, idque praecipue in codice B-B vetustiore, ut
> dicetur, sive quod exempla recitavit Aphraates, propriisque
> verbis aliquando non expressit; sive etiam quod versionis
> antiquioris lectiones affert; . . .[75]

Gwynn's brief statement on the citations also allows for more

than inaccurate quoting as a cause for the deviations from P:

"He follows the Peshitto rather than the Greek, but not seldom

departs from both; and he shows a knowledge of the Chaldee Para-

phrase."[76]

It seems certain that none of these early evaluations

34

was based on a systematic, empirical investigation of Aphr's
citations in their own right. Nevertheless, a consensus was
developing concerning the OT citations that continued to prevail,
with only a few opponents, in the twentieth century. "The general conviction about his free manner of handling the text of
the Scriptures has possibly prevented scholars from making
really thorough investigations into his text of the Old Testament."[77] (In contrast, study of Aphr's NT--especially Gospel--
quotations was pursued more vigorously from the beginning.[78])

Of the several major studies of the Syriac text of OT
books outside the Pentateuch that have been published in the
twentieth century,[79] only three have attempted to make use of
Aphr's citations. Barnes, in preparing his critical edition of
Psalms, referred to Aphr's citations a number of times, but did
not ever approach a full utilization of this material; he also
failed usually to make clear the exact reading of the few Aphr
citations to which he did refer. F. C. Burkitt, in a review,
criticized Barnes specifically on this count (" . . . the evidence of Aphraates becomes of great importance, and it is the
one serious omission in Dr. Barnes's book that he has not given
the evidence of Aphr more fully") making at the same time the
important observation that such an early witness as Aphr is
valuable "for confirmation as well as for correction;" that is,
Aphr's agreements with P are as important as his unique readings.[80] Diettrich, on Isaiah, cited a few readings from citations in Wright's edition; Running, relying apparently on

Parisot's index, made rather more extensive use of Aphr, empha-
sizing at the same time the need for distinguishing "allusions
and loose quotations by memory, from genuine variant readings
in the quotations."[81] In neither case was a systematic investigation of Aphr's citations prepared nor were discussions of the
individual citations utilized included in the work.

It is only within the context of study of the P Pentateuch that Aphr's quotations have received much attention, and
even here the work has not been satisfactory. Only three attempts
to deal with Aphr's Pentateuch citations can be found. In 1914,
John Pinkerton published "The Origin and Early History of the
Syriac Pentateuch,"[82] in which, on the basis of a collation of
all Pentateuch mss in the British Museum prior to the tenth century, he sought to establish the outline of the history of the
P Pentateuch. Of special concern to him was B.M. Add. MS 14425
(= ms 5b1, referred to above) in which, only two years previously, W. E. Barnes had discovered the text of Gen-Exod that was
different in many readings from other Pentateuch mss and was
generally closer to the MT. After completing his collation,
Pinkerton compared Aphr's Pentateuch quotations (and those in
Ephraem's commentary on Gen-Exod). He explicitly referred to
only nine quotations from the Dems, actually citing six of them,
but he seems to have done some kind of wider survey (relying on
Parisot's index), for he stated: "Aphraates . . . makes numerous quotations from Genesis and Exodus, but only a small number
of these can be used to determine what type of text he had before

him, because in the majority of the passages quoted by him no variant exists."[83] Pinkerton's deduction was that Aphr "used a text which followed the Hebrew more closely than did the text in common use in the sixth century, i.e. his text belonged to a more literal type than that found later."[84] This formed one of the bases for his general conclusion in the article that the earliest form of the Syriac Gen-Exod was a primarily literal rendering of the Hebrew and that the version gradually became less literal with the passage of time, a view that Koster's more thorough work has now firmly substantiated.

Although I can find no fault with Pinkerton's use of the six quotations as textual witnesses, the small number of quotations employed makes apparent the limitations of the article as a reliable assessment of the type of Pentateuch text known to Aphr. Pinkerton did not provide a discussion of the total corpus of citations with which he worked, thus leaving the thoroughness of his study in doubt. Also, Koster has pointed out that Pinkerton failed to compare the six quotations with the MT and other versions, an oversight that prevented him from drawing completely accurate conclusions from those citations.[85]

The most extensive treatment of Aphr's Pentateuch citations was published in 1943 by Anton Baumstark.[86] In that article, in which reference was made to thirty-two citations involving seventeen different biblical passages (Gen 1:28; 6:14; 7:1; 9:2-3; Lev 17:13; 19:8; 23:22; 25:20; Deut 6:10; 12:16; 22:6-7; 24:19; 31:29; 32:21; 34:5-6; plus Dan ch 9 and Rom 10:19),

Baumstark took up Aphr's citations with the explicit expectation
that they would provide corroboration for his view (advanced
earlier by J. Perles and J. Prager[87]) that the Syriac Pentateuch
originated from a Jewish targum.

> Dass die P(ešitta) zum Pentateuch aus einem . . . in ost-
> aramäische Sprachform umgegossenen ältesten palästinensischen
> Targum hervorgegangen ist, kann heute keinem Zweifel mehr
> unterliegen. . . . Dass von jenem Targum rund des NTlichen
> Zeitalters zum endgültigen P-Text eine allmähliche Entwick-
> lung geführt hat, liegt in der Natur der Dinge. Dass Spuren
> dieser Entwicklung an Zitaten, die von der späteren P im
> Sinne einer noch grösseren Targum-Nähe abweichen, sich in
> ältesten Schichten syrischer Literatur noch erhalten haben
> sollten, wäre ohne weiteres zu erwarten. . . . Das Hierher-
> gehöriges bei einer genaueren Prüfung auch die ungenauen
> zahl- und teilweise recht umfangreichen Bibelzitate Afrahaṭs
> ergeben würden, liess sich von vornherein vermuten.[88]

What interested Baumstark in the citations of Aphr especially
was their expansionistic and paraphrastic character: "In aller-
weitestem Umfange bekunden diese zunächst eine Auffüllung des
Textes aus verwandten bzw. parallelen Stellen."[89] Although he
acknowledged the possibility that such mixtures of text-forms
could be due to accidental memoriter conflation, Baumstark was
impressed by the fact that the Sam, the LXX, and the Palestinian
targum also contain expansionary readings and concluded from
this similarity that Aphr's citations evidence a primitive text
that was far more paraphrastic than later P mss:

> Dass eine entsprechende Neigung vielleicht in noch erheblich
> höherem Grade als Erbe des pälastinensischen Targums bzw.
> des diesem zugrundeliegenden vulgären Urtexts, dem von
> Afrahaṭ gelesenen syrischen Text eigentümlich gewesen wäre,
> gehört daher nicht nur durchaus dem Bereiche der Möglichkeit
> an, sondern es ist auch alles eher als unwahrscheinlich.[90]

Baumstark's study is deficient in several respects,

particularly in the glaring bias of its approach. The many
earlier warnings by reputable scholars about the _memoriter_ and
inexact nature of Aphr's citations notwithstanding, he chose to
avoid a comprehensive critical assessment of the textual value
of the Pentateuch citations and simply to assume (in practice,
if not in word) that even the most deviant citation must be an
accurate reproduction of Aphr's bible text. By treating only
those citations which present drastic differences from P, he
fostered the false impression that Aphr's Pentateuch text was
quite different from P; this ignored the fact (already mentioned
in passing by Pinkerton) that most of the citations reflect a
text identical to P. A third difficulty is that Baumstark's
general statements which describe Aphr's citations, the Sam,
the LXX, and the targum as all being expansionistic are quite
misleading. Although one can certainly find examples of "doublet" readings in the versions mentioned, rarely do such drastically deviant text-forms occur as one finds in the more wild
of Aphr's citations. Nor is there usually a close agreement
between the specific citations from Gen-Exod that Baumstark discusses and the corresponding vss in the targums. The citations
that Baumstark seizes upon as examples of the wild, primitive
Syriac text are usually unsupported by the other ancient witnesses. More detailed critique of his use of the Gen-Exod citations is presented below for citations 010-011, 064-070, 073,
191, and 198-205. In the light of the relatively small number
of citations treated and of the defectiveness of Baumstark's

overall approach to them, it is regrettable that B. J. Roberts
chose to transmit uncritically Baumstark's view in his widely
used manual, The Old Testament Text and Versions,[91] where it
constitutes the entire discussion of the textual significance
of the citations of Ephraem and Aphr.

Following along the lines laid down by Baumstark, in
1958 Arthur Vööbus produced Peschitta und Targumim des Pentateuchs,[92] in which he presented an elaborate defense of the view
that the oldest form of the P text was much wilder than that
evidenced in the surviving P mss: "Die Peschitta, nämlich die
Ur-Peschitta, enthielt noch etwas, von dessen Umfang und Muster
wir bisher keine Kenntnis hatten. Unsere Studie beleuchtet nun
in beträchtlichem Umfange die alte targumische Grundsicht."[93]
This "Ur-Peshitta" text, displaying considerable paraphrastic
freedom, was a targum whose explanatory and homiletical additions were later suppressed.

To substantiate this view, Vööbus was naturally forced
to seek textual evidence outside the standard P mss, and, pre-
dictably, he turned to the citations of the Syriac Fathers. His
"Einleitung" denounced Leo Haefeli's negative assessment of the
value of the patristic citations[94] and praised Baumstark for
recognizing that Ephraem and Aphr preserved an ancient text of
great worth. He voiced unqualified approval of Baumstark's
"Ps.-Jonathan zu Dtn 34:6 und die Pentateuch-zitate Afrahaṭs,"
and he lamented the fact that earlier students of the Syriac
Pentateuch had generally neglected the Fathers.

Vööbus made an examination of Exod ch 15 and Deut ch 32
the centerpiece of his work, supplemented by collations of evidence for selected additional vss. He cited Aphr only six times,
in connection with Gen 49:10; Exod 32:32; Num 35:33; and Deut
32:39. It is not within the purpose of my study to assess the
general validity of Vööbus's book, which has already been evaluated in the most complete detail by Koster.[95] My interest is
limited to his utilization of Aphr's quotations, and in that
regard much the same criticism must be registered as was directed
to Baumstark. Vööbus nowhere undertook a complete analysis of
all (or even a large group) of Aphr's Pentateuch citations before
drawing upon them for textual evidence. Not only did he fail
to see that the majority of the readings are identical to P, but
he also failed to account scientifically for his deductions from
specific citations. Goshen-Gottstein justifiably has criticized
Vööbus's ad hoc selection of patristic quotations, pointing out
that "it is only meaningful to talk of 'mehr targumnahe,' if all
the quotations in a given source are examined and evaluated. The
atomistic selection of one or two examples from a given writing
. . . is hardly enough."[96]

Vööbus cited only two quotations from the Dems that are
from Gen-Exod. One of these, of Gen 49:10, was treated properly,
although Vööbus did not note all the citations of that vs that
occur in the Dems.[97] The other one, however, of Exod 32:32, was
treated entirely incorrectly; its use by Vööbus may serve as a
prime example of the error into which one can fall who attempts

to use patristic quotations selectively, without first under-
taking a systematic and comprehensive analysis of all the related
quotations in a source. Vööbus contrasted the reading of P for
Exod 32:32 (ܐܠܗܐ   ܟܬܒܐ ܡܢ ܚܠܐ‍ܝ--so MT) with one
from the Liber Graduum (ܚܝܐ ܕ   ܟܬܒܐ ܡܢ ܚܠܐ‍ܝ). Noting
that Aphr also appears to have known the latter reading, he
cited a passage from column 85 of Parisot.[98] What one finds at
that point (actually 84:27-85:3), however, is but an allusion to
Exod ch 32: "For Scripture declares about Moses that, on behalf
of his people, he gave his own life and was willing to be blotted
out of the book of life if only his people would not be blotted
out." Even by itself this allusion could not reasonably be taken
as an exact reproduction of Aphr's bible text. But the most
important fact is that in two other passages (see #217-#218
below) Aphr presents formal, direct quotations of Exod 32:32, in
both of which his text exactly corresponds to P. By failing to
study all three passages before reaching a decision about Aphr's
text of Exod 32:32, Vööbus fell completely into error.

This survey of past attention to Aphr's OT citations
points up the need for a comprehensive study of the citations in
their own right before an attempt is made to use them in defense
of any theory about the history of the P Pentateuch. Not only
must the value of each citation as a textual witness be tested
rather than merely assumed, all of the citations from a given
book or section of scripture need to be examined as a group.
Only then can an assessment of the underlying bible text
justifiably be ventured.

CHAPTER II

CITATIONS FROM GENESIS

Note on Format

        In chs II and III the format is as follows. All cita-
tions of a given bible passage are presented together in the
order of their occurrence within the Dems. Under each biblical
reference, the Syriac text of the pertinent citation(s) is reproduced exactly, preceded first by my reference number (#001, etc.),
then by notation of its location in the editions of Wright and
Parisot. This notation consists of the Dem number (upper-case
Roman numeral), then the section number in Wright (Arabic numeral)
and the section number in Parisot (Arabic numeral in parentheses),
and finally the page and line in Wright (e.g., 125:5-6) and the
column and line in Parisot. Ms variations in the Syriac text
of each citation are shown within braces { }, with the preferred
reading placed on the line. Interpunction and diacritical points
are given according to mss B-B, unless otherwise marked.
        The significance of the citation as a witness to Aphr's
bible text is then discussed. Those passages are identified in
which Aphr shows himself to be merely alluding to his text or
paraphrasing it, or in which the literalness of his quotation
is otherwise called into serious doubt. When there is not significant question about the general literalness of a citation,
following the discussion the bible text which it attests is reproduced (marked by *). Any portion of the citation which has been
identified in the discussion as of uncertain literalness is placed
within brackets []. Ellipsis points within brackets indicate
that, in quoting only a portion of a vs, Aphr leaves the remainder
of the vs unattested.
        Beneath the text that is reproduced from the citation,
a brief apparatus is presented to show its affinities. When this
text = all of the Syriac mss collated in Preface, Genesis-Exodus,
the notation is simply "Aphr = P," and no other comparisons are
made. (Note: In these apparatuses in chs II and III the sign
"P" thus has the special meaning of all P mss.) Careful attention has been given to the "Discussion of the Specific MSS" in
Preface, Genesis-Exodus, and where omissions and illegibilities
are listed for a Syriac ms in a particular vs, that ms has not
been included in my comparison. (Ms 12a1, because of its frequent
illegibility, has never been cited.) When the attested text

differs from at least one Syriac ms, comparisons are then shown
with Ephraem (Comm) (where available), MT, Sam, TO, TJ[1], TN[1],
TF (where available), TG[A-G] (where available), TSam, LXX, and
Vg. Witnesses in agreement with Aphr are listed immediately following the text-portion at issue within the closed bracket];
those differing are listed after this bracket. If the testimony
of a witness cannot be related to the reading in Aphr, the P mss,
or the MT, it is usually omitted.

Gen 1:2

#001 VI.13(14). 125:5-6; 292:26-293:1

ܘܬܐ ܪܚܫܐ ܘܗܘܐ. ܡܪܚܦܐ ܠܥ ܡܝܐ.

Not a formal quotation, this allusion to a clause from
Gen 1:2 occurs in a description of the activity of the Holy Spirit
at Christian baptism. The textual significance of the allusion
is uncertain, because Aphr's language here may well reflect a
priestly baptismal invocation rather than his text of Gen.[1] Even
if Aphr is alluding to scripture directly, the loss of the prepositional ܐܦܝ may be due to his own economizing rather than
to his bible text itself. It seems least likely that a text is
reflected here that is related to the LXX (ἐπάνω του ὕδατος; contrast α' σ' θ': ἐπὶ προσώπον ὕδατος/ων) and Vg (super aquas),
both of which are doubtless simply idiomatic renderings of the
MT (עַל-פְּנֵי הַמַּיִם; cf. Sam, Tgs, TSam). P and Ephraem (Comm I.7
lines 7-10) read ܠܥ ܐܦܝ̈ ܡܝܐ.

Gen 1:6-7

#002 XIV.18(34). 278:16-17; 660:2-3

ܘܬܒ ܪܩܝܥܐ ܒܡܨܥܬ ܡܝܐ ܘܦܪܫ ܒܝܬ
ܡܝܐ ܠܡܝܐ.

#003 XIV.21(36). 282:14-16; 668:20-22

$\left\{\begin{array}{l} \text{B} \\ \text{A} \end{array}\right.$ ܪܩܝܥܐ} ܐܠܗܐ܂ ܕܗܘܐ ܒܗ ܐܡܪ

ܒܡܨܥܬܐ ܕܡܝ̈ܐ ܕܗܘܐ ܦܪܝܣ ܠܬ ܒܝܢܬ ܡܝ̈ܐ ܠܡܝ̈ܐ.

#002 is a paraphrastic allusion to Gen 1:7, also echo-
ing various poetic passages (e.g., Ps 104:2; Job 9:8; Isa 44:24)
which speak of God "stretching out" (ܡܬܚ) the heavens. P
ܦܪܝܣ is echoed in its ܦܪܝܣܐ .

#003 is a formal quotation which actually consists of
a mixture of elements of Gen 1:6 and 7. In the process of
explaining how God manipulated the cosmos to produce the flood,
Aphr refers to the Gen ch 1 creation account for its details
about the arrangement of cosmic waters, sky, and dry land. The
Gen creation account is not itself the object of attention, however, and one may reasonably expect a reference to it to be presented as economically as possible. Accordingly, Aphr here mixes
the words of the creative command (1:6) with the narration of
the creative act (1:7). Such a conflation affords no certain
textual witness, but the text of P seems to be reflected in #003,
at least for much of Gen 1:6. The use of _dalath_ on ܕܗܘܐ,
in contrast to _waw_ in P, Ephraem (Comm I.17 line 26), and all
other witnesses, is most probably Aphr's own alteration of his
scripture text. The manner of citation ("For the firmament was
set for a boundary between the waters above the firmament and
the waters below, as it is written . . .") tends to cast the

46

final portion of vs 6 into the form of a purpose clause (". . .
that it may divide . . ."), which in fact may be the correct
understanding of the clause as it stands in P and MT. Dalath
more explicitly marks a purpose clause and is a natural substitution in Aphr's paraphrastic citation of the vs.

No textual significance attaches to the orthographic
variation ܪܩܝܘܠܪ/ܪܩܝܘܠܪ. Ms B consistently writes the
word without the prefixed aleph; ms A does so elsewhere eleven
times, but it uses the longer spelling four times.[2]

Gen 1:9-10

#004   XIV.21(36). 282:16-18; 668:23-26

ܡܠܚ ܚܢܐ ܡܢ ܐܝܟ ܐܘ ܒܢܬܐ ܠܐܬܘܬ ܥܠ.
ܠܟܢܐ ܕܡܝܐ ܩܝܐ ܠܚܡܐ ܡܫܝܬܐܘ
ܩܝ ܐܪܩܐ

Not a formal quotation, this paraphrase of parts of
Gen 1:9-10, while reflecting the text of P in places, nevertheless is too free to provide a clear textual witness. In the
second sentence, Aphr transposes the clauses of vs 10 from their
order in P and all witnesses. This is certainly his own construction, not that of his bible text. In the Gen narrative,
vs 10 mentions the dry land first because the appearance of dry
land is the immediately antecedent element at the end and climax
of vs 9. But in Aphr's paraphrase of vs 9, which occurs in a
discussion of the flood, it is the waters which are the focus
of attention; therefore, the waters are mentioned first in his

paraphrase of vs 10.

Gen 1:27

#005 LETTER. 4:18; 4:10-11

ܘܗܘ ܥܒܕ ܠܐܢܫܐ ܒܨܠܡܗ

#006 I.15(19). 22:14; 44:15-16

ܘܗܘ ܥܒܕ ܠܐܕܡ ܒܨܠܡܗ.

These appear to be allusions to Gen 1:27. However, each is paraphrastic, reflecting the influence of 1:26 (cf. Gen 9:6) as well, and provides no textual witness. That Aphr's bible text actually has the verb ܒܪܐ at 1:27, instead of ܥܒܕ, is indicated by #008 below.

Gen 1:28

#007 XIII.3(7). 336:13-15; 553:20-23

ܡܛܠ ܕܒܗ̇ܘ ܘܒܢܐ ܒܪ̈ܝܟܝܢ ܗܘܘ ܒ̈ܢܝ ܐܕܡ
ܕܦܪܘ ܘܣܓܘ ܒܬܘܠܕ̈ܬܗܘܢ. ܐܝܟ
ܕܬܡܠܐ ܡܢܗܘܢ ܥܠܡܐ.

#008 XVIII.1(1). 345:6-8; 817:9-11

ܘܐܡܪܝܢ ܠܡ ܕܐܠܗܐ {B omits / A ܠܡ} ܟܕ ܒܪܝܗܝ،
ܠܐܕܡ ܗܟܢܐ ܒܪܟܗ ܘܐܡܪ ܠܗ. ܕܦܪܘ
ܘܣܓܘ ܘܐܘܠܕܘ ܘܡܠܘ ܐܪܥܐ

#009 XVIII.2(2). 346:12-13; 820:19-20

ܠܐܕܡ ܟܕ ܕܒܪܝܗ ܐܠܗܐ {B ܐܡܪ / A ܘܐܡܪ}
ܠܗ. ܕܐܘܠܕܘ ܘܣܓܘ ܒܐܪܥܐ.

Because of the identification of #008 and #009 as God's directive to Adam, and of #007 as to the sons of Adam (prior to Noah), Gen 1:28 appears to be the intended source of the three citations. However, the variation among the three, the considerable difference between each of them and P (and other witnesses), and the strong reminiscences of parallel vss in P all suggest that Aphr here is quoting from memory and inexactly so.

#008 is the most literal to P and has the best claim to be a careful quotation; the absence of the final "and subdue it" (in all witnesses) has obviously been omitted simply because it is irrelevant to Aphr's argument here, which concerns only the propriety of Christian asceticism. Two variants to P occur within the citation: the initial verb ܣܓܝܘ (contrast P ܦܪܘ), and an additional verb (ܘܐ‍ܠܕ‍ܗ) inserted after ܘܣܓܘ.

It is entirely possible that Aphr's bible text reads an initial ܣܓܝܘ. P alternates between ܣܓܝ and ܦܪܐ in translating the Hebrew פרו, and there could be no surprise at a ms which contained ܣܓܝܘ here. On the other hand, there is no trace of such a reading among the P mss at 1:28, and Ephraem too (Comm I.30 lines 8-9) = P. If, as I think likely, Aphr is quoting *memoriter* and does not retain a clear distinction between the various biblical injunctions to fruitfulness, then the initial verb in #008 will be the result of influence from such passages as Gen 17:20; 28:3; Lev 26:9; and Jer 23:3, all of which begin with ܦܪܝ followed immediately by ܣܓܝ. The ease with which one, quoting from memory, could mix elements from similar vss is evident from the following list:

Gen 1:22 ܦܪܘ ܘܣܓܘ ܘܡܠܘ ܡܝܐ ܕܒܝܡܡܐ

1:28 ܦܪܘ ܘܣܓܘ ܘܡܠܘ ܐܪܥܐ

8:17 ܘܢܬܝܠܕܘܢ ܒܐܪܥܐ ܘܢܦܪܘܢ ܘܢܣܓܘܢ
ܥܠ ܐܪܥܐ

9:1 ܦܪܘ ܘܣܓܘ ܘܡܠܘ ܐܪܥܐ

9:7 ܘܐܢܬܘܢ ܦܪܘ ܘܣܓܘ ܘܐܬܝܠܕܘ
ܒܐܪܥܐ ܘܣܓܘ ܒܗ̇

17:6 ܘܐܦܪܝܟ ܘܐܣܓܝܟ ܛܒ ܛܒ

17:20 ܗܐ ܒܪܟܬܗ ܘܐܣܓܝܬܗ ܘܦܪܝܬܗ
ܛܒ ܛܒ

28:3 ܘܢܦܪܝܟ ܘܢܣܓܝܟ

35:11 ܦܪܝ ܘܣܓܝ ܛܒ

47:27 ܘܐܚܕܘ ܒܗ ܘܦܪܘ ܘܣܓܘ ܛܒ

Exod 1:17 ܦܪܘ ܘܐܬܝܠܕܘ ܘܣܓܘ ܘܥܫܢܘ
ܛܒ ܛܒ ܘܐܬܡܠܝܬ ܐܪܥܐ ܡܢܗܘܢ

Lev 26:9 ܘܐܦܪܝܟܘܢ ܘܐܣܓܝܟܘܢ

Jer 23:3 ܘܢܦܪܘܢ ܘܢܣܓܘܢ

Ezek 36:11 ܘܢܦܪܘܢ ܘܢܣܓܘܢ

The addition of ܘܐܬܝܠܕܘ gives longer pause, but it also is probably to be explained as Aphr's confusion of different vss. This memoriter citation of Gen 1:28 is contaminated

by Gen 9:7 P (and perhaps also by 8:17 and Exod 1:7), in which
the verb ܣܲܓܰܘ is again immediately followed by ܐܘܚܪܒ that
is also the third verb in the series. That Aphr tends to confuse
1:28 and 9:7 is further indicated by #073.

#007 obviously is paraphrastic, and, while the text of
P is echoed, no firm textual conclusions can be drawn from it.
It is, of course, noteworthy that his citation agrees with #008
in the use of ܓܒܪ, but the freedom displayed makes it certain
that Aphr's eyes are not on a bible text as he writes. Here
again his memory is faulty, confusing the verbal pattern in parallel vss, as in #008.[3]

The unreliability of Aphr's recall of this vs is vividly
demonstrated by #009, which, despite its ostensible derivation
from Gen 1:28 (the addressee is Adam), is clearly reflective of
Gen 9:7, albeit in telescoped form. Cautiously, one can conclude
that there is no evidence in these citations that indicates a
text before Aphr that differs from P in the injunction in 1:28.
The recurrence of a form of ܦܪܘ in each of the three appears
to echo the opening compound sentence of 1:28 P (only Syriac
ms 1111 omits the verb). But Aphr's introductory statements are
usually quite free, and little weight can be placed on them as
textual witnesses.

Gen 1:29; 9:2-3

#010   XV.4(3). 309:15-20; 733:26-736:7

ܣ ܐܪܒܢ ܚܝ ܕܘ ܒܪܚܡ ܚܒ ܠܒܪ ܐܠܐ

#011 XV.4(3). 310:3-5; 736:12-14

These citations purport to give God's directive to Adam
and Noah to eat any kind of meat, despite the fact that such a
directive is found only in Gen 9:2-3 (to Noah), not in 1:29-30
(to Adam). There is no reason to suppose that Aphr knows a text
of Gen 1:30 that differs drastically from all extant witnesses,
however. Rather, he is simply being careless as he seeks to
show that Jewish kashrut distinctions were not imposed by God
in the beginning, but only after the Egyptian sojourn. The verbal similarities between Gen 1:29-30 and 9:2-3 have led to confusion of the two passages; Aphr's memory is faulty.

Analysis of #010 shows that it is in fact a mixture of

elements from Gen 1:29; 9:13; Deut 12:16, 23, 27; 15:23; and possibly Lev 17:23. Such a memoriter mixture of related vss allows very little to be deduced concerning the specific readings in Aphr's bible text, even though most of the component vss can be identified.

ܗܐ ܝܗܒܬ ܠܟܘܢ These are the opening words of Gen 1:29 P.

ܚܝܘܬܐ ܘܦܪܚܬܐ ܘܟܠ ܒܣܪ No such series occurs in P or other witnesses. The first pair of nouns seems to derive from Gen 9:2 or Lev 17:13 P. "All flesh" never occurs in any such series, although ܒܣܪ is used in Deut 12:15-28 and Lev 17:10-14 P. Cf. ܘܟܠ ܕܪܚܫܐ ܕܚܝ in Gen 9:3 P.

ܫܘܕ ܕܡܗ ܥܠ ܐܪܥܐ ܘܐܟܘܠ While the general structure of this sentence is somewhat reminiscent of Deut 12:27 (". . . and the blood of your sacrifices is to be poured out on the altar of the Lord your God, but eat the flesh . . ."), it does not occur in the biblical text and is Aphr's own sentence. The verb ܫܘܕ is never used of blood in P.

ܘܐܝܟ ܝܘܪܩܐ ܝܗܒܬ ܠܟ This is a paraphrase of Gen 9:3 P (ܐܝܟ ܝܘܪܩܐ ܕܥܣܒܐ ܝܗܒܬ ܠܟܘܢ ܟܠ).

ܒܠܚܘܕ ܕܡܐ ܠܐ ܬܐܟܠܘܢ ܐܠܐ ܥܠ ܐܪܥܐ ܐܫܘܕܝܗܝ ܐܝܟ ܡܝܐ This = Deut 12:16 and 15:23 P; cf. 12:24.

ܡܛܠ ܕܕܡܐ ܢܦܫܐ ܗܘ This = Deut 12:23b P.

#011, which occurs only a few lines after #010 and is a restatement of it, is equally free, mixing elements of Gen 9:3 and Deut 12:15-16, but differently from #010.

‍ܪ‍ܠ‍ܟ ‍ܩ‍ܒ‍ܬ‍ܟ‍ܐ ‍ܪ‍ܠ ‍ܪ‍ܒܢ This = Deut 12:16 P.

‍ܠ‍ܩ‍ܒܟ‍ܐ ‍ܣܩ‍ܒ ‍ܝ‍ܩ‍ܒ ‍ܠ‍ܒ This paraphrases Deut 12:15 P; cf. Acts 10:13 and 11:7 (‍ܠ‍ܩ‍ܒܟ‍ܐ ‍ܣܩ‍ܒ . . .).

The singular verb forms here in ms B are to be taken as the preferred reading, with Wright and Parisot. Although a scribe might have corrected originally plural forms to agree with either of the biblical vss mentioned, the context of Aphr's sentence itself with its other plural forms must be considered the stronger influence on a copyist; ms B therefore presents the lectio difficilior.

‍ܝ‍ܩ‍ܒ‍ܠ ‍ܙ‍ܪ‍ܘ‍ܕ‍ܠ ‍ܪ‍ܒ‍ܓܢ ‍ܪ‍ܒ‍ܝ‍ܩ ‍ܝ‍ܪ‍ܟ‍ܐ

Like the fourth part of #010 above, this appears to be a very free paraphrase of a portion of Gen 9:3. The similarity of the two citations at this point is noteworthy, and Baumstark (translating, "und wie Grüngemüse so möge es [von] euch geachtet werden") concludes from it: "In diesem Sinne abgebogen muss Afrahat das Element also an beiden Stellen vorgefunden haben."[4] He fails to specify the source-text which he reconstructs, but apparently he posits a simple substitution of Aphr's reading (but ‍ܝ‍ܩ‍ܒ‍ܠ or ‍ܝ‍ܠ? with or without ‍ܪ‍ܒ‍ܓܢ?) for Gen 9:3b P (‍ܠ‍ܒ . . . ‍ܝ‍ܩ‍ܐ), of which the most important feature is the variation between ‍ܘ‍ܒ‍ܓܪ (P) and ‍ܙ‍ܪ‍ܘ‍ܕ‍ܠ. Baumstark's analysis is not convincing.

He fails to take sufficient account of the fact that, (a) both citations comprise a mixture of different vss that indicates a very faulty recall of the text on Aphr's part, and (b) even though identifiable vs-portions are reflected, they are handled very paraphrastically at points within both citations. Very little probability of authenticity can be accorded any variation from P in such circumstances, particularly when, as here, MT, Sam, Tgs, TSam, LXX, and Vg all agree with P against Aphr. Baumstark bases his case primarily on the repetition of this reading in both citations. But this is to assume that Aphr would not paraphrase a vs in the same way--an unfounded assumption, especially in citations separated by only a few lines.

Perhaps Baumstark's translation of ܬܬܚܫܒ ܠܟܘܢ here has prejudiced his view. In both citations he has chosen to see mankind as the subject of the verb: "it should be regarded by you as vegetation."[5] Neusner's translation, however, is more attractive: "Pour out the blood . . . and eat, and it will be regarded for you as a vegetable" [emphasis added].[6] In the latter, God is the subject of the verb, and Aphr's emphasis on discarding the blood is better incorporated: "as long as you pour out the blood, the consumed meat will be no more imputed to you as sin than is consumed vegetation." ܬܚܫܒ as "impute," "reckon," or "charge" is of course a familiar term in the Pentateuchal legislation. It occurs in Lev 17:4 P, the same chapter which contains prohibitions against eating blood, and in Lev 7:18; 25:31; and Num 18:27 ("And your offering shall be reckoned to you as though [. . . ܐܝܟ . . . ܠܟܘܢ ܘܬܚܫܒ] it were the grain . . ."). Since it has already been demonstrated that Aphr's recall of Gen 9:2-4 is influenced by related texts from Deut ch 12 and Lev ch 17, the most obvious explanation of ܘܬܚܫܒ here is that it has crept into his paraphrase of Gen 9:3 through its association with this similar Pentateuchal legal material.

Therefore, although Aphr's citations do not offer sufficient basis for reconstructing his text of Gen 9:3 in its entirety, one finds no clear indications of a text different from P.

Gen 1:31

#012 XVIII.6(8). 353:7-8; 836:22-23

ܟܠ ܡܕܡ ܕܥܒܕ . ܕܗܘܐ ܐܠܗܐ ܠܢ ܕܕܚܠܝܢ

ܘܗܘܐ ܠܗ ܫܦܝܪ

This formal citation is made in support of Aphr's assertion that one should not despise anything which God has created. The final clause of the biblical vs ("And it was evening . . .") is omitted simply because it is not pertinent.

*Gen 1:31 ܚ[] ܐܠܗܐ ܠܢ ܕܥܒܕ ܘܗܘܐ

ܠܗ ܫܦܝܪ [. . .]

Aphr = P

Gen 2:7

#013 VI.13(14). 125:11; 293:8-9

This formal citation of part of Gen 2:7 occurs in a
discussion of the creative and redemptive role of the Holy Spirit
in creation and conversion, respectively. The remainder of the
vs is not quoted because it is not relevant to the subject. The
readings of ms B are to be followed in both cases; Aphr invar-
iably follows his introductory formulae with dalath. The yud
on ܠܘܝܐ in ms A reflects an orthographic tendency seen elsewhere in ms A (cf. #153 below) and known in other Syriac mss.[7]

*Gen 2:7

Aphr = P

Gen 2:16-17

#014 VIII.7(19). 168:4-5; 393:2-4

#015 XI.4(3). 204:24-205:1; 473:16-19

#016 XIV.14(22). 265:18-20; 625:24-628:1

ܕܝܕܥܬܐ ܘܕܒܝܫܬܐ ܠܐ ܬܐܟܘܠ ܡܢܗ ܕܠܐ
ܬܡܘܬ

#017 XXII.(1). 419:9-11; 992:13-17

ܐܠܐ ܟܕ ܦܩܕ ܠܗ ܐܠܗܐ ܒܦܘܩܕܢܐ ܠܐܕܡ
ܗܢܐ ܗܘܐ ܘܐܡܪ ܠܗ. ܕܒܝܘܡܐ ܕܬܐܟܘܠ ܡܢ
ܐܝܠܢܐ { B omits / A ܕܛܒܬܐ } ܕܝܕܥܬܐ ܘܕܒܝܫܬܐ
ܡܘܬܐ ܬܡܘܬ.

#014, #016, and #017 are formal quotations; #015 is patently a paraphrase. #014 is a citation of Gen 2:17 made to support Aphr's preceding statement that, even while physically alive, people can be dead in God's sight. He goes on to explain that Adam remained alive 930 years after he violated the command of Gen 2:17, but he was regarded by God as dead all that time.[8] Aphr's interest in the vs then is clearly limited to the last sentence, primarily to ܡܘܬܐ ܬܡܘܬ. One might expect freedom in citing the preceding part of the vs, and in fact the use of the participle plus independent pronoun (contrast ܬܐܟܘܠ in #017, which = P) is doubtless Aphr's own deviation from his text. He inserts ܐܝܠܢܐ for clarity, since without Gen 2:16, his reader would not know the referent of ܡܢܗ (P).

#016 is a citation of Gen 2:16b-17, made to explain Aphr's preceding summary statement that "Adam sinned concerning food from the tree and went forth from Paradise." His chief concern is to make explicit the meaning of "food from the tree";

accordingly, his primary interest is in the prohibition contained in vs 17a. The part of the quotation that reproduces vs 17a is actually the only part that is literal. What precedes and follows it is handled freely. Aphr's text of vs 16b is here shortened to ܐܠܟܘܠ ܥܘܠܟ ܕܡ; but a fuller reading in Aphr's bible is indicated by ܦܪܕܝܣܐ ܐܝܠܢ ܟܠܗܘܢ in the preceding lines, to which ܟܠܗܘܢ within the citation refers. This construct chain contrasts with the prepositional phrase in P and Ephraem (Comm II.8 line 4): ܐܝܠܢ ܕܒܦܪܕܝܣܐ (cf. LXX). But it agrees with TN[1]: אילני גנתה. TO, TJ[1], and TSam also read the construct chain, but with the nomen regens in the singular. Despite this agreement with TN[1], it seems unlikely that Aphr's text of 2:16 is related to the targum. P itself reads ܐܝܠܢ ܕܒܦܪܕܝܣܐ (so Ephraem [Comm II.16 lines 6-7]) in the parallel clause in Gen 3:1, and it is probable that the latter vs has supplied the construct chain to Aphr's memory. ܡܕܡ ܕܝܢ, unattested in other witnesses (all read waw), is clearly Aphr's own stylistic alteration of his text. ܕܠܐ ܬܐܟܘܠ is the product of abbreviation.[9]

#017 is a condensed form of Aphr's text of vs 17. This citation occurs in the midst of an exposition of Rom 5:14 and is made simply to clarify the Gen background to that passage. The reading of ms B is probably the original, Wright and Parisot to the contrary. It is consistent with the economizing style of the citation, and the addition in ms A can be readily explained as scribal conformity to P. While the textual value of the citation is quite limited, no evidence is presented of a bible text varying from P.

#015 is an allusion to Gen 2:17 which clearly echoes vs 17a P. It is too free, however, to offer significant independent testimony. The final portion of #015 is a summary reference to the events of Gen 3:16-24; it contains no reflection of Aphr's text of 2:17, and no connection can be established between his use of ܐܬܚܝܒ and the conclusion of 2:17 in TJ[1]: תהי הייב קטול.

*Gen 2:17 ܡܢ[] ܐܝܠܢܐ ܕܝܕܥܬܐ ܕܛܒܬܐ
ܘܕܒܝܫܬܐ ܠܐ ܬܐܟܘܠ ܡܢܗ] . . .]ܒܝܘܡܐ
ܕܬܐܟܘܠ ܡܢܗ ܡܘܬܐ ܬܡܘܬ.

Aphr = P

Gen 2:24

#018 XVIII.8(10). 354:8-10; 840:5-7
ܚܢ ܫܡܥܢ ܡܢ ܢܡܘܣܐ ܕܢܫܒܘܩ ܓܒܪܐ ܠܐܒܘܗܝ
ܘܠܐܡܗ ܘܢܩܦ ܠܐܢܬܬܗ ܘܢܗܘܘܢ ܚܕ ܒܣܪ

#019 XVIII.8(11). 354:19-20; 840:22
ܘܐܡܪ ܕܢܗܘܘܢ ܬܪܝܗܘܢ ܚܕ ܒܣܪ.

These two citations of Gen 2:24, one apparently complete and one partial, occur within the same short section of Dem XVIII, but they present different readings: "they"/"the two of them." It is, of course, extremely doubtful that Aphr knows two different texts of Gen. All P mss read "the two of

them," and it may be that a scribe has corrected #019 to agree
with the P tradition. Whether intentional or accidental, however, such a correction of only one of two closely situated quotations is unlikely. It is more likely that Aphr quotes his
Gen text faithfully in #018 and then accidentally slips (from
memory) into the NT form of the clause (Matt 19:5; Mark 10:8;
and Eph 5:31 all read ܢܗܘܘܢ in P) in #019.

A third possibility must also be considered. Gen 2:24
forms the foundation of virtually all of Aphr's discussion in
this section of the Dem.[10] #018 begins the discussion, which
presents itself almost as a formal commentary: quotation of a
scripture vs followed by separate exposition of the text. However, Aphr treats this vs in two stages. Immediately following
#018, his discussion includes a word by word treatment of only
the first part of the vs (through ܐܢܬܬܗ). Then the last
portion of the vs is quoted again as #019, and it in turn is
discussed. It is not at all difficult to believe that in each
citation Aphr bothers to quote exactly only that portion of the
text upon which he is about to comment. Accordingly, in #018
he quotes carefully up through ܐܢܬܬܗ and then resorts to
some abbreviation in the final clause, omitting "the two of
them." When he is ready to treat this final clause of the vs,
however, he quotes it again, now doing so exactly. If this
explanation is correct, Aphr's bible text reads ܢܗܘܘܢ
(so Ephraem [Comm II.13 line 28]). It is impossible to reach

a conclusion concerning the presence of the reading "the two of them" in Aphr's bible, because these last two explanations are equally possible. Elsewhere, Aphr frequently condenses his text as he cites, and he also confuses a text with its slightly different NT form on a number of occasions. While the Syriac mss and most other witnesses attest the longer reading, MT and TO read simply "they."

In all other features Aphr's text appears to correspond to P. In #018 Aphr understandably omits the initial ܡܛܠ ܗܢܐ which is surely in his text. In P this phrase functions only to relate vs 24 to vs 23, which is not cited here.

<u>Gen 3:9</u>

#020 VII.3(8). 138:7-8; 324:6-7

ܟܕ ܚܛܐ ܐܕܡ. ܩܪܐ ܠܗ ܠܬܝܒܘܬܐ. ܟܕ ܐܡܪ
ܠܗ ܐܝܟܐ ܐܢܬ ܐܕܡ.

This formal quotation of God's question in Gen 3:9 is apparently exact. The text = Ephraem (Comm II.26 line 29).

*Gen 3:9 [. . .] ܐܝܟܐ ܐܢܬ ܐܕܡ.

Aphr = P

<u>Gen 3:12</u>

#021 XIV.26(42). 293:6-7; 696:6-9

ܐܕܡ ܟܕ ܚܛܐ ܩܪܐ ܠܗ ܡܪܗ ܕܢܬܘܒ ܘܠܐ ܩܒܠ.
ܘܐܫܬܥܝ ܒܡܠܬܐ ܕܚܘܐ ܠܡ ܐܛܥܝܬܢܝ

Although ܠܡ gives the final words, "Eve deceived me,"

the appearance of a literal citation from Gen 3:12, Aphr here is presenting only a free paraphrase, borrowing the verb from Eve's reply in Gen 3:13 P (cf. 1 Tim 2:14 P). No such verb is used in 3:12 in any of the witnesses, and Ephraem (Comm II.27 lines 6-7) = P. Aphr employs this same verb again in a second allusion to Gen 3:12 at 324:7-9 (ܗܐܪ‎), which illustrates the fact that on occasion he may depart from his bible text in the same way in different places.

<u>Gen 3:14-15</u>

#022 IX.6(8). 182:19-183:2; 424:25-425:4

#023 XIV.9(12). 255:7-11; 597:26-600:6

Both of these are paraphrastic and interpretative

allusions to Gen 3:14-15; neither is a formal citation. Although
both echo P, which Ephraem (Comm II.29 lines 24, 29, 1, 6-8) also
knows, neither is sufficiently literal to offer independent witness to Aphr's text. They deserve notice, however, because they
resemble TJ[1] in presenting haggadic expansions along with the
biblical text itself. Does Aphr know a text that is related to
TJ[1]?

Such a conclusion is unwarranted. There is simply no
evidence within #022 and #023 which indicates that the interpretative elements were a part of Aphr's text itself. Also, there
are substantial differences between these elements and the haggadic expansions in TJ[1]. In TJ[1], after ". . . on your belly you
will crawl" in vs 14, the text reads, "and your feet will be cut
off, and you will shed your skin every seven years, and the poi-
son of death will be in your mouth." Aphr's two allusions, however, contain the following different features:

(a) The serpent originally had feet, which were removed
in the curse.

(b) The serpent's feet were taken away because they
were the instruments by which he moved against man.

(c) The serpent fell upon the ground at the removal of
his feet.

(d) The serpent originally ate desirable food, which
was replaced by dust in the curse.

(e) The serpent's food was taken away because food was
the instrument of his deception of Eve.

Only (a) is shared with TJ[1].

Aphr's allusions also lack any trace of the targumic

version[11] of vs 15:

> And I will set hostility between you and the woman, between
> your descendants and her descendants, and when the descend-
> ants of the woman keep the commands of the Law, they will
> aim at you and will strike you on your head. And when they
> forsake the commands of the Law, you will aim and strike them
> on their heels. Nevertheless, for them there will be a rem-
> edy, but for you there will not be a remedy.

It cannot be finally excluded that Aphr's text contains haggadic expansions interwoven with literal translation, after the fashion of TJ[1]. Given the significant differences, however, it is impossible to establish close resemblance to or dependency upon TJ[1] or the other extant targums. The originality of such haggadic material within the targums is itself always question-able,[12] and there remains the possibility that the interpreta-tive elements of these two allusions are simply the product of Aphr's own independent exposition. Even if #022 and #023 do reflect acquaintance with Jewish hermeneutical tradition,[13] that acquaintance need not have been mediated to Aphr through the text of a Jewish targum.[14]

Gen 3:16-18

#024 VI.6(6). 113:16-19; 265:10-14

This allusion to Gen 3:16-18 is too paraphrastic to afford a clear view of Aphr's bible text. It appears, however, to echo the following texts in P:

3:16 ܘܒܟܐܒܐ ܬܐܠܕܝܢ ܒܢܝܐ

3:17 ܠܝܛܐ ܐܪܥܐ ܒܥܠܠܬܟ

3:18 ܟܘܒܐ ܘܕܪܕܪܐ ܬܘܥܐ ܠܟ

There is, of course, no question of the curse on the ground having been part of the woman's curse in Aphr's text. In accordance with his ascetic viewpoint, he is content simply to attribute all of the dislocations of the "Fall" to Eve as the chief protagonist. Cf. 1 Tim 2:14.

Gen 4:4-5

#025 LETTER.(2). 4:19; 4:11-12

ܘܗܘܩ ܕܩܒܠ ܩܘܪܒܢܗ ܕܗܒܝܠ.

#026 I.10(14). 18:4-5; 33:8-9

ܗܒܝܠ ܓܝܪ ܡܛܠ ܚܘܒܘܬܗ ܐܬܩܒܠ ܩܘܪܒܢܗ.

#027 III.2(2). 45:12; 101:1-2

ܠܩܘܕܡܝܢ ܗܘ، ܢܘܩܒܐ ܕܒܢܐ ܗܒܝܠ ܒܩܘܪܒܢܗ:

#028 IV.2(2). 60:16-61:10; 140:3-20

ܠܩܘܕܡܝܢ ܒܒܘܪܬ ܠܒܗ ܕܗܒܝܠ ܐܬܩܒܠ
ܩܘܪܒܢܗ ܩܕܡ ܐܠܗܐ. ܘܕܩܐܝܢ ܐܬܛܠܠ.
ܘܐܢܝܐ ܒܬܢܒ ܠܗ ܠܒܘܫܬܐ. ܕܐܬܩܒܠ
ܩܘܪܒܢܗ ܕܗܒܝܠ ܘܐܬܛܠܠ ܕܩܐܝܢ. ܘܒܢܐ
ܗܒܝܠ ܕܐܬܩܒܠ ܩܘܪܒܢܗ. ܘܐܦ ܩܐܝܢ ܬܘܒ

$$\left\{ \begin{array}{l} \text{B} \quad \text{ܗܘ ܐ\/ܐ} \\ \text{A} \quad \text{ܐܢܘܗ} \end{array} \right\} \ldots \text{ܪܬܚܠܘ ܒܠܬܗ. ܒܕ ܕܪܐܬܘܠܕ ܒܕ}$$

ܕܬܒܥܢܕܐ ܗܘܐ ܡܢ ܡܟ ܐܠܗܐ . . . ܒܕ ܒܪ . . . ܒܝܒ ܗܢ ܗܘ
. . . ܡܚܝܒܝܬܗܘܢܗ ܐܡܚܒܝܣܡ ܐܣܘܐ ܐܟܡܣ ܠܒܕ ܝܢܝ
ܣܟ ܣܟ ܗܢ ܒܕ ܒܪ ܡܢ ܠܡܝ ܕܐܪܒܠܕ ܡܗܒܝܬܗܡ.

$$\left\{ \begin{array}{l} \text{B} \quad \text{ܩܐ} \\ \text{A} \quad \text{ܗܐܩ} \end{array} \right\} \text{ܡܣ ܟܣ ܣܒܡ ܒܕ ܒܪ ܕܪܬܚܠܘ ܒܠܬܗ.}$$

#029 IV.3(3). 62:13-17; 144:9-14

ܣܒܡ ܕܩ ܐܠܟ ܒܒ ܒܕ ܒܕ ܡܣ ܒܕ ܗܣܘ. ܘܠܗ ܪܐܬܗ ܫܘܠܬ
$$\left\{ \begin{array}{l} \text{B} \quad \text{ܩܐܪܬܠܬܡ} \\ \text{A} \quad \text{ܩܠܬܘܚܬܡ} \end{array} \right\} \text{ܐܪܬܚܠܘܒܐ ܗܡܝܒܪܗ ܐܪܐ ܪ̈ܐܕ ܕܗܡܒܝ.}$$

ܘܗܒܒܘܫ̈ ܒܠܬܗ ܐܪܬܚܠܐ ܐܪܐ ܗܘ . ܗܣܐܕ ܗܘܐ . ܡܗ . ܐܗܡ
ܡܡ ܒܣ ܐܡܗ ܕܬܒܬܝܬ ܠܝ ܠܟ ܒܠ ܗܘܝܐ . ܗܪܕܬܚ
$$\left\{ \begin{array}{l} \text{B} \quad \text{ܗܒܒܝܪܬܡ} \\ \text{A} \quad \text{ܠܗܒܝܪܬܡ} \end{array} \right\} \text{ܠܟ ܒܠܗܐ . ܗܪܘܒܐ ܐܪܐ ܐܪܬܚܠܘ}$$

. ܕܗܒܡܝ

#030 VII.3(8). 138:11-12; 324:11-13

ܐܪܩ ܐܪܩܠ ܝܐܠ ܕܗܒܠܐ ܗܘܐ ܐܠܝܢ . ܗܩܐܒܝܪܚ
. ܐܝ ܣܒ ܡܟ ܗܒܝܪܡ.

These are all paraphrastic allusions to Gen 4:4-5; none
is a formal quotation. They are too free to serve as independent witnesses to Aphr's text as a whole, but they deserve notice
because of their consistent use of the verbs ܩܒܠܬ and ܣܐܠ.
The former is also used by TN[1] and TG[B] in Gen 4:4b-5a.

TN[1] וקבל ייי ברעווא ית הבל ואת קרבניה ולקין ולקרבניה

לא קבל ברעווא

TG^{B} וקבל מאמרא דאדני ברעוה ית הבל ואת-דורון דידה
ולקין ולדורון-דידה לא-קבל ברעוה

Ephraem also uses these verbs in paraphrasing the same vss (Comm III.3 lines 8-10): ܐܬܩܒܠ ܗܒܝܠ ܘܩܘܪܒܢ ܗܒܝܠ . ܩܐܝܢ ܠܐ ܦܪܘܫܘܬܗ ܕܗܒܝܠ . ܘܐܫܬܠܛ ܐܦ ܕܩܐܝܢ ܩܐܝܢ ܠܐ ܒܚܣܡܗ. Whereas the similarity to the targums is not particularly close, the fact that Aphr and Ephraem employ the same verbs is striking, and some possibility must be admitted that Aphr knows a text which reads these two verbs; perhaps: ܘܩܒܠ ܡܪܝܐ ܗܒܠ ܘܩܘܪܒܢܗ ܘܩܐܝܢ ܘܩܘܪܒܢܗ ܐܫܠܛ.

Nevertheless, only the most limited weight can be placed on such paraphrastic allusions (Ephraem also does not quote literally in the passage cited above). The verb ܩܒܠ is a completely natural choice for describing the Cain and Abel incident. It is used in P itself in the same narrative in Gen 4:7, and it is frequently used in P for the divine acceptance of sacrifices (e.g., Lev 7:18; 19:7; 22:21, 23, 25, 27; 23:11; Ezek 20:41; Rom 12:1; Phil 4:18; 1 Pet 2:5). Common creedal or liturgical usage may have further suggested ܩܒܠ to Aphr, if the Symbols in the Letter and Dem 1.(14) do reflect a confessional formula, as has been suggested.[15]

#031 VII.3(8). 138:13-14; 324:14-16

ܐܡܪ ܠܩܐܝܢ ܕܐܢ ܬܛܝܒ ܩܒܠܬ ܩܘܪܒܢܟ .
ܘܐܠܐ ܬܛܝܒ . ܚܛܝܬ ܗܘ ܫܠܐ ܠܟ .

Although this might be taken for a formal quotation, it is clearly an interpretative paraphrase of Gen 4:7. Accordingly, its textual value is very limited. The final clause is unquestionably a summary of the final three clauses of the biblical vs; no other witness (including Ephraem [Comm IV.4]) has a similar reading.

Given this apparent tendency to paraphrase in the citation, the addition of "your sacrifice" in the apodosis of the first sentence is probably Aphr's own addition to his text, in which, as in P, the direct object of the verb ܡܩܒܠܬ is not expressed: "I will accept (it)." Cf. Ephraem (Comm IV.4 line 28): ܒܪܡ ܕܝܢ ܐܢ ܬܫܦܪ ܥܘܠܬ. Nevertheless, it cannot be finally ruled out that Aphr's bible contains the noun. The absence of initial ܗܐ (P) will probably be a further mark of Aphr's freedom in the direction of clarity and conciseness.

<u>Gen 4:9</u>

#032 VII.6(16). 144:3-4; 337:2-4

ܕܟܕ ܐܬܪܥܝ ܕܩܛܠ ܠܐܚܘܗܝ. {B ܐܡܪ / A ܘܐܡܪ}

ܕܠܐ ܝܕܥܐ ܐܢܐ ܗܒܠ. ܡܛܠ ܕܠܐ

ܗܘܬ ܢܛܪܗ.

#033 XIV.26(42). 293:8-9; 696:10-13

ܘܩܐܝܢ ܟܕ ܩܛܠ ܠܐܚܘܗܝ، ܡܠܠ ܒܥܘܗ ܐܝܟ

ܕܬܘܬܐ ܘܬܘܒ. ܘܐܫܬܐܠ ܒܡܠܬ ܕܢܟܠܬܐ.

.ܠ ܐܝܢ ܡܠ ܐܕܗ

What Aphr presents in #032 as a formal quotation of
Cain's reply to God is Aphr's paraphrastic condensation of his
bible text. Although it is impossible to be certain of the
exact form of his text, nothing here gives indication that it
differs from P.

Also in #033 Aphr presents in the form of a literal
citation (ܡܠ) what is his own restatement of Cain's reply,
differently here than in #032. This occurs in a discussion
where he sets forth Adam and Cain as examples of the kind of
dissimulation before God to avoid: "And also do not be like
Cain, who when he was accused of killing his brother. . . ." To
emphasize Cain's evasion of God, in #033 Aphr recasts Cain's rhetorical question (P = MT) into the form of a direct denial. He
places on Cain's lips a response of his own composing, one that
communicates the essence, but not the words, of Cain's actual
statement. Ephraem (Comm III.6 lines 27-28) = P.

Gen 4:8, 12, 14, 15

#034 V.3(3). 80:8-9; 185:17-19

. ܡܠܠܗܘ ,ܗܘܝܐ ܠܡܗ ܠ ܥܠܩ ܐܒܪܐܬܐܪ
. ܐܝܪܟܐ ܗܪܠܘ ܥܠܝ ܐܗܡܐ {B ܐܬܬܐܪܘ}
                              [A ܐܬܐܪܘ]

#035 VII.3(8). 138:14-15; 324:16-17

. ܐܬܐܪܘ ܡܠܠܗ ܐܠܘܝ ,ܗܘܝܐܠ ܠܠܗܘ
. ܐܝܪܟܐ ܗܪܠܘ ܥܠܝ ܐܗܡܐ

#036 IX.6(8). 183:2-3; 425:4-6

ܘܩܐܝܢ ܕܩܛܠ ܠܗܒܝܠ ܒܚܣܡܗ. ܡܛܠ ܠܩ̈ܛܠܬܐ
ܠܥܒܕ ܕܝ̈ܢ. ܘܗܘܐ ܙܥ ܘܢܐܕ ܒܐܪܥܐ.

#037 XIV.7(10). 252:17; 592:18-19

ܘܩܐܝܢ ܒܪܫܥܘܬܗ ܩܛܠ ܠܐܚܘܗܝ ܘܗܘܐ
ܙܥ ܘܢܐܕ ܒܐܪܥܐ

None of these is a formal citation; all are allusions which appear to echo Aphr's text to some extent. Although all four allude to the final sentence of Gen 4:8, none is sufficiently literal to afford a clear textual witness. #034 is a possible exception; it reproduces that sentence from P exactly, except for the use of the verb ܐܫܬܒܗܪ instead of ܩܡ. This substitution is surely due to Aphr's deliberate interpretation of his bible text, however. #034 occurs in a passage where he illustrates the prevalence of self-glorification among scriptural figures; the verb ܐܫܬܒܗܪ is used repeatedly there as a key word. Whether or not Aphr is consciously quoting the sentence from Gen 4:8, this reflection of P may be taken tentatively as evidence that he knows a text = P, as does Ephraem (Comm III.5 line 14).

The clause that is repeated in each of these allusions, "and he was a wanderer and a fugitive in the land," is a nearly literal quotation of the clause that occurs in Gen 4:12 and 14, with only a variation in the verb form. Despite the lack here of a formal quotation of either of those vss, one can assume

that Aphr probably knows a text identical to P in that clause
in both passages.

#036 is of special interest because of its resemblance
to the targums in reading "for seven generations." "Cain . . .
received curses for seven generations" is an allusion to Gen
4:15 and raises the question of a targumic bible text in front
of Aphr at this point. The parallel sentence in the targums is
as follows:

TO   כל קטוליא קין לשבעה דרין יתפרע מניה

TJ[1]   כל דקטיל קין לשבעא דרון יתפרע מיניה

The meaning of these almost identical texts is clear: "Anyone
who kills Cain will be punished for seven generations." The
meaning of TN[1] and TG[B] is not so clear:

TN[1]   כל דיקטול קין עד שובעה דרין יתלי ליה

TG[B]   כל-דקטל לקין עד-שבעה דרין יתלא-לה

The most natural translation of these texts, given the context
and the parallel use of יתפרע in TO and TJ[1] is: "Anyone who
kills Cain, for seven generations it [i.e., the consequent
guilt] will be attached to him."[16] Díez Macho,[17] however, followed by Le Déaut and Robert,[18] translates יתלי in vs 15 exactly
as in vs 24, which is not an exact parallel: [Lamech speaking]
"If Cain, who killed Abel, unto seven generations had [judgment]
suspended [איתלי] for him. . . ." He renders vs 15: "Anyone
who kills Cain unto seven generations shall (judgement) be suspended for him."[19]

Unfortunately, this translation by Díez Macho is

ambiguous as it stands. Does it promise seven generations of
reprieve for Cain's murderer? So it would seem; yet such a dec-
laration is non-sensical in the context. Does it constitute an
aside by God, who remembers that a murderer of Cain would have
to wait seven generations for punishment in the Noahic flood
and who therefore gives Cain the protective mark? Possibly,
but this too is very awkward. Perhaps this translation suffers
from a lack of punctuation, which would have identified the
opening words as a vocative: "(To) anyone who would kill Cain:
For seven generations is judgment to be suspended for him (i.e.,
Cain)."

Whatever the correct translation of TN[1] and TG[B], the
main point is that none of the four targumic texts speaks of
seven generations as the duration of Cain's punishment. This
is different from Aphr, who says that Cain, not his would-be
murderer, was cursed with punishment for seven generations.
Aphr appears, therefore, to be interpreting a text of vs 15 that
differs from these targums. There is in fact no indication that
his text differs appreciably from P. Apparently, Aphr understands the syntactic structure of vs 15 quite differently from
what is suggested by a knowledge of the MT. His exegesis of
the vs is described by Ephraem (Comm III.8 lines 6-12):

> For although some say that Cain protested the death sentence,
> others say that he was asking for death [i.e., at the end
> of vs 14] and that because of this [request] God said to
> him: "No! For it will be as you have said for murderers
> who come after you [chronologically]; as for the murderers
> who come after you, in the very hour that they are found
> they will die. But Cain will be punished seven-fold"

[ܣܝܘܕܝ ܪܐܙܪܐ ܙܘ ܝܪܩܐ ܪܐܪ]. For because
he asked for death, so that men would not gloat over his
humiliation, seven generations [ܝܚܪܢ ܝܪܝ] will come
and will witness his humiliation. Then he will die.

Aphr is apparently among those "others" who interpret
vs 14, not as a complaint by Cain, but as a wish: ". . . and
let anyone who finds me, kill me." Accordingly, he understands
the first words of vs 15 as God's answer to this plea: "But the
Lord said to him, 'No!'" The interpretation mentioned by Ephraem
further shows that the next three words of vs 15 are read as a
syntactic unit: "Thus [i.e., experiencing a prompt death] every
["other" understood] murderer." Perhaps Aphr's text adds lamad
to ܠܒ. Or perhaps his text agrees with mss 11/9b1 → (ܠܒ
ܝܝܘܕܝ ܪܐܩܒܐ), a reading whose addition in any case
confirms the interpretative tradition described by Ephraem and
shows that ܪܐܩܒܐ ܠܒ ܪܘܣܩ were read as a unit, as
does the point placed after ܪܐܩܒܐ in ms 7a1.

This leaves the next four words of P to be read as a
syntactic unit, again with the points in ms 7a1, which is the
basis for the statement Aphr makes in #036. "Cain will be punished seven-fold"; ܣܝܘܕܝ ܪܐܙܪܕ ܙܘ ܝܪܩܐ. One
looks for a contrastive particle at the beginning of this clause.
Ephraem quotes the clause exactly as in P but with initial
ܪܐܪ added; this, however, may be his own stylistic addition,
especially since he makes the quotation within a larger paraphrastic sentence of his own.

Although Aphr may know a text of vs 15 that has minor

additions to P (and this remains entirely uncertain), one can say confidently that his "seven generations" does not signal knowledge of a text of one of the extant targums. "For seven generations" is in all probability simply Aphr's interpretation of a text reading ܥܕ ܠ/ܫܒܥܐ, one which is by no means unique to him.[20]

*Gen 4:8 [. . .] ܘܐܡܪ ܠܗܒܝܠ ܐܚܘܗܝ ܘܩܛܠܗ

Aphr = P

Gen 5:1

#038 XXIII.(44). 480:14-19; II 84:17-24

ܡܢ ܐܕܡ ܒܪܝܐ ܕܟܠ ܢܘܚ ܠܡܒܘܠܐ ܗܘܝ

ܫ̈ܢܝܐ ܐܠܦ ܘܫܬܡܐܐ ܘܚܡܫܝܢ ܘܚܕܐ ܐܝܟ

ܡܕܡ ܕܒܣܦܪ ܬܘܠܕ̈ܬܐ ܟܬܝܒ. ܘܡܢ {A,B ܟܕ | C ܕܟܕ}

ܢܦܩ ܢܘܚ ܡܢ {A,B ܩܒܘܬܐ | C ܡܩܒܘܬܐ} {B ܒܒܪܝܐ | A,C ܘܒܒܪܝܐ}

ܠܒܢܝܐ ܕܐܡܠܠ ܐܠܗܐ ܡܪܝܐ ܥܡ ܐܒܪܗܡ

ܗܘܝ ܫ̈ܢܝܐ ܬܠܬܡܐܐ {A,B ܘܬܡܢܝܢ ܘܫܒܥ | C ܘܦܙ}

ܫ̈ܢܝܢ ܐܝܟ ܡܕܡ ܕܒܣܦܪ ܬܘܠܕ̈ܬܐ ܟܬܝܒ.

This passage is of interest because of its two references to "the book of generations." There is no question of a direct quotation here. The two figures listed, 1651 years and 387 years, do not appear in the Gen text of any ancient version; they are Aphr's own calculations, arrived at by adding together

the various ages given in Gen for various characters at the birth
of each's eldest son or at some other noteworthy event. The
foundation for these calculations has been already laid down by
Aphr in sections (22)-(43) of Dem XXIII, to which section (44)
serves as a preliminary conclusion. I can locate no extra-bib-
lical chronographic table which Aphr might be citing here instead
of computing directly from the biblical text.

Actually, Aphr does not claim that his two totals are
themselves written anywhere. Despite the misleading translations
of Parisot ("sicut in libro Generationum conscriptum est") and
Bert ("wie im Buch der Geschlechter geschrieben steht"[21]), the
expression that Aphr uses literally says, "according to that
which is written in the Book of Generations,"[22] by which he
claims only that his figures are consistent with or dependent
upon data found in the source referred to.

Assuming that this reference here is to Gen, the question remains whether he knows a text which has such an expression as its formal title or as the formal title for some section.
No such formal title is evidenced elsewhere in Hebrew or Syriac
sources. The Greek equivalent (ἡ βίβλος τῶν γενέσεων) is used
as a title, however, in LXX ms 129. The one time that Aphr
unquestionably refers to Gen by a title (496:2), he uses the
expected ܪܬܝܒ. While he may have known more than one title
for Gen, it seems more reasonable that ܪܬܝܠܝܕܘܬܐ ܣܦܪ
simply represents Aphr's informal descriptive name for Gen as
a whole or perhaps for its genealogical tables (especially

chs 5 and 11). Such a title could be derived quite naturally from Gen 5:1 P (ܗܢܐ ܣܦܪ ܬܘܠܕܬܗ ܕܐܕܡ) and the similar formula (ܗܠܝܢ ܬܘܠܕܬܐ ܕ) in Gen 2:4; 6:9; 10:1; 11:10, 27; etc.

<u>Gen 5:3-5</u>

#039 XIII.4(6). 236:3-4; 553:5-6

ܐܦ ܐܕܡ ܕܒܪ ܡܐܐ ܘܬܠܬܝܢ ܫܢܝܢ ܐܘܠܕ
ܠܫܝܬ.

#040 XXIII.(22). 474:6-11; II 68:8-14

ܘܟܕ ܗܘܐ ܐܕܡ ܒܪ ܡܐܐ ܘܬܠܬܝܢ ܫܢܝܢ
ܐܘܠܕ ܠܫܝܬ. ܘܚܝܐ ܐܕܡ ܡܢ ܒܬܪ ܕܐܘܠܕ
ܠܫܝܬ ܬܡܢܡܐܐ ܫܢܝܢ ܫܒܥܐ {A,B omit / C ܕܝܢ}
ܕܫܢܘܗܝ ܬܫܥܡܐܐ ܘܬܠܬܝܢ ܫܢܝܢ. ܒܫܢܬܐ
ܠܫܝܬ ܬܠܬܝܢ ܘܫܒܥܐ ܠܚܢܘܟ ܠܩܝܢ ܕܐܘܠܕ ܠܠܡܟ
ܚܝܐ ܐܕܡ. ܘܡܝܬ ܒܕܪܐ ܬܫܝܥܝܐ.

#040 is part of an extended chronographic presentation in which Aphr exhaustively details synchronisms of the births, deaths, and other important events (especially the flood and the exodus) in the biblical history. More precisely, #040 is one section of a complex genealogical table that comprises sections (22)-(42) of Dem XXIII. There can be no doubt that Aphr has patterned this material after Gen 5:3-31 and 11:10-26. Not only is the verbal format quite similar, the names included are essentially the same. Sections (22)-(30) trace the line from

Adam-Seth to Lamech-Noah, as does Gen 5:3-31, including precisely
the same intervening persons. Sections (32)-(42) follow Gen
11:10-26 exactly, with the exception that Aphr adds Abraham-Isaac
and Isaac-Jacob at the end. This addition is made in order to
complete the reckoning from Adam to the sojourn in Egypt. Aphr's
interest is primarily chronological, not genealogical.

While there can be no doubt that the text of Gen 5:3-31
and 11:10-26 is Aphr's source, he adds material from other biblical passages to supply additional information, usually of synchronic relevance. Each component of sections (32)-(42) follows
approximately this pattern, which mirrors almost exactly that of
Gen 5:3-31, with modifications based on 11:10-26:

> N^1 lived X years and fathered N^2. After he fathered N^2,
> N^1 lived X years. The total of his years was X years.
> [Often an additional synchronic note is added here.] And
> he died [sometimes an additional synchronic note is added
> here] in the Xth generation.

The reckoning of the number of the generation is Aphr's own addition. The omission of the bible's "and had other sons and daughters" is deliberate economizing; such information is irrelevant
to Aphr's chronological calculations.

It is impossible to tell whether Aphr is working from
memory or actually has before him a text of Gen. It is clear
that he uses a free hand in conforming the biblical vss to the
slightly different pattern of his own table in sections (22)-
(42).[23] For that reason, #040 and the other quotations from
these sections cannot be regarded as formal citations. Their

primary value lies in their testimony to the chronological readings in Aphr's text of Gen chs 5 and 11, readings which, in at
least one case, may be different from P.

In #040 the sentence begins, "When Adam was . . .";
this is different from P and other witnesses and is certainly
Aphr's stylistic accommodation to the preceding sentences with
which he has initiated the entire presentation in section (22).

#039 is one element of a much simpler, briefer chrono-
graph in section (6) of Dem XIII that is inserted there to prove
that Noah could not have had a wife and fathered sons before
being told about the coming flood. This material is derived
from chs 5 and 11 of Gen also, but the various components are
even less reflective of the actual text of the corresponding
biblical vss than is the case with the chronograph in Dem XXIII.
Only the numeral itself is of textual importance.

    *Gen 5:3   ܫܢܝ̈ܢ ܕܬܠܬܝܢ ܐܝܟܐ ܒܪ ܐܕܡ [. . .]
           ܠܫܝܬ [. . .] ܘܐܘܠܕ[]

    Aphr = P

    *Gen 5:4   ܘܐܘܠܕܗ ܫܝܬ ܡܢ ܐܕܡ ܗܘܐ
           [. . .] ܫܢܝ̈ܢ ܠܬܡܢܡܐ ܠܫܝܬ

ܐܕܡ ܗܘܐ   7a1 7h5 7k4 915.6 10b1 10g1 11/9b1
1114.5 12b1] ܕܐܕܡ ,ܘܚܝܐ ܘܡܗ 8/5b1 MT
Sam(כל ימי) TO TJ1 TN1(כל יומי) LXX Vg

    *Gen 5:5 [ܘܡܝܬ]   ܫܢܝ̈ܢ ܕܬܠܬܝܢ ܕܟܬܒܘ [. . .]

    Aphr = P

          Gen 5:6-8

#041 XIII.4(6). 236:4-5; 553:6-7

ܘܒܫܢܬ ܒܪ ܡܐܐ ܘܚܡܫ ܫܢܝ̈ܢ ܐܘܠܕ ܠܐܢܘܫ .

#042 XXIII.(23). 474:11-16; II 68:15-22

ܘܚܝܐ ܫܝܬ ܡܐܐ ܘܚܡܫ ܫܢܝ̈ܢ ܘܐܘܠܕ ܠܐܢܘܫ:
ܘܚܝܐ ܫܝܬ ܡܢ ܒܬܪ ܕܐܘܠܕ ܠܐܢܘܫ .
ܬܡܢܡܐܐ ܘܫܒܥ ܫܢܝ̈ܢ . { ܫܢܐ A,B | ܒܡܢܐ ܕܫܢܐ C }
ܕܚܘܒܗܝ ܬܫܥܡܐܐ { ܘܬܪܬܥܣܪܐ B | ܘܝܒ C | ܘܬܫܥܣܪܐ A } ܫܢ̈ܝܢ .
ܒܡܢܐ ܠܡܢܐ { ܘܬܡܢܐܝܢ A,B | ܘܬܡܢܝܢ C } ܠܫܢ̈ܝ
ܠܡܢ. ܚܝܐ ܬܫܥܝܢ ܫܢ̈ܝܢ ܡܢ ܩܕܡ ܡܠܟܗ
ܕܢܘܚ ܘܡܝܬ ܒܪܐ ܡܬܘܫܠܚ .

These two passages occur, respectively, in the chronographic passages discussed above. In #042, the reading "twelve" in mss B and C is to be followed, with Parisot and against Wright. The reading in ms A ("nineteen") is surely the result of dittography of the first element in the immediately preceding numeral.

*Gen 5:6 ܘܚܝܐ ܫܝܬ ܡܐܐ ܘܚܡܫ ܫܢ̈ܝܢ .
ܘܐܘܠܕ ܠܐܢܘܫ .

Aphr = P

*Gen 5:7 ܘܚܝܐ ܫܝܬ ܡܢ ܒܬܪ ܕܐܘܠܕ ܠܐܢܘܫ
ܬܡܢܡܐܐ ܘܫܒܥ ܫܢ̈ܝܢ [. . .]

Aphr = P

*Gen 5:8 [. . .]ܬܫܥܡܐܐ ܘܬܪܬܥܣܪܐ ܫܢܝ̈ܢ
[ܘܡܝܬ]

Aphr = P

Gen 5:9-11

#043 XIII.4(6). 236:5; 553:7-8

ܘܐܢܘܫ ܒܪ ܬܫܥܝܢ ܫܢ̈ܝܢ ܐܘܠܕ ܠܩܝܢܢ.

#044 XXIII.(24). 474:16-21; II 68:23-69:4

ܘܚܝܐ ܐܢܘܫ ܬܫܥܝܢ ܫܢ̈ܝܢ ܘܐܘܠܕ ܠܩܝܢܢ.
ܘܚܝܐ ܐܢܘܫ ܡܢ ܒܬܪ ܕܐܘܠܕ ܠܩܝܢܢ
ܬܡܢܡܐܐ ܘܚܡܫܬܥܣܪܐ ܫܢ̈ܝܢ ܣܟܐ ܕܫܢܘܗ̇،
ܬܫܥܡܐܐ ܘܚܡܫ ܫܢ̈ܝܢ ܘܚܝܐ ܐܢܘܫ ܥܕܡܐ
ܠܫܢܬ ܫܬ̈ܝܢ ܘܬܫܥ ܫܢ̈ܝܢ ܠܝܬܪ ܢܘܚ ܥܕܡܐ
ܠܫܢܬ ܬܫܥܡܐܐ ܘܥܣܪܝܢ ܘܚܕܐ ܡܢ ܩܕܡ
ܡܒܘܠܐ. ܘܡܝܬ ܒܪܐ {ܬܡܢܝܐ B,C / ܕܬܡܢܝܐ A}.

These two passages also occur, respectively, in the chronographic tables discussed above.

*Gen 5:9 ܘܚܝܐ ܐܢܘܫ ܬܫܥܝܢ ܫܢ̈ܝܢ
ܘܐܘܠܕ ܠܩܝܢܢ.

Aphr = P

*Gen 5:10 ܘܚܝܐ ܐܢܘܫ ܡܢ ܒܬܪ ܕܐܘܠܕ
ܠܩܝܢܢ ܬܡܢܡܐܐ ܘܚܡܫܬܥܣܪܐ ܫܢ̈ܝܢ
[. . .]

Aphr = P

*Gen 5:11 [. . .]ܬܫܥܡܐܐ ܘܚܡܫ ܫܢ̈ܝܢ

[ܘܡܝܬ]

Aphr = P

Gen 5:12-14

#045 XIII.4(6). 236:5-6; 553:8-9

ܘܩܝܢܢ ܒܪ ܫܒܥܝܢ ܫ̈ܢܝܢ ܐܘܠܕ ܠܡܗܠܠܐܝܠ.

#046 XXIII.(25). 474:21-475:4; II 69:5-13

ܘܚܝܐ ܩܝܢܢ ܫܒܥܝܢ ܫ̈ܢܝܢ ܘܐܘܠܕ ܠܡܗܠܠܐܝܠ

ܘܚܝܐ ܩܝܢܢ ܡܢ ܒܬܪ ܕܐܘܠܕ ܠܡܗܠܠܐܝܠ

{A,B ܬܡܢܡܐܐ ܘܐܪ̈ܒܥܝܢ / C ܬܬܡ} ܫ̈ܢܝܢ {A,B ܗܟܐ / C ܘܗܟܐ}

ܕܚܝܘ̈ܗܝ. {A,B ܬܫܥܡܐܐ ܘܥܣܪ / C ܬܬܩܝ.} ܫ̈ܢܝܢ. ܘܚܝܐ

ܡܢ ܒܪܝܐ ܠܥܠܬ ܕܡܐܐ ܘܥܣܪ̈ܝܢ ܘܬܠܬ

ܠܬܝܢ ܠܘܬ ܒܪܝܐ ܠܥܠܬ {ܐܪ̈ܒܥܡܐܐ / ܬܠܬܐ}

ܘܟܠܗܘܢ {A,B ܘܚܝܐ / C} {ܡܢ ܩܕܡ ܡܒܘܠܐ A,C / B omits}

ܘܡܝܬ ܒܕܪܐ ܥܒܝܕܐ.

These two passages also occur, respectively, in the chronographic tables discussed above.

*Gen 5:12 ܘܚܝܐ ܩܝܢܢ ܫܒܥܝܢ ܫ̈ܢܝܢ ܘܐܘܠܕ ܠܡܗܠܠܐܝܠ

Aphr = P

*Gen 5:13 ܘܚܝܐ ܩܝܢܢ ܡܢ ܒܬܪ ܕܐܘܠܕ ܠܡܗܠܠܐܝܠ ܬܡܢܡܐܐ ܘܐܪ̈ܒܥܝܢ

ܫ̈ܢܝܢ [. . .]

Aphr = P

*Gen 5:14 [. . .] ܬܫܥܡܐܐ ܘܥܣܪ ܫ̈ܢܝܢ
[ܘܡܝܬ]

Aphr = P

Gen 5:15-17

#047 XIII.4(6). 236:6-7; 553:9-10

ܘܡܗܠܠܐܝܠ ܒܪ ܫܬܝܢ ܘܚܡܫ ܫ̈ܢܝܢ ܐܘܠܕ ܠܝܪܕ.

#048 XXIII.(26). 475:4-10; II 69:14-22

ܘܚܝܐ ܡܗܠܠܐܝܠ ܫܬܝܢ ܘܚܡܫ ܫ̈ܢܝܢ ܘܐܘܠܕ
{ܠܝܪܕ B,C | ܠܝܪ̈ܕ A} ܘܚܝܐ ܡܗܠܠܐܝܠ ܡܢ ܒܬܪ
ܕܐܘܠܕ ܠܝܪܕ ܬܡܢܡܐܐ {ܘܬܠܬܝܢ B,C | ܘܬܠܬ A} ܫ̈ܢܝܢ
ܗܘܘ ܕܝ̈ܘܡܘܗܝ، {ܬܡܢܡܐܐ ܘܬܫܥܝܢ ܘܚܡܫ A,B | ܬܬܝܢ ܗ C}
ܫ̈ܢܝܢ ܘܚܝܐ ܡܗܠܠܐܝܠ ܥܕܡܐ ܠܫܢܬ
ܡܐ̈ܬܝܢ ܘܐܪܒܥܡܐ̈ܐ ܫ̈ܢܝܢ ܠܫܢ̈ܝ ܢܘܚ
ܥܕܡܐ ܠܫܢܬ {ܬܠܬܡܐܐ ܘܬܡܢܝܢ | ܫܒܥ}
ܘܫܬ {A,B | C} ܡܢ ܡܢܩ ܥܠܡܐ. ܘܫܢܬ ܒܪܝܐ
ܫܬܬܐ.

These two passages also occur, respectively, in the chronographic tables discussed above. Mechanical error clearly is responsible for the two readings in ms A (in #048) which differ from mss B and C. The double pointing of the final letter in the second occurrence of "Yarad" in ms A is surely the result of a corrected scribal error. The numeral "three" in ms A, which is incompatible with the total given in the same ms for the life span of Malalael, is the result of accidental haplography (cf. the plural ending on the following word, ܫܢ̈ܝܢ).

*Gen 5:15 ܘܚܝܐ ܡܗܠܠܐܝܠ ܫܬܝܢ ܘܚܡܫ
ܫܢ̈ܝܢ ܘܐܘܠܕ ܠܝܪܕ.

Aphr = P

*Gen 5:16 ܘܚܝܐ ܡܗܠܠܐܝܠ ܡܢ ܒܬܪ
ܕܐܘܠܕ ܠܝܪܕ ܬܡܢܡܐܐ ܘܬܠܬܝܢ ܫܢ̈ܝܢ
[. . .]

Aphr = P

*Gen 5:17 [. . .] ܬܡܢܡܐܐ ܘܬܫܥܝܢ ܘܚܡܫ
ܫܢ̈ܝܢ [ܘܡܝܬ]

Aphr = P

<u>Gen 5:18-20</u>

#049 XIII.4(6). 236:7-8; 553:11-12

ܘܝܪܕ ܒܪ ܡܐܐ ܘܫܬܝܢ ܘܬܪܬܝܢ ܫܢ̈ܝܢ ܐܘܠܕ ܠܚܢܘܟ.

#050 XXIII.(27). 475:10-15; II 69:23-72:4

ܘܚܝܐ ܝܪܕ ܡܐܐ ܘܫܬܝܢ {ܘܬܪܬܝܢ A,B / ܘܒ C} ܫܢ̈ܝܢ
ܘܐܘܠܕ ܠܚܢܘܟ. ܘܚܝܐ ܝܪܕ ܡܢ ܒܬܪ ܕܐܘܠܕ

[Syriac text with bracketed variant markers:]

,ܡܕܪܝ ܪܣܡ ܒܪ‍ {A,B ܪܪܣܪܣܕ} ܢܘܠܠ
 C

These two passages also occur, respectively, in the
chronographic tables discussed above.

*Gen 5:18   ܝܕܪܘ ܝܕܪܘ ܪܪܣ ܒܪ‍ ܪܘܐ
Aphr = P

*Gen 5:19   ܒܘܐܪܘ ܝܕܘ ܣ ܒܪ‍ ܪܘܐ
Aphr = P

*Gen 5:20   ܝܕܪܘ ܝܕܪܘ ܪܪܣܪܕ [. . .]
Aphr = P

<u>Gen 5:21-24</u>

#051 XIII.4(6). 236:8-9; 553:12-13

#052 XXIII.(28). 475:15-24; II 72:5-15

ܕܫܢܘܗ̈ܝ {A,B / C omits} ܬܠܬܡܐܐ ܘܫܬܝܢ ܘܚܡܫ ܫܢ̈ܝܢ

ܘܫܢܬ ܬܠܬܡܐܐ ܕܡܬܘܫܠܚ {A,B ܒܪܗ / C omits}.

ܘܫܢܬ ܡܐܐ {A,B ܘܬܠܬܥܣܪܐ / C ܘܬܢ} {B omits / A,C ܫܢ̈ܝܢ}

ܠܫܬ ܠܟܘܢ ܥܣܪܝܢ ܘܬܫܥ ܫܢ̈ܝܢ ܡܢ ܩܕܡ

ܡܘܠܕܗ ܕܢܘܚ ܬܫܥܡܐܐ ܘܥܣܪܝܢ ܘܬܫܥ ܫܢ̈ܝܢ

ܡܢ ܩܕܡ ܡܒܘܠܐ ܫܢܝܗ ܐܠܗܐ {B ܠܐܬܪܐ / A,C ܠܒܪܐ}

ܕܢܫܐ ܒܒܪܐ ܬܠܬܝܐ.

#053 XXIII.(31). 476:22-477:1; II 73:25-76:2

ܒܫܢܬ {A,B ܫܬܝܢ ܘܬܫܥ / C ܚܡܫ} ܫܢ̈ܝܢ ܡܢ ܩܕܡ

{C ܕܐܬܠܕ / A,B ܕܝܠܕ} ܢܘܚ ܐܬܕܒܪ ܚܢܘܟ ܘܠܐ

ܐܫܬܟܚ ܒܡܘܬܗ ܬܫܥܡܐܐ {A,B ܫܬܝܢ ܘܬܫܥ / C ܘܚܡܫ}

ܫܢ̈ܝܢ ܡܢ ܩܕܡ ܡܒܘܠܐ.

These three passages occur within the same two chronographic tables discussed above. #051 and #052 are typical elements within those respective tables and conform to Aphr's fairly consistent pattern. Accordingly, their testimony to his text of Gen 5:21-23 is as reliable as that of the above citations (#039-#050) to his text of Gen 5:3-20. #053, however, is simply

Aphr's own synchronic calculation and occurs outside of the pre-
vailing pattern in Dem XXIII.(22)-(42), within a passage that
interrupts the genealogical chain from Adam to Noah. It deserves
notice only because it may contain an allusion to Gen 5:24.

As noted above (see Gen 5:3-5), in composing his table
in Dem XXIII.(22)-(42), Aphr follows the text of Gen 5:3-32 and
11:10-32 rather closely. Within each section his presentation
follows the order and wording of Gen, although not without some
minor variations. It is not surprising, therefore, to find that
in #052 Aphr departs from his usual formulaic conclusion (". . .
and [N] died in the Xth generation"), apparently following his
bible text which itself reports an end to Enoch's life that deviates from what is said about the death of the other individuals
in the Gen genealogy. Of course, at this point Aphr is not quoting his text of vs 24 literally; the reference to "the place
of the living" is clearly his own interpretative comment.[24]
But there is the definite possibility that his use of ܪܠܝ
(cf. ܀ܩܘܠ in P) reflects such a verb in his text of vs 24.
Indeed, whenever Aphr speaks of God's termination of Enoch's
earthly life, he uses ܪܠܝ rather than ܀ܩܘܠ (cf. 4:12-13;
33:9-10; 473:19-21; 996:11-13). Perhaps Aphr knows a text of
vs 24 which resembles the LXX: καὶ εὐηρέστησεν Ἐνὼχ τῷ θεῷ
καὶ οὐχ ηὑρίσκετο, ὅτι μετέθηκεν αὐτὸν ὁ θεός (cf. Sir 44:16
Ἐνὼχ εὐηρέστησεν κυρίῳ καὶ μετετέθη . . .). The likelihood
of this may be increased if #053 also alludes to Gen 5:24,

because this allusion uses not only the verb ܐܫܟܚ, but also
ܐܫܟܚ (cf. LXX ηὑρίσκετο).

These considerations cannot be judged conclusive, however, because of the strong possibility that Aphr's language in
both #052 and #053 is influenced by Heb 11:5 P: (Syriac)
(Syriac)
(Syriac)
The main clause in #053 more closely resembles the Heb text than
Gen 5:24, and the fact that Ephraem knows a text of the first
part of Gen 5:24 that agrees with P rather than LXX (Comm V.2
line 6: (Syriac))
makes it less likely that a fourth-century Syriac text of Gen
5:24 was available that read (Syriac) instead of
(Syriac). If those are correct who see in the Letter and
in Dem I.(14) the reflection of a creedal or liturgical composition, then the language of Heb 11:5 will have had an additional
vehicle by which to dominate Aphr's memory of the account of
Enoch's life. The verb (Syriac) is used in both of those passages
(4:12-13; 33:9-10) in connection with Enoch. It is impossible
to find here a clear witness to Aphr's text of Gen 5:24.

*Gen 5:21   (Syriac)
(Syriac)

Aphr = P

*Gen 5:22   (Syriac)
[. . .] (Syriac)

Aphr = P

*Gen 5:23   ܘܗܘܐ ܟܠܗܘܢ ܝܘܡܬܗ [. . .]

.ܫܢܝܢ

Aphr = P

Gen 5:25-27

#054   XIII.4(6). 236:9-10; 553:13-15

ܘܚܝܐ ܡܬܘܫܠܚ ܘܐܘܠܕ ܠܠܡܟ ܘܡܝܬ .

#055   XXIII.(29). 475:23-476:6; II 72:16-27

$\begin{cases} \text{A,}\underline{\text{B}} \\ \text{C} \end{cases}$ ܘܗܘܐ ܡܬܘܫܠܚ ...

$\begin{cases} \text{A,}\underline{\text{B}} \\ \text{C} \end{cases}$ ...

$\begin{cases} \text{A,}\underline{\text{B}} \text{ omit} \\ \text{C} \end{cases}$ ...

... $\begin{cases} \text{A,}\underline{\text{B}} \\ \text{C} \end{cases}$ ...

These two passages also occur, respectively, in the chronographic tables discussed above.

*Gen 5:25

Aphr = P

*Gen 5:26 ܘܚܝܐ ܡܬܘܫܠܚ ܡܢ ܒܬܪ ܕܐܘܠܕ
ܠܠܡܟ. ܫܒܥܡܐܐ ܘܬܡܢܝܢ ܘܬܪܬܝܢ
ܫܢܝܢ [. . .]

Aphr = P

*Gen 5:27 [. . .]ܬܫܥܡܐܐ ܘܫܬܝܢ ܘܬܫܥ
ܫܢܝܢ [ܘܡܝܬ]

Aphr = P

Gen 5:28-31

#056 XIII.4(6). 236:10-11; 553:15-16

ܘܠܡܟ ܐܒܘܗܝ ܕܢܘܚ ܒܪ ܡܐܐ ܘܬܡܢܝܢ
ܘܬܪܬܝܢ ܫܢܝܢ ܐܘܠܕܗ.

#057 XXIII.(30). 476:7-14; II 73:1-12

ܘܚܝܐ ܠܡܟ ܡܐܐ ܘܬܡܢܝܢ {ܘܬܪܬܝܢ A,B | ܘܒ C}

ܫܢܝܢ ܘܐܘܠܕ ܠܢܘܚ ܘܚܝܐ ܠܡܟ ܡܢ ܒܬܪ
ܕܐܘܠܕ ܠܢܘܚ. ܚܡܫܡܐܐ {ܘܬܫܥܝܢ | ܘܨܗ}

ܘܚܡܫ {A,B | C} ܫܢܝܢ ܗܘܐ ܕܫܢܘ̈ܗܝ، ܫܒܥܡܐܐ

{ܘܫܒܥܝܢ ܘܫܒܥ A,B | ܘܥܙ C} ܫܢܝܢ ܘܚܝܐ ܠܡܟ

ܒܬܪ ܠܢܘܚ ܚܡܫܡܐܐ ܘܬܫܥܝܢ ܘܚܡܫ
ܫܢܝܢ ܠܒܢ̈ܝ ܢܘܚ ܒܪܗ. . . ܘܡܝܬ ܡܢ ܒܬܪ

ܐܪ̈ܒܥ ܫܢܝܢ {ܗܢ A,C / B omits} ܩܕܡ ܡܒܘܠܐ

ܒܪܐ ܕܬܪ̈ܝܢ.

These two passages also occur, respectively, in the chronographic tables discussed above. Apparently, in #057 Aphr has chosen not to follow the text of Gen 5:28 exactly, in order to maintain a consistent verbal pattern throughout his own table. Gen 5:28-29 deviates somewhat from the pattern found elsewhere in the ch 5 genealogy in order to include the aetiological note on ܢܘܚ. All witnesses agree with P in concluding vs 28 with "a son" rather than "Noah" and in including vs 29. It is difficult to think that Aphr knows a drastically deviant text which is entirely unique at this point. His reference later on in #057 to "Noah his son" may well echo a bible text that = P at the end of vs 28.

*Gen 5:28 ܘܚܝܐ ܠܡܟ ܡܐܐ ܘܬܡܢܝܢ
ܘܬܪ̈ܬܝܢ ܫܢ̈ܝܢ ܘܐܘܠܕ [. . .]

Aphr = P

*Gen 5:30 ܘܚܝܐ ܠܡܟ ܡܢ ܒܬܪ ܕܐܘܠܕ
ܠܢܘܚ ܚܡܫܡܐܐ ܘܬܫܥܝܢ ܘܚܡܫ
ܫ̈ܢܝܢ [. . .]

Aphr = P

*Gen 5:31 [. . .]ܫܒܥܡܐܐ ܘܫܒܥܝܢ ܘܫܒܥ
ܫ̈ܢܝܢ [ܘܡܝܬ]

Aphr = P

Gen 6:3; 7:6

#058 II.8(9). 32:1-4; 65:16-21

[Syriac text, three lines]

{A [Syriac text]
{B omits

#059 XXIII.(31). 477:5-6; II 76:7-8

[Syriac text, two lines]

#058 contains two allusions to Gen 6:3b. It is not
clear whether Aphr intends the first to be taken as a formal
quotation. The second is obviously a loose citation in which
only the numeral, "one hundred and twenty years," has value as
a textual witness. Whatever his intention, Aphr has reproduced
the text of Gen 6:3b P almost exactly in the earlier reference.
The addition of [Syriac] is doubtless his own alteration of
his bible text for clarity. He has begun his sentence with reference to [Syriac], a plural noun phrase. To follow
that with [Syriac], which has a _singular_ pronominal suffix,
would be awkward and possibly confusing. Therefore, Aphr retains
the term [Syriac] as it is remembered from his scripture text,
but adds [Syriac] to form a prepositional phrase in which
the pronominal suffix is anticipatory of the added noun. No

other witness reads a noun in this position in the vs, and Ephraem (Comm VI.4 lines 22-23) knows P. Despite the clear echo of Gen 6:3b P here, apart from the numeral, no certain reflection of Aphr's bible text is afforded. The lengthy omission in ms B in #058 is an error resulting from homoioteleuton; the passage which ms B omits extends beyond the citation reproduced above and ends with ܢܘܚ.

#059 agrees with #058 in showing that Aphr's text of Gen 7:6 reads a numeral = P, although no witness to the rest of the text of this vs is provided. Ephraem's text (Comm VI.11) includes the identical numeral.

*Gen 6:3 [. . .] ܡܐܐ ܘܥܣܪܝܢ ܫ̈ܢܝܢ .

Aphr = P

*Gen 7:6 [. . .] ܫܬܡܐܐ ܫ̈ܢܝܢ [. . .]

Aphr = P

Gen 6:7; 7:4

#060 XIII.4(5). 235:9-10; 552:8-10

ܘܐܡܪ ܠܗ ܕܡܚܐ ܐܢܐ ܠܒܢܝܢܫܐ ܡܢ
ܐܦ̈ܝ ܐܪܥܐ. ܥܠ ܕܣܟܠܘ ܐܘܪܚܬܗܘܢ.

#061 XIII.4(7). 236:19-21; 556:2-5

ܐܠܐ ܟܕ ܚܙܐ ܕܐܠܗܐ ܡܠܠ ܥܡܗ ܘܐܡܪ
ܠܗ. ܕܟܠ ܐܢܫܐ ܡܚܐ ܐܢܐ ܡܢ ܐܦ̈ܝ ܐܪܥܐ.
ܘܠܟ ܒܠܚܘܕ ܡܫܘܙܒ ܐܢܐ

#062 XIII.6(11). 241:20-242:1; 568:2-3

ܐܡܪ ܕܐܬܬܘܝܬ ܕܒܪܝܬ ܐܢܫ.

#063 XVIII.2(2). 346:17; 820:25-26

.ܩܘܪ ܕܢܐܚܐ ܕܠܐܕܕܝܪܐ ܝܪܘܪܐ

#060 and #061 both purport to give God's speech to

Noah in Gen 7:4 and are formal quotations. In each case, how-

ever, Aphr is quoting loosely, certainly from memory, and he

introduces into the quotations elements from related vss. In

#060, ܪܬܝܘܚܐ\ derives from the parallel statement in Gen

6:7 (contrast "all that exists which I have made" in 7:4), and

"because they have corrupted their way" is an addition which

Aphr derives from Gen 6:12. No other witness agrees with this

form of the quotation for either Gen 6:7 or 7:4. Aphr's use

of the participle plus cognate infinitive in #060 is unattested

in any P ms and disagrees with the reading in #061. Perhaps

he is influenced here by the same emphatic construction in the

similar sentence in Exod 17:14 (which he remembers well enough

to cite, though inexactly, at 121:17): ܪܠܚ ܪܠܝܘܚܐ . . .

ܪܝܪ ܕܝܘܕ ܩ ܐܠܝܚܐ ܩܝܪܘܚܐ ܪܝܪ.

#061 presents a free handling of Aphr's bible text, in

which its word order is rearranged. Again here conflation of

Gen 6:7 and 7:4 is evident, and again Aphr adds explanatory mate-

rial drawn from the surrounding biblical text (i.e., "and you

only will I save"). #060 and #061 do not provide a clear wit-

ness to Aphr's text of Gen 6:7a or 7:4b.

In contrast, #062 and #063 are both formal, literal

citations of Gen 6:7b. The text which they witness = Ephraem

(Comm VI.7 line 3).

*Gen 6:7 [. . .]ܕܐܬܬܘܝܬ ܕܥܒܕܬ ܐܢܘܢ.

ܕܐܬܬܘܝܬ 8/5b1 915 11/9b1mg 1114.5 →]ܕܐܬܬܘܝܬ 7a1 914 10b1 10g1 12b1

Gen 7:1; 6:9, 14

#064 IX.1(1). 175:4-6; 408:6-8

ܐܝܟ ܕܟܬܝܒ. ܕܐܡܪ ܠܗ ܐܠܗܐ {ܕܠܟ ܚܙܝܬ
ܠܢܘܚ ܠܟ}

B ܕܙܕܝܩ
A ܚܙܝܬ ܙܕܝܩ
ܘܬܡܝܡ ܒܕܪܐ ܗܢܐ.

#065 XIII.4(5). 234:12-13; 549:6-8

ܐܠܐ ܗܟܢܐ ܐܡܪ ܠܗ ܐܠܗܐ ܠܢܘܚ. ܕܠܟ
ܚܙܝܬ ܙܕܝܩ ܘܬܡܝܡ ܒܕܪܐ ܗܢܐ.

#066 XIII.4(5). 234:16-18; 549:12-15

ܗܘܐ ܠܗ ܢܘܚ ܒܪ ܫܬܡܐܐ ܫ̈ܢܝܢ. ܒܗ ܡܠܠ
ܥܡܗ ܐܠܗܐ ܘܐܡܪ ܠܗ. ܕܠܟ ܚܙܝܬ ܙܕܝܩ
ܐܢܬ ܘܬܡܝܡ ܩܕܡܝ ܒܕܪܐ ܗܢܐ.

#067 XIII.4(5). 235:1-3; 549:24-27

ܗܕܝܢ ܡܠܠ ܥܡܗ ܒܪ ܐܠܗܘܬܗ، ܒܪ ܫܬܡܐܐ
ܫ̈ܢܝܢ. ܘܐܡܪ ܕܠܟ ܚܙܝܬ ܕܙܕܝܩ ܐܢܬ ܩܕܡܝ ܒܕܪܐ ܗܢܐ.

#068 XIII.4(5). 235:5-7; 552:3-6

ܕܡܠܠ ܥܡܗ ܐܠܗܐ ܘܐܡܪ ܠܗ. ܕܠܟ ܚܙܝܬ
ܕܙܕܝܩ ܐܢܬ ܩܕܡܝ ܒܕܪܐ ܗܢܐ. ܗܫܐ ܠܟ
ܥܒܕ ܠܟ ܩܒܘܬܐ ܕܩܝܣܐ ܕܬܬܛܪ ܒܗ.

#069 XIII.4(7). 237:10-12; 556:23-27

ܗܕܝܢ ܒܫܢܬ ܫܬܡܐܐ ܫ̈ܢܝܢ ܠܚܝܘܗܝ، ܕܢܘܚ

ܡܛܠ ܗܟܢܐ ܐܠܗܐ ܘܐܡܪ ܠܗ. ܥܘܠ
ܠܩܒܘܬܐ ܐܢܬ ܘܐܢܬܬܟ. ܘܒܢܝܟ ܘܢܫܐ
ܕܒܢܝܟ ܥܡܟ.

#070 XXIII.(14). 463:2-4; II 40:18-21

ܘܟܕ ܚܒܠ ܟܠ ܒܣܪ ܐܘܪܚܗ ܥܠ ܐܪܥܐ
ܐܬܦܪܥܬ ܒܡܒܘܠܐ ܓܒܪܐ {ܕܚܣܝܐ B / ܘܕܚܒܐ A,C}
ܒܗܘܢ {ܕܐܫܬܒܩܘ B,C / ܘܐܫܬܒܩܘ A} ܘܕܗܒ ܘܬܒܥܘ
ܒܕܪܐ ܕܡܒܘܠܐ.

All of these contain or purport to contain portions of Gen 7:1; they are therefore discussed together. #069 is a formal citation of God's command to Noah to enter the ark. The use of the numeral ("600th year") and the preceding discussion make it plain that Aphr has in mind here not God's initial appearance to Noah when the building of the ark is commanded and the coming flood first described, but the actual final command to enter the completed vessel when the flood is about to begin. This points to Gen 7:1 as the source of the citation. However, Aphr's form of the command differs from the text of Gen 7:1 in P and all other witnesses, including Ephraem (Comm VI.9 lines 13-14). While it cannot be totally ruled out that #069 accurately reflects a variant bible text at this point, a more convincing explanation is that Aphr here is quoting from memory and that he produces a faulty reproduction of his text of Gen 7:1, one that is contaminated by Gen 6:18 P (. . . ܠܩܒܘܬܐ ܐܢܬ

ܠܐܬܗܩܐ . . .) and 8:18 (ܡܠܒܐ ,ܡܐܒܬܗ ܐܪܝܐܘ
,ܡܐܬܘܐ ܡܗܗܘܠܐܪܐ . . .), the latter as in ms 7a1 and
others, against ms 5b1. Such a conflated form does not afford
a clear witness to Aphr's text of any of the three vss.

The last half of Gen 7:1 is cited in #064-#068, each
of which is a formal citation. The most striking feature of
this cluster is their addition of the second adjective ܦܘܗܐ.
Does Aphr's bible in fact contain this expanded reading? Baumstark insists that it does, arguing that Aphr at this point has
before him a primitive, "targumic" Syriac text. For him this
second adjective is a "Doppelwiedergabe eines einzigen Wortes
des Urtexts, wie sie in palästinensischem--und samaritanischem--
Targum nicht selten ist."[25] The repetition of the reading in
more than one citation is conclusive for Baumstark.

Baumstark's view is not unreasonable and must be given
serious consideration. There are three factors, however, which
suggest that Aphr's citations should not be taken as evidence
of a scripture text that reads both adjectives in Gen 7:1.
First, Baumstark pays insufficient attention to the fact that
in these five citations (#064-#068), three different text-forms
are presented for the same vs.[26] This lack of consistency leaves
little doubt that these citations are from memory. The variations do not suggest conflicting bible texts before Aphr, coming
as close together as most of them do within Dem XIII. Nor does
secondary scribal correction adequately account for the

differences. Baumstark himself concedes that the abbreviated
readings in #064 and #065 are probably to be regarded as resulting from Aphr's failure of memory.

Once the memoriter nature of these citations is recognized, an additional fact must be considered--one which Baumstark
totally avoids. Gen 6:9 presents a parallel description of Noah
that could very easily supply the compound adjective phrase in
Aphr's citations: ,ܡܘܪܟܒ ܟܘܗ ܦܘܝܕܡܐ ܚܝܕ ܪܒ
ܢܘܢ (so ms 7a1 and others; ms 914 concludes with ܡܪܝܒ,
which increases the resemblance of the vs to 7:1). Memoriter
confusion of parallel passages is difficult to avoid, and Aphr's
tendency toward such conflation is witnessed frequently.

The third factor which Baumstark has ignored, and which
sheds additional light upon these citations, is the context in
which they stand within Aphr's discussions. Examination of their
respective contexts suggests that Aphr may have some special
attraction to the term ܦܘܝܕ in connection with Noah; this
attraction will have facilitated his conflation of Gen 6:9 and
7:1. In Dem IX.(1), the passage in which #064 occurs is one in
which Aphr generally extols humility as a basic virtue which
bears fruit in many other qualities, integrity (ܟ ܕ ܐܘܪܝܕܐ)
among them. Thus, shortly before #064: "Humility gives birth
to many virtues; integrity [ܟܕܐܘܪܝܕܐ] is brought forth by
it" (408:4-5). And again several lines after #064, he quotes
Prov 11:5: "Again, thus it says, 'The righteousness of a man
of integrity [ܟܘܪܝܕ ܗ] goes before him'" (408:16-17).

Clearly, in such a passage Aphr's selection of Noah as an illustration is determined primarily by the latter's identity as a
man of integrity. Aphr's argument will have inclined him to
choose or shape his citation of scripture so as to include the
adjective ܬܡܝܡ.

It is equally clear that in section (5) of Dem XIII
the primary term that Aphr associates with Noah is ܬܡܝܡܘܬܐ,
prior to and apart from any specific scripture citation. The
connotation that the term has here may be somewhat different
from Dem IX, however. Noah is discussed in Dem XIII.(5) primarily as an example of godliness and righteousness that was demonstrated apart from sabbath observance. As he mentions Noah,
Aphr becomes interested in detailing the precise nature of his
virtue, explaining:

> It was not in keeping the Sabbath that he was justified,
> but because he kept his innocence [ܬܡܝܡܘܬܐ] in the
> generation of destruction, as the force of the Scripture
> makes clear. It is not written that he took part in the
> world [i.e., married]. Noah was five hundred years old
> when God spoke with him and said to him, "You have I seen
> righteous and innocent [ܬܡܝܡ] before me in this genera-
> tion." And his innocence [ܬܡܝܡܘܬܗ]--so it seems
> to us--was in this regard: . . . he determined that he
> would not marry a wife nor have children. . . . When God
> saw that his heart was pure [ܕܟܐ] and innocent [ܬܡܝܡ]
> . . . .[27]

Neusner's translation of the term here as "innocence" (so Parisot)
is correct in view of the ascetic orientation of Aphr's exegesis.
Noah figures quite prominently in Dem XIII (and, to a lesser
extent, in Dem XVIII) as a hero worth imitating in his refusal
to follow the inferior path of marriage in favor of the higher

holiness of celibacy. (Aphr argues in Dem XIII that Noah finally married only because God instructed him to in order to repopulate the earth after the flood. And he waited until the last possible moment to take a wife.)

Given this preoccupation with the sexual purity--<u>innocence</u> from carnal corruption--of Noah, it becomes obvious that in his scripture citations in Dem XIII.(5) Aphr is under some compulsion to quote a text that will corroborate his assessment of Noah as ܟܐܢܐ. The strength of this tendency is seen in #067 and #068, where ܟܐܢܐ is the only adjective included; ܓܡܝܪ here is so secondary as to be forgotten altogether.

These considerations make it extremely dangerous to conclude from this cluster of citations that Aphr's text of Gen 7:1 contains both adjectives. No other witness reads both adjectives there, including Ephraem (Comm VI.9 lines 14-15), who = P. Apparently, Aphr's reproduction of his text in these citations is not exact; his citation of 7:1 is influenced by 6:9.

Baumstark's treatment of these citations includes an even more daring proposal, based on #068. Noting that the second sentence in this citation is identical to part of Gen 6:14 P, he assumes that this is evidence of a text known to Aphr which includes an expanded reading in Gen 6:14 that is essentially identical to what Aphr writes: "I have seen that you are upright before me in this generation; now make for yourself an ark of wood. . . ." Furthermore, he proposes ("so unbegreiflich dies

scheinen mag") that the concluding verbal clause of the citation
(ܗ̇ܬ ܗܣܘܚܕܗ̇ ܒܡ) is also an exact reproduction of the conclusion of Aphr's text of Gen 6:14:

> Sollte etwa hier in P Älteres sich erhalten und der von
> Afrahaz [sic] gelesene Text auf einer paraphrastischen
> Weiterbildung beruht haben, deren Urheber aus dem tatsäch-
> lichen Pflanzennamen ܟܘܣܪ etwas von der Wurzel ܣܪܟ
> "(ent)fliehen" herausgelesen hätte?[28]

The only evidence that Baumstark can cite in support of this last
proposal is the fact that the Hebrew term גפר posed difficulty
for the ancient translators and received a variety of renderings.

Neither aspect of Baumstark's analysis is convincing,
however. His reconstruction of Aphr's text of Gen 6:14 can stand
only if one completely ignores Aphr's exegetical tendencies in
the discussion of which #068 is a part. Here as elsewhere, he
takes Aphr's citation prima facie as exact without subjecting
it to critical evaluation.

Baumstark assumes at the outset that #068 must cite a
different Gen passage than #064-#066 simply because #068 contains only the single adjective ܟܣܘܚ. It has already been
pointed out, however, that the quotation of #064-#067 is motivated by the same preoccupation with Noah's sexual innocence as
is reflected in #068. More important, #067, which Baumstark
entirely overlooks, agrees with #068 in using the single adjective for Noah. Baumstark is wrong in assuming #068 to be unique
among Aphr's citations in this respect. The usage of the single
adjective cannot be taken as evidence of a different source for

this citation. Actually, Aphr introduces #068 almost in passing, merely to identify a particular point in God's various dealings with Noah. He has no interest in a close reading of the text itself and can well be expected to refer to it in condensed fashion.

Concerning the combination of an element from Gen 7:1 with one from 6:14, it must also be pointed out that Baumstark has entirely missed what Dem XIII.(5) reveals in a number of ways—that Aphr's recall of the events of Gen ch 6 is hazy; he does not accurately remember the sequence of vss in the chapter, although his mind is full of its various clauses and phrases. The passage within which #068 occurs (549:27-552:11) makes it plain that Aphr telescopes his text of Gen 6:5-9, 11-21:

> Now as yet he had no son, as the fact itself shows and as
> I wrote above, for Noah had not taken a wife in that entire
> time until God spoke to him and said to him, "You have I
> seen to be innocent before me in this generation. Now make
> for yourself an ark of wood that you may be saved in it"
> [conflation of Gen 7:1; 6:9, 14]. Now when Noah heard these
> things, that God commanded him to make an ark, saying to him,
> "I am surely going to destroy mankind from off the face of
> the earth, for they have corrupted their way" [Gen 6:7],
> then, in his five hundredth year, Noah took a wife. . . .

Taking this passage at its face, one would have to conclude that Aphr's bible not only contains a vs that includes elements of Gen 7:1 and 6:14, but also that it places this expanded vs directly adjacent 6:7. Of course, such a radically rearranged text of Gen ch 6 is out of the question.

It seems obvious that Aphr's recollection is sufficiently vague as to allow him to mix together the two parallel accounts

of God's appearance to Noah in Gen ch 6: vss 7-8 and vss 13-14
(and ff.). This explains why Aphr can juxtapose 6:7 and 6:14
as he does in the passage quoted above. (Baumstark fails to
offer an explanation of this. He seems not to notice that Aphr
speaks of 7:1; 6:9, 14; and 6:7 as together constituting "these
things.")

Inexact recall can also credibly account for Aphr's conjunction of parts of 7:1; 6:9; and 6:14 in #068. In both passages in Gen ch 6 (vss 7-8 and vss 13-14), it is evident that
Noah has found God's favor and will be spared, despite the dec-
laration that God is about to destroy the world; this is plain,
if only implied. This implication is one of the three components of the telescoped version of Gen ch 6 that Aphr has in his
mind: (a) God will destroy the earth; (b) Noah has found God's
favor and will be spared; and (c) Noah is to build an ark. Given
this _memoriter_ version of the chapter, it is not surprising that
when Aphr quotes the instructions to build an ark from 6:14 in
#068, he also includes indication of God's favor toward Noah,
since the latter is associated with God's revelation of the coming flood in 6:7-8 and 13-14. That he does this by means of a
partial quotation of 6:9 (actually 7:1 mixed with 6:9) is a log-
ical--almost predictable--error, inasmuch as 6:9 will have been
associated with 6:7-8 (parallel to 6:13-14) in Aphr's memory.
In short, #068 reflects the telescoped version of Gen ch 6 which
Aphr remembers; it does not reflect a bible text known to him

which contains a greatly expanded form of Gen 6:14.

Baumstark's suggestion that the final verb clause in #068
is an actual part of Aphr's text of Gen 6:14 must also be judged
highly unlikely. Certainly, his idea of a development from P
ܐܘܪ is ingenious. The fact is, however, that there is no
trace of a Syriac text which reads ܡܢ ܕܬܗܕܪܝܢ, which one
would expect if Baumstark's theory were correct. Indeed, no witness presents any rendering of this part of the vs that is not
a name for some sort of physical material, and Ephraem (Comm VI.8
line 27) = P. It is much more reasonable to assume that Aphr
is simply making an interpretative addition to his text here;
his overriding concern throughout this part of the Dem is to show
that Noah was justified and saved apart from sabbath observance.
Perhaps there is also an echo here of Heb 11:7, where two ideas
occur in succession that resemble these in the last half of #068:
". . . and he made an ark for the saving of his household." It
has already been observed that Aphr's quotation of 6:14, indeed
his entire recollection of ch 6, is not exact. This tendency
to make explicit what is only implicit in his text is evident
also in #061, where he expands a quotation of Gen 6:7 similarly
with "and you alone I will save."

The use of ܗܘܐ in this addition may simply be Aphr's
own individual style, but it seems probable that this particular
verb will have been associated with Noah in creedal or liturgical formulae. If those are correct who see in the Letter and

in Dem I.(19) a reflection of a Syriac liturgical piece, then
it is noteworthy for our purposes that in each of these passages
there is a reference to Noah:

Letter.(2). 4:13-14   ܘܟܠ ܢܘܚ ܣܗܕܘ ܗܘܐ ܐܠܗܐ ܐܚܬܗ

I.(14). 33:10-11   ܘܗܘܐ ܢܘܚ ܟܠ ܕܗܡܟܢ ܐܚܬܗ ܡܢ ܡܒܘܠܐ

Pass notes a similar item in the <u>Acts of Philip</u>: "and he deliv-
ered Noah from the flood,"[29] and Murray finds a parallel in the
first Macarian homily: ". . . protected Noah in the ark."[30]
Therefore, in place of Baumstark's rather fanciful proposal, it
is much more reasonable to think that Aphr merely adds on to his
citation of Gen 6:14 his own explanatory clause for the sake of
explicitness and emphasis, and that in so doing he resorts to
a verb commonly used of Noah in liturgical recitations. He will
have omitted ܕܩܝܣܐ in the interest of economy and directness; this additional detail about the ark is not relevant to
his argument.

    *Gen 6:9   [. . .] ܘܬܡܝܟ ܗܘܐ [. . .]
    Aphr - P

    *Gen 6:14   [. . .]ܕܩܡܐ ܩܒܘܬܐ ܠܟ ܥܒܕ
    Aphr = P

    *Gen 7:1   ܐܢܬ ܗܝܕܗ ܫܘܝ ܠܟܗ [. . .]
                    ܗܘܐ ܕܟܝܪ ܩܕܡ.

    Aphr = P

Gen 7:11; 8:14

#071 XXIII.(31). 477:6-9; II 76:9-13

،ܠܐ ܐܡ} ܟܗܐ ܐ ܢܘ ܟܡܘ

ܟܠܘ ܟܢ ܟ ܝ {A,B ܡܗ
C omits

ܟܢ ܝ ܟܐ { B ܟܐ}}
 [A ܟܐ}]

ܝܗ ܟܗܐ ܟܐ {A,B ܟܠܘ
C omits

. ܝܗ ܟܐ ܝ

This reckoning by Aphr of the total time Noah spent inside
the ark (cf. also 557:4-5) includes references to the dates of
Gen 7:11 ("seventeenth day in the second month") and 8:14 ("twen-
ty-seventh day in the second month"). Because this is not a
direct quotation, however, one cannot determine the precise verbal form of these numerals in Aphr's bible text, even though the
numerals themselves = P and Ephraem (Comm VII.11 line 1; VII.12
lines 14-15) in substance. The large omission in ms C is an
accident due to homoioteleuton.

Gen 9:6

#072 III.3(5). 48:12; 108:23-24

. ܟ ܟ ܟ ܐ ܝ ܠ ܗ ܗ
. ܐ ܗ ܡ

This formal quotation of the first part of Gen 9:6 is made within a discussion of Jezebel in order to substantiate the appropriateness of her violent death. Aphr's point is to emphasize the principle of retribution--he who kills will be killed; he has no interest in the further deduction that could be made from the text in P (= MT), that he who kills will be killed by man. Therefore, it is difficult to be entirely certain that Aphr is not simply abbreviating his text in omitting ܒܐܢܫܐ (P).

*Gen 9:6 ܡܢ ܕܐܫܕ ܕܡܐ [ܕܐܢܫܐ] ܕܡܗ
ܢܬܐܫܕ [. . .]

ܡܢ ܕܐܫܕ TN[1]] ܗܘ, ܗܘ ܕܐܫܕ Ephraem(Comm VI.15 line 2); שפך MT Sam TSam LXX(ὁ ἐκχέων); ܡܢ(ܘ) ܕܐܢܫܘܕ P TO TJ[1] | ܕܐܢܫܐ LXX Vg] add ܒܐܢܫܐ P Ephraem MT Sam TN[1] TSam | ܢܬܐܫܕ TN[1mg] TG[E]] ܢܬܐܫܕ P Ephraem MT Sam TO TN[1] TSam

Gen 9:7

#073 XVIII.1(1). 345:8-9; 817:11-13

ܘܐܦ ܠܟܘܢ ܒܗ ܒܒܘܪܟܬܐ ܐܡܪ ܠܗ. ܕܦܫܘ
ܒܐܪܥܐ ܘܐܬܝܠܕܘ ܒܗ.

This passage has the appearance of a formal citation of Gen 9:7, although it is partial and presents a transposition of the final two verbs in P. Aphr is surely quoting loosely, and there is little basis here for reconstructing a text different from P. One recalls the conflation of parallel vss that is evident in #007-#009 above. Baumstark disregards the indications of free citation here and ventures the suggestion that #073 actually reflects a text which lacks the second verb (ܘܦܫܘ) in

the vs in P. The fact that Aphr here omits not only the latter
verb (the same verb would not occur twice in succession, of
course), but also the preceding ܩܝܦ ܢܐܘܪܐ , calls into
question Baumstark's reasoning. If the citation is to be taken
as literal and complete, then logically one should postulate an
even more drastically shortened form of the vs in Aphr's bible.
Baumstark does not do this, however, and such a severely altered
text would indeed be extremely improbable; it is totally without
support in the other witnesses. One suspects that Baumstark is
motivated here less by an objective appraisal of Aphr's citation
than by a prior discomfort (shared by others--cf. the critical
apparatus in BHS) with the MT of Gen 9:7.

As pointed out above, #009, although ostensibly a citation of Gen 1:28, probably reflects Aphr's text of Gen 9:7 to
a greater degree (cf. "in the earth") than it does 1:28. If so,
then its order of the verbs will tend to confirm that Aphr's text
= P and that a simple memoriter transposition has occurred in
#073. The most convincing explanation of #073 remains that it
is partial and a slightly rearranged form of Aphr's scripture
text. It is partial because Aphr is presenting it as one in a
series of proof-texts in his discussion and is content with a
condensed reference. It is rearranged because his memory is
faulty or because he quotes carelessly.

Gen 9:25

108

#074 III.8(13). 56:1-12; 128:4-5

#075 XIV.7(10). 252:18-19; 592:19-21

#076 XIV.25(40). 290:1-2; 685:21-22

#075 and #076 are allusions which echo Gen 9:25 P more
or less closely. #074 has the appearance of a formal quotation
but in fact is Aphr's own paraphrase, in which he has recast his
text into direct address. The readings of #074 and #076 confirm
that Aphr's text reads the plural "brothers"; the absence of
seyame in ms B in #075 must be an error. The spelling of "Ham"
in ms A in #076 is also surely a mechanical error; such a variant spelling is not attested elsewhere. Although Ham is placed
under the curse in #075 and #076, Canaan is the recipient of
Noah's malediction in #074 (cf. 128:3 and II 41:5). There seems
little question, therefore, that Aphr's text reads "Canaan"; the

the reference to Ham is Aphr's interpretative substitution. The

use of various forms of the verb ܗܘܐ in all three passages

makes it all but certain that Aphr's text reads, with P, ܗܘܐ.

This is not explicitly witnessed in the citations, however.

*Gen 9:25   [ܗܘܐ] ܥܠܝ ܠܐܚܘܗܝ ܕܥܒܕ̈ܝܢ [. . .]

ܠܐܚܘܗܝ.

ܥܠܝ ܠܐܚܘܗܝ 5b1 7a1 7h5 9l4-6 10b1 10g1 11/9b1
12b1.2 Ephraem (Comm VII.3 lines 9-10) MT Sam Tgs TSam
LXX(παις οἰκετης) Vg] ܠܐܚܘ̈ܗܝ 11l4 LXX⁵⁹(οἰκετης)

Gen 9:27

#077   XXIII.(14). 463:9-10; II 41:3-5

ܐܡܪ ܬܘܒ ܕܢܦܬܐ ܐܠܗܐ ܠܫܡ. ܘܢܫܪܐ
ܒܡܫܟܢܘ̈ܗܝ ܕܫܝܡ.   ·{ A,B omit / C ܠܥܠܡ }

This formal quotation reproduces the first part of Gen

9:27. The absence of the final clause is surely Aphr's own econ-

omizing. His purpose in the context is to show that Shem was

the inheritor of the divine promise and favor that had been con-

ferred on Noah; the final clause of the vs is not necessary to

that argument. The addition of "for ever" in ms C is probably

to be rejected as secondary, although one cannot be certain. It

is the lectio difficilior in relation to the text of P, and mss

A and B could possibly have suffered scribal correction at this

point. On the other hand, ms C is extremely late and generally

inferior in other respects as a witness. The addition of "for

ever" is unattested in all other witnesses, including Ephraem

(Comm VII.4 line 4); even if it were the original reading in the text of Dem XXIII, it would most reasonably be regarded as Aphr's embellishment of his scripture text rather than a feature of his text itself.

*Gen 9:27 ܟܢܫܐ . ܠܥܠ ܐܠܗܐ ܠܗܘ

[. . .] ܕܢܫܪܐ ܒܡܫܟܢܗ

Aphr = P

Gen 9:28

#078 XXIII.(14). 463:13; II 41:8-9

ܚܝܐ ܝܢ { A,C ܡܢ ܒܬܪ / B ܒܬܪ } ܛܘܦܢܐ . ܬܠܬܡܐܐ

ܘܚܡܫܝܢ ܫܢܝܢ

#079 XXIII.(31). 477:10-11; II 76:14-15

ܘܚܝܐ { B,C ܢܘܚ / A omits } ܡܢ ܒܬܪ ܛܘܦܢܐ

ܬܠܬܡܐܐ ܘܚܡܫܝܢ ܫܢܝ̈ܢ .

Neither of these is a formal quotation; both are components of the large chronograph discussed above. Whether consciously or not, Aphr reproduces the text of Gen 9:28 P almost exactly in each passage, and one can be confident that his text = P. Nevertheless, the variations among the mss of the Dems and the small differences between #078 and #079 obstruct a clear witness to Aphr's bible text of the first portion of the vs.

*Gen 9:28 [. . .] ܒܬܪ ܛܘܦܢܐ ܬܠܬܡܐܐ

ܘܚܡܫܝܢ ܫܢܝ̈ܢ .

Aphr = P

Gen 10:10

#080 V.10(11). 88:23-89:1; 208:4-5

ܐܝܟ ܕܟܬܝܒ. ܕܗܘܬ ܪܫ ܡܠܟܘܬܗ
ܕܢܡܪܘܕ ܒܒܠ.

This formal quotation of Gen 10:10 is made in conjunction with several citations from Dan to confirm the appropriateness of Babylon's king being symbolized by the head of gold in the vision in Dan ch 2. Because Aphr quotes the vs here apart from its Gen context, in which the referent of the suffix on "kingdom" is plain (i.e., "Nimrod" in vs 9), he is forced to insert "of Nimrod" in the quotation for the sake of clarity.[31] This addition is most certainly not a part of his text, however; no other witness reads such an insertion, and it appears quite redundant within the Gen narrative. The final portion of the vs is not relevant to Aphr's purposes at this point in the Dem and so is omitted.

*Gen 10:10 [. . .] []ܗܘܬ ܪܫ ܡܠܟܘܬܗ ܒܒܠ

Aphr = P

Gen 11:10-11

#081 XIII.4(6). 235:17-20; 552:20-24

ܫܝܡ ܒܪ ܒܘܟܪܗ ܕܢܘܚ ܬܪ̈ܬܝܢ ܫ̈ܢܝܢ ܡܢ
ܒܬܪ ܛܘܦܢܐ ܗܘܐ ܠܗ ܒܪܐ ܐܪܦܟܫܕ.
ܘܗܘ ܫܝܡ ܒܪ ܡܐܐ ܗܘܐ ܫ̈ܢܝܢ ܟܕ ܐܘܠܕ.

ܠܐܪܦܟܫܕ. ܬܪܬܝܢ ܫ̈ܢܝܢ ܡܢ ܒܬܪ
ܛܘܦܢܐ

#082 XXIII.(32). 477:15-17; II 76:21-24

ܫܝܡ ܒܪ {ܡܐܐ A,C / B omits} ܫ̈ܢܝܢ ܐܘܠܕ
ܠܐܪܦܟܫܕ ܬܪܬܝܢ ܫ̈ܢܝܢ ܡܢ ܒܬܪ ܛܘܦܢܐ.
ܘܚܝܐ ܫܝܡ ܡܢ ܒܬܪ ܕܐܘܠܕ ܠܐܪܦܟܫܕ
ܚܡܫܡܐܐ ܫ̈ܢܝܢ.

These passages come, respectively, from the two chronographic tables discussed earlier (see above under Gen 5:3-5). #082 is part of a section from the last half of the longer table, which, it will be recalled, Aphr has constructed from the genealogical material in Gen chs 5 and 11. Although incorporating the biblical vss almost exactly in his own table, he consistently omits the biblical notice "and had other sons and daughters"; this is irrelevant to his chronological calculations. The omission of ܡܐܐ in ms B is an obvious mechanical error; the sentence is nonsensical without it. #081 does not reproduce any one vs of Aphr's text, but it is worthy of notice because it evidences the numerals which he reads in Gen 11:10-11.

*Gen 11:10 [. . .] ܫܝܡ ܒܪ ܡܐܐ ܫ̈ܢܝܢ ܐܘܠܕ
ܠܐܪܦܟܫܕ ܬܪܬܝܢ ܫ̈ܢܝܢ ܡܢ ܒܬܪ
ܛܘܦܢܐ.

ܡܐܐ 7a1 7h5 9l4 10b1 10g1 11/9b1 MT Sam] add ܗܘܐ 10/5b1 LXX^{mss} | ܐܘܠܕ 7a1 7h5 9l4 10b1 10g1 11/9b1 Vg] pr ܟܕ 10/5b1 TJ^{1} LXX(ὅτε); pr waw MT Sam TSam TO TN^{1}

*Gen 11:11 ⲁ︤ⲗⲁⲕ︦ⲁ ⲓⲇⲟ ⲥⲟ ⲡⲩⲝ ⲕⲱⲁ
[. . .] ⲡⲝ ⲕⲕⲁⲭⲁⲩ ⲓⲉⲁⲱⲓⲣⲁⲗ

Aphr = P

Gen 11:12-13

#083 XXIII.(33). 477:21-478:1; II 77:5-8

ⲡⲝ ⲝⲁⲩⲁ ⲭⲇⲇⲟ ⲕⲱ {A,B ⲓⲉⲁⲱⲓⲕⲁ}
                      {C   ⲓⲝⲁⲱⲕⲁ}

ⲥⲟ ⲓⲉⲁⲱⲓⲕ ⲕⲱⲁ . ⲩⲗⲝⲗ ⲁⲗⲁⲕⲁ
ⲇⲗⲟⲟ ⲕⲕⲁⲭⲝⲓⲕ ⲩⲗⲝⲗ ⲁⲗⲁⲕⲁ ⲓⲇⲟ
ⲡⲝ

This passage also occurs in the large chronographic table discussed above and reproduces most of the text of Gen 11:12-13.

*Gen 11:12 ⲝⲁⲩⲁ ⲭⲇⲇ ⲕⲱ ⲓⲝⲁⲱⲓⲕⲁ
            . ⲩⲗⲝⲗ ⲁⲗⲁⲕⲁ ⲭⲝ

Aphr = P

*Gen 11:13 ⲓⲇⲟ ⲥⲟ ⲓⲝⲁⲱⲓⲕ ⲕⲱⲁ
 ⲡⲝ ⲇⲗⲟⲟ ⲕⲕⲁⲭⲝⲓⲕ ⲩⲗⲝⲗ ⲁⲗⲁⲕⲁ
                                      [. . .]

ⲇⲗⲟⲟ 7a1(ⲇⲗⲟⲟ ⲕⲁⲭⲝⲓⲕ) 7h5 914 10b1 10g1 10/5b1 11/9b1 12b2 MT TO TJ¹] ⲭⲇⲗⲟⲟ 12b1 → TN¹ Vg; 303 years Sam TSam Vg

Gen 11:14-15

#084 XXIII.(34). 478:4-7; II 77:13-15

ⲁⲗⲁⲕⲁ ⲭⲝ ⲭⲇⲇⲟ {A,C ⲕⲱ ⲩⲗⲝⲁ}
                 {B   ⲩⲗⲝ ⲕⲱⲁ}

ܢܬܘܠܕ ܕܐܘܠܕ ܒܬܪ ܡܢ ܐܝܠܝܢ ܘܗܘܐ { B,C ܠܬܪܝܢ }
{ A ܠܥܣܪܝܢ }

{ A,B ܚܡܫ } ܘܗܘܐ ܐܪܦܟܫܪ { B,C ܠܬܪܝܢ }
{ C omits }   { A ܠܥܣܪܝܢ }

This passage also occurs within the large chronographic
table discussed above. It is difficult to know which of the two
readings is original for the opening two words. Wright and
Parisot follow ms B, but this simply represents their general
preference for the older mss B-B and probably also for the text
which agrees with the Peshitta text in the Urmia and Mosul editions. Two facts point to the alternate reading, however, as
being the original. First, it is supported by two mss (A and
C), which, unless they can be shown to be dependent upon one
another, must carry more weight than the single witness of ms B.
Second, the reading of mss A and C conforms to the pattern which
Aphr follows at the beginning of the first two sentences in each
section of the last half of the large chronograph (sections [32]-
[40]):[32]

. . . ܚܝܐ ܘܒܬܪ
. . . ܘܒܬܪ ܘܗܘܐ

Because Aphr follows this pattern so consistently, in
contrast to P (= MT) which begins both sentences in each section
with ܘܗܘܐ ܘܒܬܪ,[33] no conclusions can be drawn from #084
regarding the reading of Aphr's bible text for the first two
words of Gen 11:14, where the P mss themselves offer conflicting

readings. The earlier mss generally read ܘܬܠܬ ܫܢܝܐ, while the later mss read ܘܫܢܝܐ ܬܠܬ.

It is also difficult to be certain about the spelling of the name ܥܒܘܪ/ܥܒܪ in Aphr's Gen text. Although no P mss attest the longer spelling, it occurs not only here in ms A, but also in ms C in #085. This alternation suggests that both forms of the name were known and accepted. It is not impossible that Aphr's own text of Gen fluctuates in its spelling of the name, but, given the heavy predominance of ܥܒܪ in all mss of the Dems (see also II 65:18), it is probable that the shorter form of the name occurs in Aphr's bible. The omission of "years" in ms C is certainly the inferior reading. It violates the pattern which Aphr follows throughout the chronographic table, and it reflects the general abbreviating tendency of ms C (cf. #089 below).

*Gen 11:14 [...] ܬܠܬܝܢ ܫܢܝܢ ܘܐܘܠܕ [ܠܥܒܪ]

Aphr = P

*Gen 11:15 ܘܚܝܐ ܫܠܚ ܡܢ ܒܬܪ ܕܐܘܠܕ
ܠܥܒܪ ܐܪܒܥܡܐܐ ܘܬܠܬ ܫܢܝܢ [...]

Aphr = P

<u>Gen 11:16-17</u>

#085 XXIII.(35). 478:9-11; II 77:20-23

ܘܥܒܪ ܚܝܐ ܬܠܬܝܢ ܘܐܪܒܥ ܫܢܝܢ. ܘܐܘܠܕ ܠܦܠܓ.

ܘܚܝܐ {ܥܒܪ A,<u>B</u> / ܥܒܘܪ C} ܡܢ ܒܬܪ ܕܐܘܠܕ ܠܦܠܓ.

116

This passage also occurs in the large chronographic table discussed above. In the word order at the beginning of the first sentence, Aphr now seems to be governed primarily by a tendency toward consistency within his own table rather than by strict adherence to his scripture text. As in #084, therefore, it is impossible to find here a reliable witness to his text for the beginning of vs 16.

*Gen 11:16 [. . .]

Aphr = P

*Gen 11:17 [. . .] [. . .]

Aphr = P

Gen 11:18-19

#086 XXIII.(36). 478:14-16; II 80:1-3

A,B C A,B C omits A,B omit C

This passage also occurs in the large chronographic table discussed above. The rather considerable departure in ms C from Aphr's otherwise consistent pattern in the table is interesting. Being the more difficult reading, it deserves consideration;

perhaps Aphr is not as consistent as he first appears. On balance, however, the later (and in many ways clearly inferior) ms C cannot be preferred over the combined witness of mss A and B. No certain reflection of the beginning of vs 18 in Aphr's Gen text is provided.

*Gen 11:18 ܐܫܝܠ ܐܘܐܪܐ ܝܝ ܝܕܠܕ [. . .]

Aphr = P

*Gen 11:19 ܐܘܐܪܚ ܝܕܒ ܝܪ ܝܠܦ ܪܘܐ
Aphr = P

Gen 11:20-21

#087 XXIII.(37). 478:18-20; II 80:7-10

ܝܝ {A,B ܝܕܝܕܐ} ܝܕܠܕ ܪܘ ܐܫܝܪܐ
{C ܝܒܐ}

This passage also occurs in the large chronographic table discussed above. Here again no reliable witness is provided of the beginning of the first sentence (vs 20) in Aphr's bible text.

*Gen 11:20 ܐܘܐܪܐ ܝܝ ܝܕܝܕܐ ܝܕܠܕ [. . .]
Aphr = P

*Gen 11:21 ܐܘܐܪܚ ܝܕܒ ܝܪ ܐܫܝܪ ܪܘܐ
Aphr = P

<u>Gen 11:22-23</u>

#088 XXIII.(38). 479:2-3; II 80:14-16

ܘܣܪܘܓ ܚܝܐ ܬܠܬܝܢ ܫܢܝܢ ܘܐܘܠܕ ܠܢܚܘܪ.
ܘܚܝܐ ܣܪܘܓ ܡܢ ܒܬܪ ܕܐܘܠܕ ܠܢܚܘܪ.
ܡܐܬܝܢ ܫܢܝܢ

This passage also occurs in the large chronographic table discussed above. Here again no reliable witness is provided of the beginning of the first sentence (vs 22) in Aphr's bible text.

*Gen 11:22 [. . .] ܬܠܬܝܢ ܫܢܝܢ ܘܐܘܠܕ ܠܢܚܘܪ.

Aphr = P

*Gen 11:23 ܘܚܝܐ ܣܪܘܓ ܡܢ ܒܬܪ ܕܐܘܠܕ
ܠܢܚܘܪ ܡܐܬܝܢ ܫܢܝܢ [. . .]

Aphr = P

<u>Gen 11:24-25</u>

#089 XXIII.(39). 479:6-7; II 80:21-23

ܘܢܚܘܪ ܚܝܐ { ܥܣܪܝܢ ܘܬܫܥ A,<u>B</u> | ܟܛ C } ܫܢܝܢ ܘܐܘܠܕ
ܠܬܪܚ. ܘܚܝܐ ܢܚܘܪ ܡܢ ܒܬܪ ܕܐܘܠܕ ܠܬܪܚ
{ ܡܐܐ ܘܬܫܥܣܪܐ A,<u>B</u> | ܩܛ C } { ܫܢܝܢ A,<u>B</u> | C omits }

This passage also occurs in the large chronographic table discussed above. Here again no reliable witness is provided of the beginning of the first sentence (vs 24) in Aphr's bible text.

*Gen 11:24 [. . .] ܥܣܪܝܢ ܘܬܫܥ ܫܢܝܢ.
ܘܐܘܠܕ ܠܬܪܚ.

Aphr = P

*Gen 11:25   ܘܗܘܐ ܫܘܪ ܚܝܐ ܡܢ ܒܬܪ ܕܐܘܠܕ

[. . .] ܠܬܪܚ ܐܪܒܥ ܘܬܠܬܝܢ

Aphr = P

Gen 11:26, 32

#090 XXIII.(40). 479:12-14; II 81:5-8

$$\text{ܘܗܘܐ ܬܪܚ} \begin{Bmatrix} A,\underline{B} & \text{ܫܢܝܐ} \\ C & \text{ܒܪ} \end{Bmatrix} \text{ܫܒܥܝܢ ܘܐܘܠܕܗ}$$

ܠܐܒܪܗܡ. ܘܗܘܐ ܬܪܚ ܒܬܪ ܕܐܘܠܕܗ

$$\text{ܠܐܒܪܗܡ} \begin{Bmatrix} A,\underline{B} & \text{ܐܪܒܥ ܘܚܡܫܝܢ ܫܢܝܢ} \\ C & \text{ܩܒܠ} \end{Bmatrix}$$

ܘܡܝܬ ܬܪܚ $\begin{Bmatrix} A,\underline{B} \text{ omit} \\ C \quad \text{ܕܚܝܐ} \end{Bmatrix}$ ܒܚܪܢ.

.ܬܪܚ

This passage also occurs in the large chronographic table
discussed above. For some reason, Aphr here departs from his
usual pattern at the beginning of the first sentence (ܘܟܠ
ܚܝܐ). Is this purely accidental? His first sentence agrees
with P. Does Aphr perhaps refer back to his bible text as he
comes to the end of the Gen ch 11 table and deviate from his
previous pattern under the influence of a text that is identical
to P? One can only guess. His consistency earlier in the table
is impressive, and one may at least suspect that his Gen text
is reflected in the word order at the beginning of the first
sentence here, a sentence which reproduces Gen 11:26.

120

It is obvious that Aphr is not following his scripture
text after the first sentence. After vs 26, the Gen table itself
abandons its previous formulaic regularity. Aphr simply maintains the pattern he has established earlier for his own chronographic table; he carries it on into sections (41) and (42), utilizing chronological and genealogical information supplied by
other biblical passages outside Gen ch 11. Because Aphr's interest is purely chronological, rather than genealogical, he chooses
to mention only the birth of Abraham in this passage. Terah's
other sons and Abraham's wife are irrelevant to his computations,
and Aphr therefore omits them as he has the younger offspring
of the other individuals in his table.

Abraham's name, as usual with Aphr except when quoting
Gen 17:5 directly, is given in its longer form--evidence that,
if he has looked at his bible text when beginning to write section (40), he has done so hurriedly and with an eye primarily
on the numerals. The variant in ms C is the poorer reading. The
addition of the proper name departs from Aphr's consistent practice earlier in the table.

*Gen 11:26

ﬡﬡ ﬡﬡ [ﬡﬡ ﬡﬡ]
[. . .] ﬡﬡﬡﬡ

ﬡﬡ 10/5b1 MT Sam Tgs TSam LXX Vg] add ﬡﬡﬡ
7a1 7h5 9̲1̲4 10b1 10̲1̲1 11/9b1 12b1.2

*Gen 11:32 [. . .] ܡܐ̈ܬܝܢ ܘܚܡܫ ܫ̈ܢܝܢ [. . .]

Aphr = P

Gen 14:18-19

#091 XI.4(3). 205:21-22; 476:20-22

ܡܠܟܝܙܕܩ ܟܗܢܐ ܗܘܐ ܕܐܠܗܐ ܡܪܝܡܐ.
ܒܪܟ ܠܐܒܪܗܡ ܟܕ ܠܐ ܓܙܝܪ ܗܘܐ ....

In this allusion to Gen 14:18-19 Aphr appears to give a literal reproduction of the final part of his text of vs 18. The inclusion of ܗܘܐ (which is not necessary syntactically in Aphr's sentence) in the clause that is followed immediately by the verb ܒܪܟ is fairly strong proof that it is the text of Gen 14:18 that is reflected, rather than the similar phrase in Heb 7:1.

*Gen 14:18 [. . .] ܟܗܢܐ ܗܘܐ ܕܐܠܗܐ ܡܪܝܡܐ.

Aphr = P

Gen 15:1

#092 II.2(2). 25:8-9; 49:14-16

ܘܐܡܪ ܠܗ ܐܠܗܐ ܕܝܢ ܒܬܪ ܗܘ ܙܒܢܐ.
ܕܐܓܪܟ { B ܛܒ ܣܓܝ / A ܣܓܝ ܛܒ } ܒܟܐܢܘܬܟ.

In this formal quotation, Aphr reproduces the final portion of Gen 15:1 in support of his description of Abraham as one who achieved "righteousness apart from the law." The addition of ܒܟܐܢܘܬܟ is obviously Aphr's interpretative addition to his text, making explicit what is only implicit in the vs (cf. Gen 15:6) for the sake of his argument.[34] He is surely excerpting here from what in his text is a longer vs.

It is impossible to decide between the variant readings. That of ms A might deserve preference in the light of its difference from P. On the other hand, the two other times that Aphr uses these two words together (385:15 in a quotation of Ezek 37:10; 461:17-18), he does so according to the order of ms B here. If the presumption of consistency can be allowed, then the reading of ms B has the better claim to be the original. This is entirely uncertain, however, and no clear witness to Aphr's scripture text is afforded. Ephraem (Comm XII.1 line 2) = P.

Gen 15:4

#093 II.4(4). 27:2-3; 53:17-19

$$\text{ܡܠ ܕܐܬܐܡܪܬ . ܪܒܐ ܗܕܐ ܥܠ ܗܘ}$$
$$\text{ܘܐܬܝܕܥ ܡܠܬܐ ܩܡܪ . ܩܡܪ ܕܐܒܠ ܗܘܐ ܠܐ.}$$

Despite its appearance as a formal quotation, "You shall have a son" does not constitute a literal citation, but rather an allusion to the substance of Gen 15:4. No textual witness is provided.

Gen 15:5

#094 XVIII.1(1). 345:9-11; 817:13-16

$$\text{ܘܐܬܝܕܥܡ ܡܢܝܢ ܘܐܡܪ ܠܗ. ܕܢܗܘܝ ܙܪܥܟ}$$

[Syriac text — two lines]

This formal quotation reproduces the complete text of God's statement in Gen 15:5. It differs from P only in the addition of *dalath* on [Syriac], a feature in which Aphr may be deviating from his bible text, consciously or not.

*Gen 15:5 [Syriac text . . .]

[Syriac text]

[Syriac text]

[Syriac] Ephraem (Comm XII.1 lines 23-25)] omit *dalath* P

Gen 15:6

#095 I.10(14). 18:7-8; 33:12-13

[Syriac text — two lines]

#096 II.4(4). 27:4-5; 53:20-22

[Syriac text — two lines]

#097 XI.4(3). 205:15-16; 476:11-13

[Syriac text — three lines]

#098 XIII.4(8). 237:23-238:1; 557:16-18

[Syriac text — two lines]

These four passages, of which the latter three are formal citations, appear to reproduce Gen 15:6. There is variation
among them, however, and some or all must be inexact, possibly
contaminated by parallel NT passages:

Rom 4:3 ܗܝܡܢ ܐܒܪܗܡ ܠܐܠܗܐ ܘܐܬܚܫܒܬ
ܠܗ ܠܙܕܝܩܘ.

4:5 ... ܕܡܬܚܫܒܐ ܠܗ ܡܗܝܡܢܘܬܗ ܠܙܕܝܩܘ.

4:9 ... ܕܐܬܚܫܒܬ ܠܐܒܪܗܡ ܡܗܝܡܢܘܬܗ
ܠܙܕܩܘ.

4:22 ... ܡܛܠ ܗܢܐ ܐܬܚܫܒܬ ܠܗ ܠܙܕܝܩܘ.

Gal 3:6 ܐܝܟܢܐ ܕܗܝܡܢ ܐܒܪܗܡ ܠܐܠܗܐ
ܘܐܬܚܫܒܬ ܠܗ ܠܙܕܝܩܘ.

Jas 2:23 ܕܗܝܡܢ ܐܒܪܗܡ ܠܐܠܗܐ ܘܐܬܚܫܒܬ
ܠܗ ܠܙܕܝܩܘ ...

None of the four provides a reliable witness to Aphr's text.

#095, not being a formal citation and occurring in what
may be part of a liturgical or creedal composition, is the least
valuable as a textual witness. #096 occurs within an extended
discussion of the relationship of law and faith that depends
heavily on Rom chs 2-4. The dominating concept in this section
of the Dem is "the righteousness [ܟܐܢܘ] which is in the law,"
and ܟܐܢܘ (or ܟܐܢܘܬܐ or ܟܐܢܝ) is the term for righteousness that is used throughout the discussion. In sections
(1)-(4) of Dem II ܙܕܝܩܘܬܐ is used only once. All of this
inclines one to suspect influence from Rom ch 4 on #096, although

#096 is immediately preceded and followed by citations from Gen.

#097 occurs in a context which suggests no external influence on the choice of the noun for "righteousness." Furthermore, it is preceded by a sentence in which Aphr somewhat sarcastically paraphrases the vs: "If circumcision had been given for the acquisition of eternal life, then Scripture would have pronounced, 'Abraham circumcised, and his circumcision was reckoned to him as righteousness [ܘܗ ܙܕܩ],' but [#097]." One would expect him to use the same noun for "righteousness" in this paraphrase and in the citation itself. The fact that he changes from ܘܗ ܙܕܩ to ܘܗ ܙܕܩܘܬܐ suggests that the latter occurs in his bible text; of the various parallel vss, only Gen 15:6 contains this noun (in ms 1114 and Ephraem [Comm XII.1 lines 25-28]). The presence of ܘܗ ܙܕܩܘܬܐ in Aphr's text may also be confirmed by #098, a formal quotation that does not occur in a context which would tend to cause Aphr to modify his text. It is one of seven successive citations of Gen. The addition of ܣܘܟܠܬܗ in #097 must be recognized as an addition to Aphr's text for the sake of emphasis; his argument at this point is that it is _faith_, not circumcision, which was reckoned as righteousness. It may also reflect influence from Rom 4:5 or 9.

Although no clear attestation of Aphr's text of Gen 15:6 occurs in these passages, it is probable that it is identical to P except in the noun ܘܗ ܙܕܩܘܬܐ. Except for ms 1114, all P mss (and Tgs) read ܘܗ ܙܕܩ.

Gen 15:9-10

#099 IV.2(3). 61:18-22; 141:7-13

ܐܡܪ ܠܗ ܕܣܒ ܠܟ ܥܓܠܬܐ ܬܠܝܬܝܐ. ܘܥܙܐ
ܬܠܝܬܝܐ. ܘܫܦܢܝܢܐ ܘܒܪ ܝܘܢܐ. ܘܩܪܒ ܕܒܚ
ܐܝܟ ܐܒܪܗܡ. ܘܦܠܓ. ܘܣܡ ܗܕܡܐ
ܠܘܩܒܠ ܚܒܪܗ. ܢܦܠ ܥܠܘܗܝ ܫܢܬܐ ܘܥܡܛܢܐ
ܗܘܐ. ܘܢܚܬܬ ܢܘܪܐ ܘܒܥܪܬ ܒܝܬ ܦ̈ܠܓܐ.
ܘܐܟܠܬ ܠܩܘܪܒܢܗ ܕܐܒܪܗܡ.

This passage constitutes a summary reference to Gen 15:9, 10, 12, and 17, made by Aphr to illustrate the manner in which God typically manifested his acceptance of a sacrifice. Aphr's interest here is limited to showing that fire came down from heaven and consumed Abraham's offering. His citation of the biblical narrative is accordingly condensed. Although echoes of vss 12 and 17 are evident, no clear reflection of his text of those vss is provided.

The formal citation that begins the passage is so nearly a literal reproduction of P that it must be carefully considered. It differs from P only in the omission of ܘܕܟܪܐ ܬܠܝܬܝܐ as the second animal in the series. Is this simply memoriter error, or intentional abbreviation? One might assume so, except that Ephraem (Comm XII.2 lines 11-12) also knows a shorter text which includes only four animals. All other witnesses read five animals in the series in vs 9, although some transpose the second and third.

Aphr seems to be reproducing his text literally also in the distinctive clause, "and he laid each half over against the other," which is identical to a portion of vs 10 P.

*Gen 15:9 [. . .] ܣܒ ܠܝ ܥܓܠܬܐ ܬܠܬܬܐ
ܘܥܙܐ ܬܠܬܬܐ ܘܫܘܦܢܝܢܐ ܘܒܪ ܝܘܢܐ.

ܬܠܬܬܐ 1°] add ܘܕܟܪܐ ܬܠܬܬܐ 7a1 7h5 9l4.5 10b1 10g1 10l1 11/9b1 11l1.4 12b1.2 TJ^1 LXX^{mss}; add ܘܕܟܪܐ ܬܠܬܬܐ post ܬܠܬܬܐ 2° 5b1 Ephraem(omit ܥܓܠܬܐ ܬܠܬܬܐ)MT Sam TO TN^1 TSam LXX Vg

*Gen 15:10 [. . .] ܘܣܡ ܗܕܡܐ ܠܘܩܒܠ ܚܒܪܗ
[. . .]

comma 5b1 7a1 7h5 9l4.5 10b1 10g1 11/9b1 11l1.4 12b1.2 MT Sam Tgs TSam LXX Vg] omit 10l1

Gen 15:13; Exod 12:40

#100 II.4(4). 26:18-27:1; 53:8-17

ܘܐܬܪܫܝܡܬ ܡܠܬܐ ܕܡܘܬܒܗܘܢ. ܕܗܘܘ ܫ̈ܢܝܢ
ܐܝܣܪܝܠ ܒܐܪܥܐ ܕܡܨܪܝܢ. ܐܪܒܥܡܐ ܘܬܠܬܝܢ
ܫ̈ܢܝܢ. ܘܟܠ ܡܢܝܢܐ ܕܝܢ ... ܐܬܟܬܒ ܠܗܘܢ
ܐܪܒܥܡܐ ܘܬܠܬܝܢ ܫ̈ܢܝܢ. ܐܠܐ ܡܛܠ ܕܡܢ
ܗܝ ܫܢܬܐ. ܕܐܡܪ ܠܗ ܠܐܒܪܗܡ. ܕܡܕܥ
ܬܕܥ. ܕܥܡܘܪܐ ܢܗܘܐ ܙܪܥܟ ܒܐܪܥܐ ܕܠܐ
ܕܝܠܗܘܢ. ܘܢܦܠܚܘܢ ܒܗܘܢ ܘܢܫܥܒܕܘܢ ܐܢܘܢ.
ܐܪܒܥܡܐ ܫ̈ܢܝܢ.

#101 II.8(8). 31:1-5; 64:12-17

ܕܐܢ ܐܢܫ ܢܐܡܪ ܕܠܡܢܐ ܟܬܝܒܐ ܡܠܬܐ
ܗܕܐ. ܕܡܘܬܒܗܘܢ ܕܗܘܘ ܫ̈ܢܝܢ

[Syriac text with manuscript variants marked B and A]

In these passages Aphr discusses the contradiction between
the figures in Gen 15:13 and Exod 12:40 for the length of the
Egyptian bondage. #100 includes formal and nearly complete quotations of both vss; #101 quotes Exod 12:40 but merely alludes
to the numeral in Gen 15:13 (cf. Acts 7:6).

The variation between the mss in #101 in the phrase "in
(the land of) Egypt" is troublesome, especially since both readings are attested in other witnesses. It is not impossible that
the shorter reading in ms A is Aphr's original, which has been
corrected in ms B to the later P mss. However, virtually all
early witnesses, that is, those prior to the date of ms B in the
sixth century, show the shorter reading. More important, both
mss A and B give the longer reading in the corresponding passage
in #100. It is most reasonable to assume that the agreement of
mss A and B in #100 with ms B in #101 validates the longer reading as the original in both citations. In #101, then, the shorter
reading in ms A will be a scribal correction to the reading which
was dominant in the earlier Syriac mss of Exod. Ephraem (Comm

XII.6 lines 4-5) has the shorter reading, but the reliability of his witness is doubtful because he appears to quote the entire vs in condensed fashion.

*Gen 15:13 [. . .] ܡܕܥ ܬܕܥ ܕܬܘܬܒܐ ܢܗܘܐ
ܙܪܥܟ ܒܐܪܥܐ ܕܠܐ ܕܝܠܗܘܢ ܘܢܦܠܚܘܢ
ܒܗܘܢ ܘܢܫܥܒܕܘܢ ܐܢܘܢ ܐܪܒܥܡܐܐ
ܫ̈ܢܝܢ.

ܘܢܫܥܒܕܘܢ 5b1 7a1 7h5 91̲4̲.5 10b1 10g1 101̲1̲ 11/9b1 111̲1̲.4 12b1 Ephraem(Comm XII.4 line 21)] ܢܫܥܒܕܘܢ 12b̲2̲

*Exod 12:40 []ܡܘܬܒܗܘܢ ܕܗܘܘ ܒ̈ܢܝ ܐܝܣܪܝܠ
[ܒܐܪܥܐ ܕܡܨܪܝܢ] ܐܪܒܥܡܐܐ ܘܬܠܬܝܢ
ܫ̈ܢܝܢ.

ܒܐܪܥܐ ܕܡܨܪܝܢ 9b1 10b1.2 10j1 12al_fam_ 12b2 →] ܕܡܨܪܝܢ 5b1 7a1 7h13 8b1 91̲6̲ Ephraem MT Tgs Vg; ἐν γῇ Αἰγύπτῳ καὶ ἐν γῇ Χανάαν L̄X̄X̄; בארץ כנען ובארץ מצרים Sam TSam

<u>Gen 15:16</u>

#102 II.8(8). 31:15-16; 65:6-7

. . . ܘܕܬ̈ܪܬܝܢ ܕܢܫܠܡܘܢ ܚܘ̈ܒܝܗܘܢ ܕܐܡܘܪ̈ܝܐ.

#103 XXIII.(4). 451:19; II 13:20

. . .ܕܢܫܠܡܘܢ ܚܘ̈ܒܝܗܘܢ ܕܐܡܘܪ̈ܝܐ . . . .

Both of these allusions to the final portion of Gen 15:16 fall almost exactly into the form of the text of P. The difference in the form of the verb from that in P, Ephraem (Comm XII.4 line 28), and all other witnesses is probably to be explained by Aphr's manner of alluding to the vs. Whereas in the biblical text the verb is in the perfect aspect (ܫܠܡܘ) to express the simple present tense (". . . because the sins of the Amorites are not yet complete"), Aphr here recasts the clause in the subjunctive mood (imperfect aspect) to fit his own sentence in each case. #102: "In this God showed his patience, first, that they might be chastised because they had rebelled against Moses, and second, that the sins of the Amorites might be completed." #103: "Because the measure of their sins [i.e., the Canaanites'] was not filled up, he did not want to destroy them. He brought the descendents of Abraham into Egypt and decreed servitude for the offspring of his beloved that the sins of the Amorites might be completed. . . ." It seems probable that Aphr has here altered his text, which = P, to fit his own sentences. On the other hand, it is not impossible grammatically for a text of Gen 15:16 to have the verb ܫܠܡ in the imperfect, and it could be so in Aphr's bible. These allusions afford no clear witness to Aphr's text.

<u>Gen 16:12; 21:20; 25:18</u>

#104 XI.10(9). 211:11-14; 492:5-9

ܗܟܢܐ ܟܬܝܒ. ܕܝܬܒ ܒܡܕܒܪܐ ܘܠܦ ܗܘܐ
ܩܫܬܐ. ܕܬܗܘܐ ܐܝܕܗ ܒܟܠ. ܘܐܝܕܐ ܕܟܠ
ܒܗ. ܘܥܠ ܬܚܘܡܐ ܕܟܠܗܘܢ ܐܚܘܗܝ ܫܪܐ.

#105 XI.10(10). 213:15-17; 496:25-497:1

ܘܗܘܐ ܠܗ ܕܦܪܫܬ ܘܫܘܬܦ. ܕܬܕܥ
ܕܐܫܬܟܢ ܥܠ ܬܚܘܡܐ ܕܟܠܗܘܢ

ܐܝܪܐ . ܘܗܡܐ ܒܝܐܪ ܘ܏ܕܒܠ {
cn ,ܐܘܚܡ
A ,ܐܘܩܡ
}
. ܐܒܝܪ

#104 is a formal citation which actually consists of a mixture of elements from Gen 16:12; 21:20; and perhaps 25:18. Aphr makes this citation in support of assertions about the geographical location of the Israelites in relation to neighboring peoples. He is describing a situation in the past and therefore casts the sentence which he creates out of these Gen excerpts in the past tense. No change needs to be made in the portion quoted from Gen 21:20 ("He lived in the desert and became skilled with the bow"), since it is already in the past tense in the biblical text. The imperfect verb form in the second clause, however, must be considered Aphr's own term, despite the fact that an imperfect form of ܗܘܐ governs this clause in Gen 16:12. In #104 Aphr ties together the two portions to form a purpose clause: ". . . so that his hand would be against everyone and the hand of everyone would be against him." The verb in the third clause (ܐܒܝܪ) has apparently been altered also from its form in Aphr's text of 16:12 to fit the past tense sentence here, but the text of Gen 25:18 P will doubtless also have influenced the citation, if, as seems likely, it is from memory.

The same ambiguity attends this clause ("on the border of all his brothers he lived") in #105, which is not a formal citation but nevertheless clearly intends to cite Gen 16:12.

Aphr rearranges the elements of his biblical text and adjusts a verb form in the second clause ("and he was a wild ass among men") to conform to the past tense in which his own sentence is cast.

Although one can have no hesitancy in assuming that Aphr knows a text = P for Gen 16:12, the different word order in these citations and the several apparent departures from his bible text obstruct a clear witness. The fact of the parallel text in Gen 25:18 also complicates the picture. Because the concluding portion of Gen 21:20 is quoted intact within #104, however, it may safely be taken as a reproduction of Aphr's text.

*Gen 21:20 [. . .] []ܝܬܒ ܒܡܕܒܪܐ ܘܗܘܐ ܪܡܐ ܩܫܬܐ.

ܒܡܕܒܪܐ MT Sam Tgs TSam LXX] add ܕܦܐܪܢ P LXX^{mss} Vg

<u>Gen 17:1, 24, 25</u>

#106 XI.5(4). 206:4-6; 477:9-12

ܐܠܐ {ܟܕ cn / ܟܕ A} ܗܘܐ ܒܪ ܬܫܥܝܢ ܘܬܫܥ ܫܢ̈ܝܢ

ܐܘܕܥܗ ܡܪܝܐ ܕܠܒܬܪ ܡܐܐ ܫܢ̈ܝܢ

ܒܪܐ ܡܬܝܠܕ ܠܗ. ܗܘܝܢ ܥܕܪܗ.

#107 XI.5(4). 206:10-13; 477:19-24

ܘܓܙܪ ܐܒܪܗܡ ܒܣܪܐ ܕܥܘܪܠܘܬܗ. ܒܪ

ܬܫܥܝܢ ܘܬܫܥ ܫܢ̈ܝܢ. ܘܓܙܪ ܠܐܫܡܥܝܠ

ܒܪܗ ܒܪ ܬܠܬܥܣܪܐ ܫܢܝ̈ܢ. {ܘܐܬܓ̈ܙܪ, cn / ܘܐܬܓܙܪ, A}
ܒܫܢܬܗ ܘܩܛܝܢ ܒܣܘܦܗ ܓܙܪ ܐܒܪܗܡ
ܒܒܣܪܗ ܗܘ. ܐܝܟ ܕܡܠܠ ܥܡܗ ܐܠܗܐ.

#106 is an allusion to Gen 17:1, and #107 is an allusion to Gen 17:24-25. Both are sufficiently paraphrastic that their value as textual witnesses is limited to the chronological references alone, although #107 appears to echo the P text of vs 24 generally. It is clear from #107 that Aphr's text of vs 24 contains the numeral "ninety-nine" for Abraham's age, but the exact text-form is not reflected.

*Gen 17:1 [. . .] ܒܪ ܬܫܥܝܢ ܘܬܫܥ ܫܢܝ̈ܢ

Aphr = P

*Gen 17:25 [] ܐܝܫܡܥܝܠ ܒܪܗ ܒܪ ܬܠܬܥܣܪ [. . .]

Aphr = P

Gen 17:5

#108 XI.1(1). 202:3-5; 468:4-7

ܟܕ ܐܡܪ ܠܗ ܕܠܐ ܢܬܩܪܐ ܫܡܟ ܐܒܪܡ.
ܐܠܐ ܢܗܘܐ ܫܡܟ ܐܒܪܗܡ. ܡܛܠ ܕܐܒܐ
ܠܣܘܓܐܐ ܕܥܡ̈ܡܐ ܝܗܒܬܟ.

#109 XI.10(10). 214:3-4; 497:15-16

ܘܫܠܡܐ ܡܠܬܐ ܕܐܡܪ ܐܠܗܐ ܠܐܒܪܗܡ.
ܕܐܒܐ ܠܣܘܓܐܐ ܕܥܡ̈ܡܐ ܝܗܒܬܟ.

#110 XII.7(11). 228:10-13; 533:16-18

ܒܗ ܒܙܒܢܗ ܘܐܡܪ ܠܗ. ܕܠܐ ܬܬܩܪܐ ܬܘܒ
ܫܡܟ ܐܒܪܡ. ܐܠܐ ܢܗܘܐ ܫܡܟ ܐܒܪܗܡ.
ܡܛܠ ܕܐܒܐ ܠܣܘܓܐܐ ܕܥܡ̈ܡܐ ܝܗܒܬܟ.

#111 XVI.1(1). 320:2-3; 760:3-5

ܐܝܟ ܕܐܡܪ ܐܠܗܐ ܠܐܒܪܗܡ. ܕܐܒܐ
ܠܣܘܓܐܐ ܕܥܡ̈ܡܐ ܝܗܒܬܟ

All four of these passages contain formal quotations of Gen 17:5, although #109 and #111 are intentionally partial. The four are unanimous in their witness except for the absence of ܬܘܒ from #108, in contrast to #110. What is the significance of this variation? Neither reading can be dismissed as impossible. Virtually all witnesses include the adverb, but ms 11l5 and a few LXX mss do omit it.[35] (Ephraem does not cite this vs.)

It seems unlikely that Aphr knows two different forms of the text, nor does scribal correction provide a convincing explanation. Any such correction would most likely have been in the direction of the dominant Syriac textual tradition; thus the scribe would have added ܬܘܒ to the citations which originally lacked it. However, the manner in which Aphr utilizes #110 makes it all but certain that ܬܘܒ was an integral part of the text which he cites there.

Dem XII is concerned generally with showing that the Christian Easter celebration is the proper replacement for the older Jewish Passover feast. Accordingly, in section (11) Aphr

cites three OT passages which, for him, show that the Hebrew
scriptures themselves taught the Jews that the elements of their
religion were destined to be replaced one day. These three passages are chosen because they support his contention that tempo-
rariness--displacement of the old by the new--was an inherent
aspect of Judaism. So, Jer 3:16 at 532:24: "They will not say
anymore [ܒ ܩ ܕ] 'the ark of the covenant of the Lord,' . . .
nor shall it be done anymore [ܒ ܩ ܕ]," and Jer 31:31-32 at 533:6:
"I will complete with the house of Israel and with the house of
Judah a new covenant, not like that covenant which I gave to
their fathers . . . ," and #110. It seems probable that Gen 17:5
suggested itself to Aphr at this point because of its opening
words, "Your name will not anymore be called. . . ."   ܒ ܩ ܕ
thus becomes something of a catchword in these citations of Aphr.
It is doubtful whether the vs would have the force that Aphr
expects of it here if it lacked ܒ ܩ ܕ .

By contrast, the context in which #108 occurs will have
encouraged Aphr to omit ܒ ܩ ܕ , even if it were present in his
bible text. At the beginning of Dem XI,[36] Aphr has no interest
at all in demonstrating that any kind of change or substitution
has occurred in God's original economy. Instead Aphr seeks to
show that from the very beginning God intended Abraham to be the
forebear of many nations, not simply of the Jews. For this reason he will have shaped his citation of Gen 17:5 to suit his
emphasis by omitting ܒ ܩ ܕ . He deliberately avoids treating

the vs as describing a move on God's part from old to new; he wishes instead to see it as indicating the significance that Abraham was originally intended to have. The introduction to #108 reads: "When God blessed Abraham and made him head of all believing, righteous, and upright men, God did not make him father of only one people, as he said to him. . . ." Cf. 476:2-4: "And Abraham, when God chose him . . . he called him and chose him and named him that he should be father of all the nations." It appears from this that #110 reflects Aphr's bible text accurately, while #108 is abbreviated to accomodate his argument.

*Gen 17:5 []ܠܐ ܬܬܩܪܐ ܬܘܒ ܫܡܟ ܐܒܪܡ
ܐܠܐ ܢܗܘܐ ܫܡܟ ܐܒܪܗܡ ܡܛܠ
ܕܐܒܐ ܠܣܘܓܐܐ ܕܥܡܡܐ ܝܗܒܬܟ.

ܬܘܒ 5bl 7al 7h5 9l1 10bl 10gl 10l1 11/9bl 11l4 12bl.2 MT Sam Tgs TSam LXX Vg] omit 11l5 LXX^{mss}

Gen 17:10

#112 XI.3(2). 204:10-11; 472:22-24

ܐܝܟ ܕܐܡܪ ܠܗ ܐܠܗܐ. ܕܗܢܐ ܩܝܡܐ
ܕܬܛܪܘܢ. ܕܢ ܬܓܙܪܘܢ ܟܠ ܕܟܪܐ.

This formal quotation is made by Aphr to prove his assertion that circumcision, instead of having inherent salvific value, was enjoined in the beginning merely as a sign and covenant.[37] His point is to show the linkage between circumcision and covenant. Therefore, he cites vs 10 in abbreviated form in order to bring these two key words (ܩܝܡܐ and ܬܓܙܪܘܢ) as close

together as possible. There can be virtually no doubt that Aphr's
text contains the phrase, "between me and you and your descendants
after you," even though it is not reflected here. No other witness omits it, and a motive for condensation is evident on Aphr's
part.

*Gen 17:10 ܓܒ [. . .]ܕܗ ܡܠܘܢ

ܕܒܝܬܗ.

P Ephraem(Comm XIV.1
lines 29-30)

Gen 18:6; 22:18; 26:4

#113 II.3(3). 26:7-9; 52:17-21

A ܠܗܘܢ
B ܒܗܘܢ

#114 XII.7(11). 228:13-14; 533:19-20

#115 XX.(17). 391:13-17; 925:12-19

B
A

B
A

138

ܕܬܠܬܐ ܡܢ ܗܘܐ ܬܠܬ {B ܩܡܚܐ ܢ
                        {A ܩܡܚܐ ܢ

ܬ {A ܬܠܬ ܩܡܚܐ ܗܘܐ ܘܬܠܬ ܕܬܡܝܢ
 {B ܘܕܬܠܬ

ܬܠܬ ܩܡܚܐ ܘܕܬܠܬܐ {B ܐܪܒܥܝܢ
                      {A ܐܪܒܥܬܐ

ܕܕܒܝܗܘܢ ܐܬܚܙܝܘ ܠܗܘܢ ܠܡܐܟܠ.

#115 is part of an extended paraphrastic summary of Gen
18:1-15 in 924:23-925:19 in which Aphr alludes to Abraham's
reception of the three strangers as an illustration of Christian
hospitality. Despite strong echoes of P throughout this passage,
none of the allusions is close enough to be a reliable textual
witness. Also in the case of #115, despite Parisot's identification of it as a scripture citation,[38] the allusion to Gen 18:6
is too distant to provide a clear reflection of Aphr's text.
The abbreviating tendency particularly stands in the way of drawing any conclusions from the text-form here of the phrase, "three
measures of fine meal." Aphr's use of a single noun for "fine
meal" after ܣܐܡܝܢ is indeed intriguing, and the significance
of the variation in the mss is difficult to assess. All P mss
read ܣܐܡܝܢ ܣܡܝܕܐ ܕܢܩܝܐ at this point, and all other
witnesses except the LXX (τρία μέτα σεμιδάλεως) agree in using
a two-word phrase to denote "fine meal." Therefore, if in either
of the two mss the scribe were correcting Aphr to P, the change
would probably have involved replacing the single noun with a

two-word phrase. Is it possible then that early Syriac mss which
have not survived read only one noun for "fine meal" in Gen 18:6
and that they sometimes differed as to which noun they read? If
so, Aphr's form of the phrase "three measures of fine meal" in
#115 might in fact be a literal reproduction of his text, and his
reading (probably ܪܤܝܬܐ inasmuch as ms B seems consistently
to have the better readings in this passage) was corrected by the
scribe in ms A who was used to a different noun in the passage.

One might attempt to support such a view with a line in
Ephraem (Comm XV.1 lines 13-14: ܐܒܪܗܝܡ ܕܗ̈ܘ ܐܪܡܝܬܝ
ܘܐܡܪ ܣܡܝܕܐ ܬܠܬ ܕܐܦܬ ܗܘܐ ܠܘܬ) where
again only a single noun for "fine meal" is used--an entirely
different noun than in Aphr. Reliance upon Ephraem here is very
dangerous, however, because he too is clearly paraphrasing and
condensing in this sentence. One simply cannot know how closely
he is following his bible text; ܣܡܝܕܐ may be his own term.

Despite the fact that the two mss of Aphr agree in reading a single term for "fine meal" and that no obvious reason
exists for a scribe to have preferred one noun over another,[39]
it is entirely possible that Aphr knows a bible text identical
to P at this point. His use of a single noun for "fine meal"
will then be simply the sort of paraphrastic economizing that is
frequently encountered elsewhere in his allusions. It is equally
possible that the variation occurs in the two mss merely because
of a scribe's personal preference, a preference that was strong

enough to lead to a complete substitution. These several uncertainties make it impossible to determine whether Aphr knows a
text which reads a single noun for "fine meal," perhaps under
the influence of the LXX, or is simply quoting his bible text
here in slightly condensed form.

Nor can any conclusions be drawn from the final portion
of #115, "that in his seed all nations would be blessed." It is
obvious that Aphr is not quoting his text exactly here, and no
clear reflection of his text of Gen 18:18 is presented. #113
and #114 also purport to cite this promise to Abraham, both as
formal quotations. But their textual value is undermined by the
fact that it is impossible to determine which bible vs they are
citing. This promise to Abraham is given in nearly identical
form in no fewer than five passages: Gen 18:18; 22:18; 26:4;
Acts 3:25; Gal 3:8 (cf. Gen 28:14). The three Gen passages agree
in word order and in vocabulary; however, 18:18 reads "in you"
while 22:18 and 26:4 read "in your seed." Aphr agrees with the
latter two vss except in word order; he begins, in all three quotations, with the prepositional phrase instead of the verb. No
other ancient Semitic version, including Ephraem (who quotes only
26:4--Comm XX.3 lines 25-26), gives the text of the promise in
Gen 22:18//26:4 in any other form than with the verb in initial
position. Does Aphr alone witness an authentic ancient text in
which the word order of 22:18//26:4 is altered?

That cannot be finally ruled out, of course, but it seems

much more likely that Aphr is citing here a conflation of more
than one passage in his bible text. He quotes the essential text
of Gen 22:18//26:4 P but alters the word order under the influence of Acts 3:25 P: ܪܟܘܬ ܝܢܠ ܐܬܘܢ ܒܪܝܢܕ
ܕܐܪܝܐ. This confusion is facilitated by the fact that Gal
3:8, which also begins with the prepositional phrase (but "in
you" instead of "in your seed"), more exactly agrees with the
vocabulary of the Gen vss than does the Acts passage. It is not
at all surprising that #113 occurs in a discussion that follows
rather closely the argument and hermeneutical approach of Gal
ch 3; it is preceded and followed by citations from Gal ch 3.

There is not sufficient basis for concluding that Aphr
knows a form of Gen 22:18//26:4 that is different from P. None
of the three passages given above provides adequate basis for
identifying Aphr's text of any one of the biblical vss that contain the promise to Abraham.[40]

Gen 18:14

#116 XXI.(4). 398:1-4; 940:16-19

ܢܕ ܐܡܠܐ ܡܢ ܐܪܝܡ ܪܝܬܘܐܪܗ ܐܢܐ ܡܢ
ܐܬܘܪ ܐܬܠ ܡܗ ܐܒܪܝܕ ܐܪܠ
ܐܪܘܠ ܐܝܗ ܐܡܬܘ ܠܬܘܗ ܝܐܡܪܐ
.ܝܐܬܘܪ

This formal citation of the angel's words to Abraham is
made merely to identify a point in the biblical history from
which chronological reckonings can be figured. Aphr has no

142

interest in the details of the text itself. There can be little question that he is quoting from memory, and it is apparent that confusion of parallel passages is involved here. The angel's words may be taken from either Gen 18:10 or 18:14. The initial "at this time" in place of the initial infinitive (ܢܐܡܪ) in vs 10 P indicates that it is the text of vs 14 which Aphr has primarily in mind. Nevertheless, the citation is not exact.

Apparently he has confused the initial ܕܢܒܪ ܗ ܗܘ of Gen 18:14 with the longer phrase ܗܘ ܕܢܒܪ ܒܙܒܢܐ ܐܚܪܢܐ from Gen 17:21, a vs which also predicts the birth of Abraham's son. It is impossible to decide whether the omission of ܒܪ ܗܝ, ܚܝ after ܠܘܬܗ is an accident or conscious abbreviation. No other witness omits it. If Aphr understands this clause as meaning "next year,"[41] it would be redundant to include it along with the initial adverbial phrase ("at this time next year") which is taken from 17:21.

Although #116 appears to reflect the substance of Aphr's text of Gen 18:14, the evident confusion with 17:21 and the close similarity between 18:14 and 18:10 make it impossible to find here a clear textual witness.

Gen 18:19

#117 II.2(2). 25:12-15; 49:21-25

ܕܝܠܗܘܢ . ܐܝܟ ܦܩܕ ܐܒܪܗܡ ܕܐ
ܕܐܡܪ . ܐܝܟ ܘܗܝ ܕܗܘܐ ܗܝ ܗܘܐܬ

{B ... } ... (Syriac text with manuscript variants)

{B omits / A ...} ... (Syriac text)

... (Syriac text)

This formal quotation occurs in a series of biblical references which Aphr makes to support his argument that righteousness preceded the Mosaic law and was always attainable apart from it. Abbreviation may be expected in such a string of related proof texts (cf. #092 above), and this citation is in fact a shortened and paraphrased version of Gen 18:19. The addition of "The Lord said to Abraham" is of course Aphr's own supplement; the initial ... of vs 19 P is similarly droppped in the citation, since it serves in the biblical narrative to connect vs 19 to vs 18 and the latter is not included here.

Wright and Parisot are doubtless correct in following the shorter text of ms B. The addition of "and the members of his household" in ms A is probably a correction to P. The textform of ms B elsewhere conforms to the abbreviating tendency of the citation. It is extremely doubtful that this omission is actually a feature of Aphr's bible text, however; no other witness supports it. Aphr appears to be summarizing the remainder of his vs when he uses ... (a common biblical phrase--cf. Lev 16:15; Num 15:40; Deut 5:29). Part of the text of vs 19 that is so summarized is in fact echoed in the sentence preceding the quotation itself ("that they do righteousness and justice"). Even though this sentence is not a formal quotation, one can assume that it preserves the form of the phrase "righteousness and justice" in Aphr's bible text. The very last clause of vs 19 is omitted from the citation because it is unrelated to Aphr's theological argument.

As is the case elsewhere in the Dems, one cannot be certain which form of the participial construction ("I know") is Aphr's original. Not only do the mss differ here, neither is consistent in its handling of this type of construction generally; sometimes the independent pronoun is used, but other times the enclitic form of the pronoun occurs.

*Gen 18:19 [. . .] [ܕܝܕܥܢܐ] ܠܗ ܕܡܦܩܕ
ܠܒܢܘܗܝ [. . .] ܕܢܥܒܕܘܢ ܙܕܝܩܘܬܐ ܘܕܝܢܐ [. . .]

ܙܕܝܩܘܬܐ ܘܕܝܢܐ 5b1 7a1 7h5 911.4 1011 1111 MT Sam Tgs TSam LXX Vg] ܕܝܢܐ ܘܙܕܝܩܘܬܐ 10b1 10g1 11/9b1 12al<u>fam</u> 12b1 →

<u>Gen 18:25</u>

#118 XIV.4(5). 249:13-15; 584:15-18

ܘܐܦ ܟܠ ܕܝܢܐ {B ܕܫܠܝܐ / A omits} ܕܥܒܕܘܢ ܐܓܪ
ܪܘܫܥܗ ܢܓܐ ܐܠܗ. ܘܐܩܘܡ ܠܐܒܪܗܡ
ܪܘܫܥܗ ܕܒ ܐܡܪ ܠܗ. ܕܠܐ ܡܬܒܥܐ ܕܝܢܐ
ܒܪܘܓܙܐ.

This formal quotation is ambiguous. The saying may be either that of Abraham as a plea to God ("Let not judgment be executed in wrath") or of God as a reply to Abraham ("Judgment will not be executed in wrath"). The former is probable. Not only does it conform to the actual sense of the biblical vs in the Gen narrative, but it also coincides with the immediately following example (Aphr cites several illustrations of God's righteousness in section [5]), in which Aphr mentions that God justified himself to Ezekiel when the prophet challenged him with the words of Ezek 9:8 and 11:3.

Aphr is being free in this citation. The interpretative addition of ܟܐܢܘܬܐ is clearly an echo of Abraham's questions in Gen 18:23-24. His text there apparently agrees with P, which has misunderstood העף of the MT. No other witness supports such an addition in vs 25. Given the looseness of the citation, no clear textual witness is afforded.

Gen 18:27

#119 VII.6(16). 144:9-10; 337:10-11

ܐܡܪ ܒܝ ܐܝܟ ܐܝܪܝܡܝܢ . ܗܐܢܐ ܐܝܬ ,ܒܝܐ
ܘܥܦܪܐ.

This formal quotation occurs in a passage where Aphr extols humility (and condemns its opposite) before God, giving a series of biblical examples. He cites these words by Abraham in Gen 18:27 as a model of Christian self-appraisal; the first part of the vs is not included because it is not relevant to his theme.

Aphr's usage of the copulative particle contrasts with

with P, which repeats the personal pronoun as a copula: ܘܐܢܐ ܥܦܪܐ ܐܢܐ ܘܩܛܡܐ.[42] Does Aphr know a different bible text here, or is he merely indulging in stylistic variation? Ephraem does not cite this vs, and the other Semitic versions entirely lack a copulative here. Although it bears no sure marks of looseness, the reliability of the citation as a witness to Aphr's text is not beyond question.

*Gen 18:27 [. . .] ܐܢܐ ܐܝܬܝ ܥܦܪܐ ܘܩܛܡܐ.

ܐܝܬܝ ܥܦܪܐ] ܥܦܪܐ ܐܢܐ P

<u>Gen 19:24</u>

#120 XIV.26(42). 293:10-12; 696:13-16

ܘܠܣܕܘܡܝ̈ܐ {ܚܣ A / ܚܣܝ B} ܐܝܟ ܕܒܪ ܡܠܐܟܘܬܗ,

ܕܠܐ ܬܒܘ ܘܗܦܟ {ܒܒܪܫܘܬܗܘܢ B / ܒܒܫܘܬܗܘܢ A}

ܘܗܘ ܗܦܟ. ܘܐܚܪܒ ܘܗܦܟ ܒܢܘܪܐ

ܘܟܒܪܝܬܐ.

#121 XVIII.2(2). 347:13; 821:23-24

. . . ܠܣܕܘܡܝ̈ܐ ܕܐܬܗܦܟܘ ܒ ܢܘܪܐ

{ܘܟܒܪܝܬܐ A / ܘܒܟܒܪܝܬܐ B} ܚܛܗ̈ܘܢ.

#122 XXI.(6). 401:2-3; 948:1-4

ܕܐܠܐ ܢܚܬ ܐܠܗܐ ܡܛܪܐ ܠܣܕܘܡ

ܘܠܚܒܪ̈ܬܗ. ܠܐ ܗܘܐ ܒܢܘܪܐ ܘܒܟܒܪܝܬܐ

ܗܦܟ ܗܘܐ ܠܗܝܢ

These three allusions to Gen 19:24-25 (cf. also 185:19-22)
are quite distant and are generally without value as textual witnesses. Despite the freedom exercised in the three passages,
their consistency in the phrase from Gen 19:24, "fire and brim-
stone," suggests that they accurately reflect Aphr's text at this
point. Influence by parallel vss in P is possible, however: Ps
11:6 (ܟܒܪܝܬܐ ܢܘܪܐ); Ezek 38:22 (ܟܒܪܝܬܐ ܢܘܪܐ);
and Luke 17:29 (ܢܘܪܐ ܘܟܒܪܝܬܐ ܡܢ ܫܡܝܐ).

   *Gen 19:24   [. . .] ܟܒܪܝܬܐ ܢܘܪܐ [. . .]
ܟܒܪܝܬܐ ܢܘܪܐ 7a1 911 12b2 → LXX^{mss}(πῦρ καὶ
θεῖον)] ܢܘܪܐ ܟܒܪܝܬ 5b1 7h5 914 10b1 10g1
1011 11/9b1 12b1 Ephraem(Comm XVI.7 lines 21-22) MT Sam
Tgs TSam LXX Vg

Gen 19:29

#123 XIV.5(6). 250:12-13; 585:20-22

   Not a formal citation, this reference to the deliverance
of Lot nevertheless includes a clause that so closely resembles
part of Gen 19:29 P, one must ask if Aphr's text is literally
reproduced. The use of the verb ܦܠܛ is the only variant from
P, which employs ܫܕܪ (MT ישלח). The Tgs also employ שלח here;
cf. Old Latin mss, respectively, emittit, eiecit, exemit, and
LXX ἐξαπέστειλεν. Of the other ancient witnesses, only the Vg
agrees with Aphr: et liberavit Loth. Although the Vg never elsewhere seems to render the Pi'el of שלח with libero (the usual

choice is mitto, demitto, or emitto, even in the "liberation" passages of Exod chs 5-12), this may well be merely an interpretative translation of the MT.[43] An allusion to Lot in 2 Pet 2:7 employs a reference to his deliverance from Sodom, but Aphr does not seem to know the four minor catholic epistles and Revelation, which were not a part of the P canon. The Philoxenian version reads a different verb in 2 Pet 2:7 (ܦܨܝ).

One is left with uncertainty regarding the source of the verb ܦܠܛ in this allusion. It may be Aphr's own paraphrastic selection, but his use of it again at 925:19-21 (ܘܐܦ ܠܘܛ ܘܦܠܛܗ ܡܢ ܣܕܘܡ . . .) may perhaps indicate its presence in his Gen text. It is unfortunate that Ephraem does not cite this vs.

*Gen 19:29 [. . .] [ܘܦܠܛ] ܠܠܘܛ ܡܢ ܓܘ
[. . .] ܗܦܟܬܐ

ܘܦܠܛ Vg] ܘܫܕܪ P MT Sam Tgs TSam LXX

Gen 21:5; 25:7

#124 XI.5(4). 206:6-7; 478:12-14

ܗܝܕܝܢ ܓܙܪܗ. ܟܕ ܗܘܐ ܒܪ ܡܐܐ ܫܢܝ̈ܢ
ܐܬܝܠܕ ܠܗ ܐܝܣܚܩ.

#125 XXIII.(15). 464:6-8; II 44:4-7

ܘܟܕ ܗܘܐ ܐܒܪܗܡ ܒܪ ܡܐܐ ܫܢܝ̈ܢ . . .
{ܗܕܝܢ A,B / ܘܗܕܝܢ C} ܐܬܝܠܕ ܐܝܣܚܩ.

#126 XXIII.(15). 464:12-13; II 44:12-14

$$\left\{ \begin{array}{l} \text{A,}\underline{\text{B}} \\ \text{C} \end{array} \right.$$ ܘܨܒܪ ܐܘܪܝܟ} ܒܪ ܐܟܐ ܐܝܪ̈ܟܗ ܒܪ ܐܟܐ ܘܒܣܗ

#127 XXIII.(41). 479:18-20; II 81:14-18

ܐܣܚܘܐ ܐܩܘܢ̈ ܬܪ̈ ܐܟܐ ܐܝܪ̈ܟܗ ܘܐܟ
ܐܣܚܘܐ ܐܩܘܢ̈ܕ ܒܥ ܕܒ ܐܝܪ̈ܟܗ ܘܐܟ
ܕܪ̈ܘܗܝ, ܐܘ̈ܗ} ܬܪ̈ $\left\{ \begin{array}{l} \text{A,B} \\ \text{C} \end{array} \right.$ ܘܨܒܪ ܐܘܪܝܬ}

$$\left\{ \begin{array}{l} \text{A,}\underline{\text{B}} \\ \text{C} \end{array} \right.$$ ܬܪ̈ ܘܨܒܪ ܐܘܪܝܟܐ ܐܟܐ

None of these is a formal citation. They are of textual
value only for the numerals attested, the age of Abraham at the
birth of Isaac and at his own death. While #124 and #125 echo
P for the entire text of Gen 21:5, they do not provide a basis
on which to reconstruct Aphr's text of that vs. #127 is Aphr's
own artificially constructed component of the large chronographic
table discussed above; it has no counterpart in the table in Gen
ch 11 in any witness. Thus, Aphr is not quoting scripture at
this point, merely utilizing data from Gen 21:5 and 25:7. While
these passages provide clear witness to the substance of the
numerals in the two vss, they do not afford a clear view of the
exact text in either case. Aphr's text gives Abraham's age as
100 years in Gen 21:5 and as 175 years in Gen 27:5; both readings
agree with P.

Gen 25:23

#128 XIV.16(27). 272:14-15; 644:5-6

ܐܝܟ ܕܐܡܪ ܠܗ ܠܪܦܩܐ. ܕܪܒܐ ܢܫܬܥܒܕ ܠܙܥܘܪܐ.

Seeking to demonstrate the reason for Rebekah's partiality to Jacob, Aphr makes this formal citation of the final portion of Gen 25:23, intentionally excerpting from the overall vs.

*Gen 25:23 [. . .] []ܪܒܐ ܢܫܬܥܒܕ ܠܙܥܘܪܐ.

Aphr = P

Gen 25:26; 35:28

#129 XXIII.(15). 464:10; II 44:9-10

ܘܐܝܣܚܩ ܐܘܠܕ ܠܝܥܩܘܒ ܘܗܘܐ ܒܪ ܫܬܝܢ ܫܢܝ̈ܢ.

#130 XXIII.(15). 465:4; II 45:8-9

. . . {A,B ܡܝܬ / C ܘܡܝܬ} ܒܪ ܡܐܐ {A,B ܘܬܡܢܐܝܢ / C ܘܬܡܢܝܢ} ܫܢܝ̈ܢ.

#131 XXIII.(42). 479:22-480:2; II 81;21-24

ܘܗܘܐ ܐܝܣܚܩ ܫܬܝܢ ܫܢܝ̈ܢ ܘܐܘܠܕ ܠܝܥܩܘܒ

ܘܗܘܐ ܐܝܣܚܩ ܡܢ ܒܬܪ ܕܐܘܠܕ ܠܝܥܩܘܒ.

{A,B ܡܐܐ ܘܥܣܪܝܢ / C ܡܟ} ܫܢܝ̈ܢ ܚܝܐ {A,B omit / C ܕܝܢ}

ܕܚܝܘ̈ܗܝ {A,B ܡܐܐ ܘܬܡܢܐܝܢ / C ܡܦ} ܫܢܝ̈ܢ.

None of these is a formal citation. They are of textual

value only for the numerals attested, the age of Isaac at the
birth of his twin sons and at his own death. Aphr is not quoting scripture here, merely utilizing chronological data from
Gen 25:26 and 35:28. While these passages provide clear witness
to the substance of the numerals in the two vss, they do not
afford a clear view of the exact text in either case. Aphr's
text gives Isaac's age as 60 years in Gen 25:26 and as 180 years
in Gen 35:28; both readings agree with P.

Gen 25:27

#132 IX.9(13). 188:16-17; 440:2-4

Though not a formal citation, this sentence literally
reproduces the final clause of Gen 25:27 P. It seems best to
set aside the customary preference for the reading most different from P here, because there is no place for ܪ‍ܒܐ at this
point in Aphr's discussion without considerable awkwardness. A
mechanical error has probably produced ܪ‍ܒܐ in ms A. Only the
final portion of vs 27 is mentioned, because Aphr is concerned
with Jacob only as a model of humility.

*Gen 25:27   ܝܥܩܘܒ ܥܒܪ ܬܡܝܡ[] [. . .]
                              ܒܡܫܟܢܐ.

Aphr = P

Gen 27:40

#133 III.9(13). 55:17-18; 125:19-21

ܗܟܢܐ ܓܝܪ ܐܡܪ ܐܝܣܚܩ ܠܥܣܘ. ܕܠܝܥܩܘܒ
ܐܚܘܟ ܬܦܠܘܚ. ܘܐܡܬܝ ܕܬܬܘܒ ܬܦܪܘܩ ܢܝܪܗ
ܡܢ ܨܘܪܟ.

#134 III.9(13). 55:20-21; 125:24-128:1

ܘܠܥܩܒܐ ܕܝܢ ܫܡܥ ܐܡܪ ܐܝܣܚܩ ܠܥܣܘ.
{ܕܠܝܥܩܘܒ ܐܚܘܟ B} ܬܦܠܘܚ.
{ܕܠܐܚܘܟ ܝܥܩܘܒ A}

#135 V.18(24). 100:2-4; 233:4-5

ܐܝܟ ܕܐܡܪ ܐܝܣܚܩ ܠܥܣܘ. ܕܠܝܥܩܘܒ
ܐܚܘܟ ܬܦܠܘܚ.

All three passages contain formal quotations of part of Gen 27:40. In each case, Aphr makes the citation simply to support a statement about the divinely ordained superiority of Jacob over Isaac. For this reason, the initial "by your sword you will live" is omitted.

The text reflected agrees with P except for the addition of the name "Jacob." One might be inclined to regard this as Aphr's own clarifying addition, since, when the vs is cited out of the context of the Gen narrative, "your brother" would be ambiguous. However, such an explanation can be defended only for #133. Both #134 and #135 occur in passages where the person designated by "your brother" is quite clear. Therefore, one is compelled to assume that "Jacob" is in Aphr's bible text, even

though no other ancient witness agrees. Unfortunately, Ephraem
does not cite this vs. In #134, ms B is to be followed; the
reading of ms A is certainly an accidental transposition caused
by the scribe's familiarity with a text identical to P. It would
be most surprising to find Aphr altering the wording of a citation which has just been given a few lines previously.

*Gen 27:40 . ܝܘܠܬܕܐ ܝܩܘܪ ܢܩܘܠܒܐ[] [. . .]

. ܝܢܝܢܩܣ ܝܦ ܡܝܫܝ ܢܕܒܠ ܢܩܕܘ ܝܩܐ

ܝܩܘܪ ܢܩܘܠܒܐ] ܝܩܘܪܠܘܐ P MT Sam Tgs
TSam LXX Vg | ܝܘܠܒܕܐ 5b1 7a1 7h5 7k4 8b1 915 10b1
10g1 11/9b1 1113.5 12b1.2 MT Sam TO TJ¹ TF TSam] add
ܪܕܘܢܒܒ 1114 TN¹(תהוי פלח ומשועבד)

Gen 28:13

#136 IV.4(5). 63:8-9; 145:10-12

. ܝܩܢܝܒܢ ܡܒܠܓܢ ܢܩܕ ܪܘܕ ܡܕܘܟܪܘ
ܠܟ ܪܝܒܣܘ . ܪܕܠܒܫ ܕܘܡܒܢ ܝܢܝܬܕܘܟܪܕ
. ܡܝܒ ܠܟ ܝܩܡܣ

This allusion to Jacob's vision of the ladder extending
from earth to heaven falls into a verbatim reproduction of a portion of Gen 28:13, but the amount of material is so small as to
be of very limited value. The use of ܠܥ here may signal Aphr's
consciousness that he is at this point giving the words of scripture itself, and the phrase so designated is identical to P.
Because this clause ("and the Lord was standing at the top of
it") is imbedded in Aphr's own sentence, in a construction where
the initial ܡܩ of P would be unnecessary and intrusive, it is

impossible to determine from this allusion whether or not Aphr's bible text contains ܘܗܐ at the beginning of the clause. This is unfortunate, because the LXX, Vg, and Ephraem (Comm XXVI.1 lines 14-19) all omit ܘܗܐ (though Ephraem may be abbreviating in his citation), and the possibility exists of a variant here in the early Syriac mss.

<u>Gen 28:18</u>

#137 IV.4(4). 63:11-13; 145:15-17

ܘܩܪܝܗ̇ ܝܥܩܘܒ ܠܐܬܪܐ ܗܘ ܒܝܬ ܐܝܠ.
ܘܐܩܝܡ ܝܥܩܘܒ ܬܡܢ. ܩܝܡܬܐ ܕܟܐܦܐ
ܠܣܗܕܘܬܐ. ܘܐܫܕ ܡܫܚܐ ܒܪܝܫܗ̇.

This allusion to Gen 28:18-19 echoes P unmistakably. Aphr is too free, however, for this passage to provide a significant textual witness. He certainly falls into the exact words of P in the final clause ("and he poured oil on its top"); otherwise, no deductions about his text can be sustained.

*Gen 28:18 [. . .] ܘܐܫܕ ܡܫܚܐ ܒܪܝܫܗ̇.

Aphr = P

<u>Gen 29:1</u>

#138 IV.5(6). 64:6-7; 148:17

ܘܐܪܝܡ ܪ̈ܓܠܘܗܝ ܠܐܪܥܐ ܕܒ̈ܢܝ ܡܕܢܚܐ.

This sentence is part of a longer interpretative allusion to the events of Gen 28:12-22. Although Wright and Parisot both identify it as a scripture quotation, caution is in order in

attempting any textual deductions from it. Aphr here does not
intend a formal citation; he simply falls (probably unintention-
ally) into a close approximation of Gen 29:1 P at one point in
his discussion. His reproduction of P is not exact, and uncertainty remains concerning the bible text that is reflected here.

Aphr's text probably contains the name "Jacob," despite
its absence here. This is one of a series of successive sentences
that all have Jacob as the understood subject, the name having
been given explicitly at 148:1. The absence of ܐܝܪܠ following ܠܥܩܘܡ is more difficult. Does Aphr know a shorter
text? No other witness attests a form of the vs without the verb
(Ephraem does not cite the vs), and it is the type of economizing
omission that Aphr frequently makes. One suspects that his text
agrees with P, but no clear witness is afforded.

Gen 31:3; 32:10

#139 XXIII.(15). 464:20-22; II 44:25-45:1

ܐܡܪ ܠܗ ܐܠܗܐ {B ܒܡܥܗܘܢ / A,C ܡܥܗܘܢ} ܒܐܪܥܝ. {A,C ܐܬܪܐܒ / B ܘܐܬܪ} ܠܘ ܘܐܗܘܐ ܥܡܟ.

This formal citation occurs within a lengthy passage in
which Aphr calculates the ages of various biblical persons at
various events. The occasion of this promise to Jacob by God
is mentioned only to provide a reference point for further calculations. In such a passing citation, Aphr surely quotes from

156

memory, and some abbreviation would not be surprising. The
absence of ܘܐܛܐܒܠܟ after ܗܐܝܬܝܟ is probably the
product of Aphr's condensation of his text. The term is present
in P and all other witnesses (Ephraem does not cite Gen 31:3 or
32:10) in both possible sources of this citation, Gen 31:3 and
32:10.

It seems equally likely that Aphr is accidentally conflating the latter two vss when he includes here both of the
clauses, "and I will do good to you" (from 32:10) and "and I
will be with you" (from 31:3). No other witness attests such
an expended text for either vs, and, as already demonstrated in
other citations, Aphr has a tendency toward *memoriter* conflation
of parallel vss. Wright and Parisot are probably correct in
taking the reading of mss A and C (ܘܐܥܒܕ) as the original.
Although both the first-person singular and the first-person
plural forms are appropriate in connection with God, it is difficult to believe that Aphr would vary the form of two parallel
verbs in such close proximity. The reading of ms B is probably
a secondary alteration or mechanical error. Coincidentally, the
text of TN[1] presents a nearly exact parallel to this variation.
In Gen 32:10 the main text of TN[1] reads ואוטב לך, which is
changed to ונייטבה לך in a marginal gloss. No connection between
the mss of Aphr and TN[1] can be established, however.

Although it seems entirely probable that Aphr knows a
text of the divine promise in Gen 31:3 and 32:10 that agrees with

P, the apparently abbreviating and conflating nature of the citation here obstructs a clear view of his text of either vs.

Gen 31:38-40

#140 X.1(1). 191:8-12; 444:11-18

This formal quotation is the centerpiece of a passage
in which Aphr exhorts Christian pastors to care for their flocks
with the same zeal and faithfulness that characterized "those
righteous shepherds of old" (444:9). Although Joseph, Moses,
David, and Amos are included in the catalogue of pastoral exem-
plars (444:9-446:6), only Jacob is described at length by means
of scriptural citation.

While it is immediately clear that Aphr is conscious of
making a serious reproduction of a bible text here, he is not
interested in close analysis of it; the passage is quoted merely
to establish the general point that Jacob was dependable and
conscientious as a shepherd. Only the substance of the passage

is essential to Aphr's point, and it is not surprising, therefore, that some abbreviation occurs in the quotation. There are
two significant omissions, unattested elsewhere, which are of
such magnitude as to allow virtually no doubt that they are due
to Aphr's manner of quoting rather than to his bible text. These
are the clauses, both from vs 39, "I bore it myself" and "whether
stolen by day or stolen by night." These losses do not alter
the essential meaning of the vs and look very much like economizing changes.

A more questionable omission is that of the initial word
ܗܘܐ in vs 40. This is also probably due to Aphr's tendency
to abbreviate his text, although one cannot be certain. No other
Semitic witness omits this verb (Ephraem does not cite the vs),
and, being an auxiliary to ܐܟܠܬ, it could easily drop out
of a _memoriter_ or condensed citation.

Most troublesome are the ms variations. In both cases,
Wright and Parisot follow ms B, doubtless encouraged in this
choice by the latter's agreement or closer agreement with P.
However, the readings of ms A seem preferable. In the case of
the first set of variants, the reading of ms A conforms exactly
to the abbreviating tendency already noted in the citation. Aphr
here omits the verbal clause (ܐ ܠܒ ܠܟ ܕ) in the interest of conciseness; this does not change the basic sense of the
sentence. It is much easier to assume that such an original
reading was partially corrected by a scribe who knew P (as in

ms 5bl^{c}[vid]), thus producing the reading in ms B, than to assume that the reading in ms B was altered to produce that in ms A.

For the same reason, the reading in ms A is given preference in the second set of variants. Here too, of course, accidental transposition could lie behind the reading in ms A, but in the absence of other evidence it is safest to assume that the reading that agrees with P is secondary.

*Gen 31:38 ܗܐ ܥܣܪ̈ܝܢ ܠܝ ܫ̈ܢܝܢ ܥܡܟ .
ܥܢܟ ܘܥܙ̈ܝܟ [. . .] ܘܕܟܪ̈ܐ ܕܥܢܟ ܠܐ
ܐܟܠܬ.

ܠܝ 5bl LXX(μοι)] omit 7al 7h5 8bl 10bl 10gl 11/9bl 12bl.2 MT Sam Tgs TSam Vg | ܥܡܟ 5bl] add ܐܢܐ 7al 7h5 8bl 10bl 10gl 11/9bl 12bl.2 MT Sam Tgs TSam LXX

*Gen 31:39 [. . .] ܕܬܒܝܪܬܐ ܠܐ ܐܝܬܝܬ ܠܟ
ܕܡܢ ܐܝܕ̈ܝ، ܬܒܥ ܗܘܝܬ ܠܗ [. . .]

ܕܬܒܝܪܬܐ TJ[1]] pr waw P; omit dalath MT Sam TO TN[1] TSam LXX

*Gen 31:40 [. . .] ܒܐܝܡܡܐ ܐܟܠܢܝ ܫܪܒܐ.
ܘܓܠܝܕܐ ܒܠܠܝܐ ܦܪܕܬ ܫܢܬܝ، ܡܢ ܥܝܢ̈ܝ.

Aphr = P

Gen 32:11

#141 IV.5(6). 64:4-5; 148:14-15

ܒܚܘܛܪܗ ܗܘ ܒܠܚܘܕ ܥܒܪ ܝܘܪܕܢ

#142 IV.5(6). 64:17-18; 149:6-8

ܘܗܘܒܠܐ ܝܠ. ܘܐܘܕܝ، ܘܐܡܪ. ܕܒܚܘܛܪܝ،
ܥܒܪܬ ܝܘܪܕܢ ܗܢܐ. ܘܗܫܐ ܗܘܝܬ

ܠܐܝܠ ܡܣܪܝ.

#142 is a formal citation of the final portion of Gen
32:11 which occurs in a lengthy explication of Jacob as a type
of Christ. Only the quoted portion of the vs is relevant to
Aphr's purposes here, and there can be little question that he
is deliberately omitting the first part of the vs.

Although #142 is identical to P, notice must also be
taken of the more paraphrastic allusion to the same passage in
#141, which raises the question of a text that adds ܒܠܚܘܕ
after ܒܚܘܛܪܝ. Is it possible that Aphr's Gen text does
contain this word and that he has simply omitted it in #142?
If so, his text thus manifests a targumic influence, inasmuch
as it agrees with both TO (ארי יחידי עברית ית ירדנא) and TJ[1]
(ארום בחוטרי בלחוד עברית ית ירדנא).

The question must be raised, but my judgment is that #141
does not accurately reflect Aphr's bible text. In a situation
such as this, unless there are other factors involved, precedence
must be given to the formal quotation, particularly when it is
otherwise entirely literal and when the allusion is so obviously
paraphrastic. The idea of Jacob having only his staff when he
entered Laban's land is clearly implicit in the sentence as it
stands in P and MT (cf. RSV: "with only my staff"), and it is
natural when restating the vs, indeed even when translating it
(so TO and TJ[1]), to make this explicit. The context of Aphr's
discussion adds a further motive for adding this word in #141.

161

He stresses here that Jacob's staff was a symbol of the cross of Christ, Accordingly, given Aphr's understanding of the centrality of the cross in the salvific work of Jesus, it is natural for him to emphasize as strongly as possible that Jacob entered with <u>only</u> his staff.

On balance, there is no strong evidence for assuming that Aphr's text contains ܒܠܚܘܕ. In his paraphrase in #141 he adds the word for the sake of explicitness, paralleling but demonstrating no necessary knowledge of the text of the two targums.

*Gen 32:11 ܕܒܚܘܪ̈ܝ, ܒܠܚܘܕܝ [. . .]

ܗܢ ܘܗܐ ܗܘܬ ܠܬܪ̈ܬܝܢ ܡܫܪ̈ܝܢ.

Aphr = P

Gen 35:22-26

#143 XXIII.(43). 480:8-11; II 84:7-13

{image of Syriac text lines}

These lines come from that large chronographic table discussed earlier, which is based primarily on Gen chs 5 and 11. There can be little doubt that Aphr here is not making an exact quotation of his scripture text. Although Gen 35:22-26 is the most likely source of these lines, other passages might be used

(e.g., Gen 29:31-30:24). If the genealogical table in Gen ch 35

is Aphr's source, clearly he is handling it freely, perhaps from

memory. No textual deductions can be based on #143, therefore.

The most striking feature here is the transposition of

the sons of Bilhah and Zilpah. All three mss agree in this trans-

position, and it is surely authentic. No other witness agrees

with this change. It is impossible to know whether this is a

genuine reading from Aphr's Gen text or a result of error or

casualness in the quotation.

Gen 36:33

#144 XI.10(9). 212:21-23; 496:1-3

$$\text{ܘܡܠ̈ܟ ܗܘܐ ܒܪ ܚܝܝܐ . ܚܝܐ ܒܪ ܐܘܠܦ}$$

$$\text{ܐܪܐܕܡ. ܘܡܝܬ ܒܘܠܦܐ ܘܡܠܟ}\ \begin{cases} \text{cn} & \text{ܒܨܪܐ} \\ \text{A} & \text{ܒܨܪ} \end{cases}$$

$$\text{ܒܪ ܟܦܘܝ .ܗ}$$

This formal citation, one of the few which mention the

biblical book being quoted, is made to buttress Aphr's argument

that Bosra belonged to the Edomites. He resorts to vs 33 in the

Edomite king list in Gen 36:31-39 because of the mention there

of Bosra as the city of Jobab, king of Edom (cf. 1 Chron 1:44).

Since this is his only purpose for the quotation, having no inter-

est in the Edomite throne succession itself, Aphr excerpts the

words that he needs from their formulaic framework in Gen

(. . . ܒܨܪܐ ܒܨܪܐ ܒܨܪܐ). His text

of the entire vs probably agrees with P. Notice that the introductory "when kings ruled in Edom" echoes Gen 36:31 P.

*Gen 36:33 ܂ܘܗܝ ܒܪ ܒܕܕ ‌[. . .ܢܠܡܟܐ. . .]
ܟܕ ܡܠܟ ܗ̇ܝ.

Aphr = P

Gen 37:3; 41:46

#145 XXI.(9). 403:19; 953:9-10

ܘܥܒܕ ܐܝܟܘܬܗ ܟܡܐ, ܟܘܬܢܐ ܕܦܪܕܐ.

#146 XXI.(9). 404:23-405:1; 956:23-25

ܘܝܘܣܦ ܒܪ ܬܠܬܝܢ ܫ̈ܢܝܢ ܗܘܐ ܟܕ ܩܡ ܩܕܡ ܦܪܥܘܢ
ܘܗܘܐ ܪܒ ܥܠ ܟܠܗ̇.

These two passages are grouped together for convenience,
because they both occur within a lengthy discussion of the life
of Joseph in which Aphr makes a detailed comparison between
Joseph and Jesus. Aphr makes no effort within this discussion
to quote formally from Gen chs 37-50, but he is obviously very
well acquainted with these chs and numerous echoes of P can be
found. Except for the two passages given above, however, none
of these echoes provides a clear witness to Aphr's bible text.
Even the two presented here are of very limited usefulness.

#145 is of value only for its corroboration of the phrase
for Joseph's coat in Gen 37:3 P. Though not a part of a formal
or literal citation, this phrase is sufficiently distinctive as
to have been recalled by Aphr with exactness from his Gen text.

#146 is of textual value only for its transmission of

the numeral in Gen 41:46. This passage shows that Aphr's text agrees with P in reading "30 years" as the age of Joseph in 41:46, but it does not afford a witness to the precise text-form.

*Gen 37:3 [. . .] ܒܟܘܬܝܢܐ ܕܦܣ̈ܬܐ.

Aphr = P

<u>Gen 39:7, 9</u>

#147 II.2(2). 25:17-18; 49:27-51:1

ܐܡܪ̇ ܠܗ̇. ܐܝܟܢܐ ܐܥܒܕ ܒܝܫܬܐ ܗܕܐ
ܪܒܬܐ. ܘܐܚܛܐ ܠܐܠܗܐ.

#148 XIII.4(8). 238:4-7; 557:22-26

{ܘܥܒܕ B / ܕܥܒܕ A} ܐܢܬܬ ܡܪܗ ܐܪܝܡܬ ܥܝܢܗ̇
ܠܘܬܗ، ܐܝܟ ܕܡܫܬܥܐ ܒܟܬܒ̈ܐ ܦܢܩܝܬܐ
ܘܗܘ ܟܠܐ ܘܐܡܪ ܠܡܪܬܗ. ܕܐܝܟܢܐ ܠܡ
ܐܥܒܕ ܒܝܫܬܐ ܗܕܐ ܪܒܬܐ ܘܐܚܛܐ
ܠܐܠܗܐ.

These two formal quotations of the final part of Gen 39:9 happily are identical to one another. It is clear from the context of Aphr's discussion that only this last portion of vs 9 is of interest to him in both cases; therefore, he skips over the first half of the vs. In #148, the introductory sentence constitutes a very close paraphrase of Gen 39:7 P; Aphr's text of this vs also probably agrees with P, but the passage does not afford a clear witness.

*Gen 39:9 [. . .] []ܐܝܟܢܐ ܐܥܒܕ ܒܝܫܬܐ

ܗܕܐ ܪܒܬܐ ܘܐܚܛܐ ܠܐܠܗܐ.

Aphr = P

<u>Gen 43:32</u>

#149 XV.4(3). 310:15-19; 737:3-9

ܟܕ ܗܘܐ ܒܥܐ ܠܡܬܡܟܘ. ܟܬܒ ܕܣܡܘ
ܠܗ ܒܠܚܘܕܘܗܝ, ܘܠܐܚܘ̈ܗܝ, ܒܠܚܘܕ̈ܝܗܘܢ
ܘܠܡܨܪ̈ܝܐ ܕܐܟܠܝܢ ܗܘܘ ܥܡܗ ܒܠܚܘܕ̈ܝܗܘܢ
ܡܛܠ ܕܠܐ ܡܫܟܚܝܢ {A ܗܘܘ ; B omits} ܡܨܪ̈ܝܐ
ܠܡܐܟܠ ܠܚܡܐ ܥܡ ܥܒܪ̈ܝܐ ܡܛܠ
ܕܛܢܦܘܬܐ ܗܝ ܠܗܘܢ.

Because of its formality and its length, this citation must be taken seriously as a possible exact reproduction of Aphr's bible text, although alteration due to paraphrase or <u>memoriter</u> error cannot be ruled out. It presents only four variants to P.

(1) The addition of ܗܘܘ after ܕܐܟܠܝܢ could be considered Aphr's own stylistic adjustment of his text, but it may just as easily represent an authentic reading. Ephraem does not cite this vs, and the non-Syriac versions cannot be compared here.

(2) The addition of ܗܘܘ after ܡܫܟܚܝܢ is even more difficult than (1) because of the ms variation. Wright and Parisot follow ms <u>B</u>, probably because of its agreement with P. The reading most different from P has the better claim to be original, however. There is no way to be certain that this addition is in Aphr's Gen text and is not his own adjustment in this

166

citation.

(3) The use of the noun ‏‎,ܡܐܘܪ‍ܠܐ‎‏ in place of ‏ܠܥܡܠܐ‎‏ in P is almost as difficult to assess. This is the kind of change that Aphr sometimes makes in other citations to make explicit something that is only implicit in his text. He usually does this, however, when the antecedent of a pronoun or an internal verb subject is no longer clear because his citation has removed a single vs or clause from its context in the biblical narrative. No such necessity is present here. He has made mention of Joseph's brothers specifically just before #149 (at 737:1-2: ‏ܣܡܩܗ‎ ‏,ܡܐܘܪ‎ ‏ܬܠ‎ ‏ܐܕܪ‎ ‏ܬܐ‎); therefore, there is no greater ambiguity created by ‏ܠܥܡܠܐ‎‏ here than in the text of P itself. Certainty is impossible, but the agreement of Vg (et seorsum fratribus) is a datum which tilts the balance of probability toward this reading as a genuine feature of Aphr's bible text.

(4) The use of the final pronoun ‏ܠܥܡ‎‏ (contrast ‏ܐ‎ ‏ܕ‎ ‏ܬܒܠ‎‏ in P) is again the kind of alteration that Aphr sometimes makes in an abbreviating citation. Here, however, there are no other marks of a tendency toward condensation, and this reading finds support in LXX ms D.

Given the length and apparent carefulness of this citation, the soundest procedure is to assume that these four readings are present in Aphr's Gen text. It should be noted, however, that Neusner is wrong in considering the formal quotation to include the introductory clause, "when it was time to recline."[44] The placement of ܟܬܝܒ suggests that Aphr does not intend the clause preceding it to be understood as scripture, a signal that Parisot and Bert[45] correctly follow.

*Gen 43:32 ܘܣܡܘ ܠܗ ܠܚܘܕܘܗܝ[]

ܘܠܐܚܘܗܝ ܠܚܘܕܝܗܘܢ ܘܠܡܨܪ̈ܝܐ

ܕܐܟܠܝܢ ܗܘܘ ܥܡܗ ܠܚܘܕܝܗܘܢ

ܡܛܠ ܕܠܐ ܡܫܟܚܝܢ ܗܘܘ ܡܨܪ̈ܝܐ

ܠܡܐܟܠ ܠܚܡܐ ܥܡ ܥܒܪ̈ܝܐ ܡܛܠ

ܕܛܢܦܘܬܐ ܗܝ ܠܗܘܢ.

ܘܠܐܚܘܗܝ Vg] ܘܠܗܘܢ P MT Sam Tgs TG^E TSam LXX | ܗܘܘ 1°] omit P | ܗܘܘ 2°] omit P | ܠܗܘܢ LXX^D] ܠܡܨܪ̈ܝܐ P MT Sam TN^1 TG^E TSam LXX

<u>Gen 46:33-34; 47:2</u>

#150 XV.4(3). 310:22-311:7; 737:13-25

ܘܐܦ ܟܕ ܢܚܬ ܝܥܩܘܒ ܠܡܨܪܝܢ ܕܒܪ ܝܘܣܦ

ܥܡ ܐܚܘ̈ܗܝ ܫܒܥܝܢ ܒܢܝܢ. ܘܐܩܝܡ

ܐܚܘܗܝ ܩܕܡ ܦܪܥܘܢ. ܘܦܩܕ ܐܢܘܢ ܕܟܕ

ܢܫܐܠܘܢ ܦܪܥܘܢ ܘܢܐܡܪ ܠܗܘܢ ܕܡܢܘ

ܥܒܕܟܘܢ ܐܡܪܘ ܠܗ ܪ̈ܥܝ ܥܢܐ ܐܝܟ

ܥܒ̈ܕܝܟ {ܘܡܢ̈ܝ A / ܘܡܢ̈ܝܢ B} ܩܢܝܢܐ ܚܢܢ {ܘܐܦ B / ܐܦ A}

ܐܒ̈ܗܝܢ. ܕܡܐ ܕܐܡܪܬܘܢ ܠܗ ܗܟܢܐ

ܢܬܒ ܠܟܘܢ. ܕ̈ܬܒܘܬܐ ܐܝܬ ܕܣܢܝܬܐ

ܕܡܨܪ̈ܝܐ ܘܣܢܐ ܠܗܘܢ ܟܠ ܪܥܝܐ ܥܢܐ

ܠܐܪܥܐ (B) / ܐܪܥܐ (A) ܕܓܫܢ. ܘܣܡܠܐ ܠܟܘܢ ܕܠܐ
ܢܒܙܪ ܥܡܟܘܢ ܘܢܣܩ ܠܟ ܒܒܝܬܗ ܐܝܟ
ܕܟܬܒ ܕܡܣܠܝܢ ܐܢܘܢ ܠܡܨܪ̈ܝܐ ܟܠ
ܪ̈ܥܝ ܥܢܐ.

This passage contains, in its final sentence, a formal quotation of the concluding portion of Gen 46:34. Aphr cites only the part of the vs that is relevant to his discussion, omitting the first portion. His text is identical to P.

Earlier in the passage there are additional resemblances to P, which nevertheless fall short of providing reliable testimony to Aphr's scripture text. The statement that "Joseph took from his brothers five men and set them before Pharaoh" appears to be a close paraphrase of Gen 47:2 P; it differs from the latter only in the order of the first three words. Unfortunately, one cannot know if Aphr is reproducing his text literally here. The same is true of the clause, "When Pharaoh asks you and says to you, 'What is your work?'. . . ." This is almost identical to Gen 46:33 P, differing only in the verb ܢܫܐܠܟܘܢ (cf. ܢܩܪܝܟܘܢ in P) and, from ms 5b1, in the addition of ܠܟܘܢ. Aphr does not mark this as a formal quotation, and one cannot take it _prima facie_ as an exact reproduction of his text.

*Gen 46:34 [. . .] ܕܡܣܠܝܢ ܐܢܘܢ ܠܡܨܪ̈ܝܐ
ܟܠ ܪ̈ܥܝ ܥܢܐ.

Aphr = P

Gen 47:28

#151 XXIII.(15). 465:7-9; II 45:13-15

#152 XXIII.(43). 480:12-13; II 84:13-15

Although these two passages are not formal citations, the numerals they contain in reference to Jacob's ages doubtless come from Aphr's text of Gen 47:28

*Gen 47:28 [. . .] [. . .]

Aphr = P

Gen 49:1-4

#153 VIII.3(8). 160:18-161:1; 376:11-17

ܬܦܘܫ. ܠܐ {B ܕܣܠܩܬ / A ܕܣܠܩܬܝ} ܠܡܫܟܒܗ

ܕܐܒܘܟ. ܛܢܦܬ {B ܥܘܫܬ / A ܥܘܫܬܝ} ܬܫܘܬܝ

{B ܘܣܠܩܬ / A ܘܣܠܩܬܝ}.

This passage contains a formal quotation of Gen 49:3-4 that is noteworthy especially because of its omission of the concluding compound phrase in vs 3 (ܫܪܟܐ ܕܫܘܒܚܬܐ ܘܫܪܟܐ ܕܥܘܫܢܐ in P). This phrase, difficult in the MT (יתר שאת ויתר עז), is attested in various ways by the Sam, TSam, LXX, Vg, α', σ', θ', and Syrohexapla. Ephraem (Comm XLII.2 line 13) cites the phrase in an otherwise paraphrastic rendering of vs 3, but in a variant form: ܫܪܟܐ ܕܥܘܫܢܐ ܘܫܪܟܐ ܕܬܘܩܦܐ. Tgs and TF all abandon literal translation in the latter part of the vs to such an extent that their textual testimony is unclear. In the Göttingen edition of the LXX text of Gen, Wevers reports only Epiphanius Latinus (I 118) and ὁ Σύρος as agreeing with Aphr in this omission.

Aphr cites these vss in connection with Deut 33:6 (at 376:23-25) in support of his general theme that even before Christ the ancients looked forward to a future resurrection of the dead. For this reason Moses cancelled Jacob's decree about Reuben: "You will not abide." This context provides no clear reason for Aphr deliberately to have omitted the phrase from vs 3. If he were to be economizing and selective of only the condemnatory part of the passage, vs 3 could have been omitted entirely or drastically condensed. At the same time, this final phrase is not at all necessary to Aphr's argument, and it could easily have been dropped from the quotation as his attention focused on the important (for him) portion of the citation, which is vs 4. Given the otherwise literal, complete reproduction of vs 3 here, this omission must be taken seriously as a feature of Aphr's Gen text.

In the quotation of vs 4, the text of P seems to be reproduced exactly except for the addition of ܠܝ after ܬܦܘܫ. Aphr is entirely unsupported by the other Aramaic witnesses in this addition. The addition of final yud to several of the words in ms A is an orthographic peculiarity noted above in #013 and discussed in n. 7.

In addition to the formal citation in #153, the introductory sentence also appears to reflect a portion of Aphr's text. It closely approximates the conclusion of Gen 49:1 P. Such a passage does not afford a clear textual witness, however.

*Gen 49:3 ܪܘܒܝܠ ܒܘܟܪܝ، ܐܢܬ ܚܝܠܝ ܘܪܫ
ܬܘܩܦܝ.

ܬܘܩܦܝ Epiph ὁ Σύρος] add ܫܪܒܐ ܕܫܩܘܠܬܐ ܘܫܪܒܐ ܕܥܘܫܢܐ P MT Sam TSam LXX Vg; add ܫܪܒܐ ܕܥܘܫܢܐ ܘܫܪܒܐ ܕܬܘܩܦܐ Ephraem(Comm XLII.2 line 13)

*Gen 49:4 ܦܚܙܬ ܐܝܟ ܡܝܐ ܠܐ ܬܦܘܫ ܠܝ
ܕܣܠܩܬ ܠܡܫܟܒܗ ܕܐܒܘܟ ܫܪܝܬ
ܦܫܬ ܬܫܘܝܬܝ، ܘܣܠܩܬ.

ܟܠ] omit P

Gen 49:9

#154 IV.5(6). 63:23-64:2; 148:7-9

ܘܒܝܢܗ ܐܚܘܗܝ. ܗܘܐ ܓܘܪܝܐ ܕܐܪܝܐ
ܝܗܘܕܐ. ܕܒܗ ܓܒܪ ܗܘܐ ܡܠܟܐ ܡܫܝܚܐ.

Although not a formal citation, this passage uses the distinctive phrase, "the whelp[46] of a lion, Judah," which must come from Aphr's text of Gen 49:9. None of the rest of the vs is reflected.

*Gen 49:9 ܓܘܪܝܐ ܕܐܪܝܐ ܝܗܘܕܐ [. . .]

Aphr = P

Gen 49:10

#155 II.6(6). 29:3-4; 60:2-4

ܘܟܠ ܕܐܣܠܘ ܡܠܟܘܬܗ. ܫܒܛܗ̇ ܡܢܗܘܢ
{B ܡܠܟܘܬܐ
A ܠܡܠܟܘܬܐ}. ܡܛܠ ܕܐܬܐ ܡܢ ܕܕܝܠܗ
ܗܝ ܡܠܟܘܬܐ.

#156 V.17(23). 99:19-20; 232:23-24

ܡܐ {B ܕܐܬܐ ܓܒܪ
A ܓܒܪ ܕܐܬܐ ܗܘ} ܡܢ ܕܕܝܠܗ ܗܝ
ܡܠܟܘܬܐ {B omits
A ܕܠܥܠܡ}.

#157 V.18(23). 100:4-6; 233:5-8

ܘܟܕ ܠܐ ܬܘܒ ܐܒܫܪܘ ܒܡܠܟܘܬܐ. ܫܒܛܗ̇

ܣܒܪܗܘܢ ܕܟ̈ܠ ܥܡܡܐ. ܘܗܘܝܘ ܠܟ̈ܠ
ܥܡܐ. ܥܕܡܐ ܕܐܬܐ ܡܢ ܕܕܝܠܗ ܗܝ..

#158 XVI.1(1). 320:7-10; 760:9-14

ܘܝܥܩܘܒ {ܐܒܘܢ ܣܗܕ ܥܠ ܥܡ̈ܡܐ A | B omits}
{ܟܕ B | ܘܟܕ A} ܡܒܪܟ ܠܝܗܘܕܐ ܘܐܡܪ ܠܗ.
ܕܠܐ ܢܥܒܪ ܫܒܛܐ ܡܢ ܝܗܘܕܐ. ܘܡܚܩܩܢܐ
ܡܢ ܒܝܬ ܪ̈ܓܠܘܗܝ. ܥܕܡܐ ܕܢܐܬܐ ܡܢ
ܕܕܝܠܗ ܗܝ ܡܠܟܘܬܐ {ܘܠܗ ܥܡ̈ܡܐ | ܘܥܡ̈ܡܐ ܢܣܒܪܘܢ}
{ܢܣܒܪܘܢ B | ܒܗ A}.

#159 XVII.8(10). 340:16-17; 805:7-9

ܟܕ ܐܬܐ ܡܢ ܕܠܗ ܕܥܡ̈ܡܐ ܢܣܒܪܘܢ
ܒܗ.

#160 XIX.6(11). 374:6-8; 885:7-11

{ܐܦ B | ܘܐܦ A} ܝܥܩܘܒ ܐܒܘܢ ܐܡܪ ܟܕ ܡܒܪܟ
ܠܝܗܘܕܐ. ܕܠܐ ܢܥܒܪ ܫܒܛܐ ܡܢ ܝܗܘܕܐ
ܘܡܚܩܩܢܐ ܡܢ ܒܝܬ ܪ̈ܓܠܘܗܝ. ܥܕܡܐ
ܕܢܐܬܐ ܡܢ ܕܕܝܠܗ ܗܝ ܡܠܟܘܬܐ.

Within this cluster of quotations of Gen 49:10, only #158, #159, and #160 are formal, and only #158 reproduces the entire vs. It is clear that Aphr's text includes essentially the same form of the vs as P; most of these quotations excerpt only portions of the vs. #155, #156, and #157 all incorporate the penultimate clause of the vs into Aphr's own sentence.

The variation among the different passages in the form of the verb ܐܬ‍ܐ/ܐܬܐ is noteworthy. This variation surely does not indicate knowledge of two different bible texts by Aphr. It seems significant that the two most formal and complete citations that include this verb, #158 and #160, agree in reading ܐܬܐ. Those passages which present the participial form, #155, #156, and #157, are all fragmentary references woven into sentences of Aphr's own composition and are therefore of less reliability as textual witnesses than the formal quotations, which surely reflect Aphr's bible text. No other Semitic witness employs the participle here instead of the imperfect form.

Also in the case of the addition of ܠܥܠܡ by ms A in #156, no variant scripture text is reflected. Whether or not this reading is authentic (and it has every appearance of a theologizing addition by the scribe), its addition to the clause that echoes Gen 49:10 has certainly come about under the influence of Aphr's theme in this part of the Dem. His dominant emphasis here is upon the everlastingness of Christ's kingdom; cf. 232:25-26: "he will be king for ever and ever," and 233:1: "it will be an eternal kingdom." There is no attestation here of a text of Gen 49:10 that reads ܠܥܠܡ.

By far the most significant feature of these citations

is their testimony to the presence of ܡܠܟܘܬܐ in Aphr's text.[47] In addition to several P mss and Ephraem (and a number of later Syriac sources[48]), TO, TN^1, and TF agree in this addition, which is cited by Vööbus as one of the "targumhaften Lesarten" which substantiate his theory of "eines palästinischen west-aramäischen Targums als die Urgestalt des Pentateuchtextes der Peschitta."[49]

Determination of Aphr's text of the final clause of the vs is complicated by the ms variants in #158. The agreement of the reading of ms A in #158 with that in #159, however, leaves little doubt that it represents Aphr's text. (One must assume that ms B probably gives the authentic form of Aphr's citation; ms A will have fallen victim to a scribal correction to the biblical text.) Although the LXX agrees with the verb used in Aphr's text (ܣܒܪ "hope, trust"; cf. P ܣܟܐ), the syntax is different: καὶ αὐτὸς προσδοκία ἐθνῶν. A reading that seems to agree exactly with Aphr is found in Epiphanius Latinus (II 136): καὶ ἐπ' αὐτοῦ ἔθνη ἐλπιοῦσιν.

*Gen 49:10 ܠܐ ܢܥܒܪ ܫܒܛܐ ܡܢ ܝܗܘܕܐ
ܘܡܒܩܢܐ ܡܢ ܒܝܬ ܪ̈ܓܠܘܗܝ ܥܕܡܐ
ܕܢܐܬܐ ܡܢ ܕܕܝܠܗ ܗܝ ܡܠܟܘܬܐ
ܘܥܡ̈ܡܐ ܢܣܒܪܘܢ ܒܗ.

ܡܠܟܘܬܐ 915^{mg} 1114.5 12b2 → Ephraem(Comm XLII.5 line 20) TO TN^1 TF] omit 5b1 7a1 8a1 8b1 913-5 11/10g1 1111 12b1 MT Sam TJ^1 TSam LXX Vg | ܘܥܡ̈ܡܐ ܢܣܒܪܘܢ ܒܗ Epiph] ܘܠܗ ܢܣܟܘܢ ܥܡ̈ܡܐ P MT Sam

Gen 49:12

#161 XXIII.(9). 456:8-10; II 24:21-24

ܘܐܡܪ̇ ܟܠܢ ܕܨܗܐ ܘܐܫܬܘ ܕܠܐ ܕܡ̈ܝܢ
ܚܡܪܐ ܘܚܠܒܐ܂ ܡܢ ܗܘ ܕܙܓܢ ܥܝܢܘ̈ܗܝ
ܡܢ ܚܡܪܐ܂ ܘܚܘܪܢ ܫܢܘ̈ܗܝ ܡܢ ܚܠܒܐ܂

This formal quotation consists of a conjunction of part of Isa 55:1 and Gen 49:12. The phrase "from him who" is Aphr's own insertion to connect the two texts. The citation is literal.

*Gen 49:12 ܙܓܢ ܥܝܢܘ̈ܗܝ ܡܢ ܚܡܪܐ
ܘܚܘܪܢ ܫܢܘ̈ܗܝ ܡܢ ܚܠܒܐ܂

Aphr = P

Gen 49:29, 31

#162 VIII.3(2). 159:15-18; 373:4-7

ܝܥܩܘܒ ܓܝܪ ܐܒܘܢ܂ ܟܕ ܡܐܬ ܗܘ̣ܐ܂
ܐܘܨܝ ܠܝܘܣܦ ܒܪܗ ܘܐܡܪ ܠܗ܂ {ܕܒܡܥܪܬܐ / ܒܡܥܪܬܐ}
ܕܐܒ̈ܗܝ ܩܒܘܪܝ {B / A} ܠܘܬ ܐܒܪܗܡ
ܕܐܒܗܝܢ ܬܩܒܪܢܝ
ܘܣܪܐ܂ ܘܐܝܣܚܩ ܘܪܦܩܐ܂

This passage, which has the appearance of a formal quotation of Jacob's death-bed instructions in Gen 49:29-31, is in fact extremely paraphrastic and echoes Gen 50:25 and Exod 13:19 as well as Gen 49:29 and 31. No clear witness to Aphr's bible text is afforded. Aphr's citation here of Gen 49:31 is

sufficiently free that he falls into the natural symmetrical
pattern of husband-plus-wife, husband-plus-wife. This explains
why Leah, a second wife, is omitted from the list of names.

Gen 50:25; Exod 13:19

#163 VIII.3(8). 160:2-4; 373:16-18

$$\left.\begin{array}{l} \text{\underline{A}} \quad \text{ܐܰܫܘܳ̈ܢ,} \\ \text{\underline{B}} \quad \text{ܐܰܫܘܳ̈ܢ} \end{array}\right\} \text{ܐܳܡܰܪ ܗܘܳܐ ܐܶܠ ܟܰܕ}$$

ܘܐܡܪ ܠܗܘܢ . ܕܕܢ ܬܥܒܪܘܢܟܘܢ ܐܠܗܐ .

ܐܣܩܘ ܓܪ̈ܡܝ, ܥܡܟܘܢ ܡܢ ܗܟܐ .

This formal quotation of Joseph's instructions is of
almost no value as a textual witness. Aphr's interest here is
solely in Joseph's determination that his remains be taken back
to Palestine someday. Accordingly, he quotes literally only
the heart of Joseph's command: "Take up my bones with you from
this place," treating more freely the preceding part of the vs.
In both Gen 50:25 and Exod 13:19 all witnesses render the preceding statement ("and God will surely visit you") by an infinitive followed by cognate participle or by an infinitive followed
by cognate imperfect. Aphr condenses somewhat and is more direct
with his use of the imperfect alone (ܬܥܒܪܘܢܟܘܢ). This
is probably a departure from his text. Because it is impossible
to know which of the two possible biblical passages supplies the
text for this citation, no clear textual witness is provided.

CHAPTER III

CITATIONS FROM EXODUS

Exod 1:22

#164 XI.9(8). 210:14-15; 489:4-6

אֵיךְ דָּבַר יוֹסֵף דֶּרֶךְ עַל דֶּרֶךְ לֵאמֹר אָמַר
דָּל כָּל בְּרָא מָא דְּיַלְדָּא דַּהְוָא בַּבְּרֵיהּ וּמַיָּא נֶהֱרָא.

    This formal quotation of Pharaoh's command to his people
is neither complete nor exact, and its departures from P may be
due to Aphr's own freedom or error. He cites this vs as he discusses how Pharaoh's daughter could have known that the infant
Moses, found in the basket in the river, was a Hebrew rather than
an Egyptian child. He rebuts those who contend that it was the
child's circumcision which revealed his ethnic identity, pointing
out that, according to Jeremiah, the Egyptians too circumcised
their children. Rather, Aphr says in the sentence preceding #164
(488:25-489:5): "When Pharaoh's daughter found Moses and saw
that he was floating on the water, she knew that he was from the
sons of the Hebrews, because it had not been commanded concerning
the Egyptians that they should be thrown into the river. . . ."

    This usage of the vs explains why it appears in shortened
form. The final clause, "but you shall let every daughter live,"

is omitted simply because it is not necessary to establish Aphr's argument at this point. He is interested here only in the substance of the command to cast Hebrew babies into the river, not in the detailed qualifications of the command. No other witness omits the final clause.

The citation departs from P and all other witnesses also in using a passive, third-person plural form of the verb (ܪ‍ܡ‍ܕ‍ܠ‍ܛ‍ܝ) in contrast to the second-person imperfect (= imperative) form of P (ܡ‍ܢ‍ܐ‍ܪ‍ܬ‍ܘ). This is probably Aphr's departure from his bible text, resulting from two influences. On the one hand, Aphr may unconsciously pattern the citation after the sentence with which he introduces it: ". . . it had not been commanded concerning the Egyptians that they should be thrown [ܠ‍ܢ‍ܕ‍ܠ‍ܛ‍ܝ] into the river." Such parallelism comes about naturally as Aphr poses a simple opposition in his argument: it is not the Egyptians, but the Hebrews, about whom the command was given. On the other hand, because Aphr's attention is focused on the substance of the command rather than on its recipients, he introduces the command in #164 without mention of the latter. (Contrast the beginning of vs 22 in P: "And Pharaoh commanded all his people and said. . . .") With the subject of the imperative verb form thus lost from view, it becomes especially easy to shift the verb to third-person form.

Aphr's reading ܪ‍ܝ‍ܒ‍ܕ‍ܗ ܪ‍ܝ‍ܒ is the most difficult and potentially important variant in the citation. The agreement of

TJ[1] and TN[1] (ביר/בר דכר) may increase the possibility that Aphr
here knows a text different from P. That he may accurately cite
his bible text at this point cannot be ruled out. However, in
view of the freedom apparent elsewhere in the quotation and of
its possible _memoriter_ nature, it seems equally likely that
ܗܒܪܐ ܒܪܐ represents Aphr's deviation from his text under
the influence of the similar vs in Exod 1:16. Such influence
is apparently at work in mss 12b1 and → which entirely replace
ܒܪܐ in vs 22 with ܗܒܪܐ. There is simply no way to reach
a final determination. Although contextual factors are lacking
in Aphr's discussion which would by themselves encourage the
addition of ܗܒܪܐ in the citation, the citation is otherwise
not sufficiently literal to warrant confidence in it as a textual
witness.

Exod 2:14

#165 II.8(8). 31:10-11; 64:24-26

ܐܢܫܝܢ ܕ̈ܠܡܐ ܗܘ ܝܕܥ ܠܢܒ̈ܝܐ ܣܒܠ ܐܩܛܠܢܝ
ܠܟ ܥܒܕ ܫܠܝܛܐ ܘܕܝܢܐ܂ ܡܢ ܠܟ܂

Aphr makes this formal citation, presumably of Exod 2:14,
in order to illustrate his extended reference to Moses' flight
from Egypt following his intervention in the fight between two
Hebrew men. Aphr calculates the length of Moses' stay in Midian
as thirty years, and he refers to these events of Exod ch 2 simply
to explain that there is no discrepancy between the length of
the Egyptian bondage as predicted to Abraham (400 years) in

Gen 15:13 and as described in Exod 12:40 (430 years). His view is that the original intention of God was a period of 400 years, but that he lengthened it to 430 years when Moses was forced to flee from Egypt to Midian.

The textual form of the citation is both fascinating and troublesome. It defies sure analysis, presenting a baffling combination of similarities to and differences from other witnesses, a list of which demonstrates the difficulties:

Exod 2:14 P (most mss) ܘܐܡܪ ܠܗ. ܡܢܘ ܥܒܕܟ
ܓܒܪ ܪܒ ܘܕܝܢ ܥܠܝܢ . . . .

Exod 2:14 P (ms 8b1) ܘܐܡܪ ܠܗ. ܡܢܘ ܐܩܝܡܟ
ܓܒܪ ܪܒ ܘܕܝܢ ܥܠܝܢ . . . .

Exod 2:14 Ephraem (Comm II.5 lines 21-22) ܡܢܘ ܠܟ
ܐܩܝܡܟ ܥܠܝܢ ܪܫܐ.

Exod 2:14 TO ואמר מן שויך לגבר רב ודיין עלנא. . . .

Exod 2:14 TJ[1] ואמר ליה דתן מאן הוא דמני יתך לגבר רב ודיין
עלנא. . . .

Exod 2:14 TN[1] ואמר מן שוי יתך לגבר רב ושליט עלין. . . .

Exod 2:14 MT ויאמר מי שמך לאיש רש ושפט עלינו. . . .

Luke 12:14 P ܝܫܘܥ ܕܝܢ ܐܡܪ ܠܗ. ܓܒܪܐ. ܡܢܘ
ܐܩܝܡܢܝ ܥܠܝܟܘܢ ܕܝܢܐ ܘܡܦܠܓܢܐ. . . .

Acts 7:27 P . . . ܘܐܡܪ ܠܗ. ܡܢܘ ܐܩܝܡܟ ܥܠܝܢ
ܪܫܐ ܘܕܝܢܐ.

Acts 7:35 P . . . ܟܕ ܐܡܪܝܢ: ܕܡܢܘ ܐܩܝܡܟ
ܥܠܝܢ ܪܫܐ ܘܕܝܢܐ. . . .

Assuming that Aphr is accurately reproducing some one
biblical passage here and is not quoting freely or paraphrasing,
two alternative conclusions are possible. On the one hand, Aphr
may indeed reflect here a unique, early Syriac reading that has
disappeared from the later mss. In support of this view it can
be observed that (a) Ephraem and Aphr agree against most P mss
in the use of ܐܘܣܦ and in the placement of ܠܢ ; (b)
ms 8bl, which often attests an earlier textual tradition,[1] also
agrees with Ephraem and Aphr in the use of ܐܘܣܦ against
the other P mss; (c) Aphr's concluding compound noun phrase
(ܫܠܝܛ ܘܕܝܢ) is entirely unique to him and cannot be
the result of _memoriter_ confusion of parallel vss in any known
witness.

On the other hand, there is no less a possibility that
Aphr's quotation here comes not from his text of Exod 2:14 but
from his text of Acts 7:27//35. The following arguments can be
made in behalf of this conclusion. First, the position of ܠܢ
agrees exactly with the P Acts text (and also with the similar
P Luke 12:14). That Aphr might have dominant in his memory the
NT quotation of an OT vs is of course not at all unlikely, and
examples of such confusion have already been seen. His familiarity with Acts is sufficiently illustrated by the twelve citations from it which Parisot identifies in his index. (Both
Parisot and Wright designate #165 as a citation of Exod 2:14.)
Second, the use of ܐܘܣܦ also agrees exactly with the Acts

text (cf. ܐܡܝܡܢܝ in Luke 12:14). Third, despite similarities among Aphr and Ephraem and ms 8bl that are not shared with
the other P mss, close analysis reveals other significant differences among the three that make it impossible to cite them
as mutually corroborating witnesses.

So, in the case of the use of ܐܡܝܡܣ by ms 8bl, it
has to be noted that this ms otherwise agrees exactly with the
other P mss __against__ Aphr and Ephraem. Therefore, the use of
ܐܡܝܡܣ by the scribe in ms 8bl may simply be the result of
accidental contamination from Acts 7:27//35.[2] Furthermore, critical analysis of Ephraem's citation shows it to be an abbreviation of his biblical text, an intentional excerpt. This being
so, one can reasonably assume that Ephraem's text, like other
witnesses, had two nouns at the end of the quoted sentence, the
second one surely being ܗܕܝܢܐ. Ephraem's citation thus
reflects a text identical to the Acts vss, and the most logical
explanation of this fact is that Ephraem here accidentally reproduces his Acts text rather than his text of Exod 2:14. That both
Aphr and Ephraem should make this same error is a striking coincidence, but not an impossible one.

At the same time it is important to recall that Aphr and
Ephraem do not agree with one another exactly in their citations.
While both resemble Acts 7:27//35 P more closely than Exod 2:14 P,
only Ephraem appears to cite the former exactly. Aphr is entirely
alone in his form of the final noun-phrase ܗܕܝܡܐ ܡܝܠܝܛ.

This disagreement makes it impossible to assert that Aphr and Ephraem stand together in witnessing to a primitive text of Exod 2:14.

The hypothesis that best accounts for Aphr's closer resemblance to Acts 7:27//35 than to Exod 2:14 P and also for his difference from the former is that Aphr's text of the Acts vss preserves an "Old Syriac" reading. The study by Kerschensteiner[3] has shown it to be probable that Aphr knows such a text for Acts, and Matthew Black agrees that "the conclusion at any rate stands that an 'Old Syriac' text of Acts did once exist and is cited by Ephraem, the Liber Graduum and almost certainly also by Aphraates."[4] It is unfortunate that Kerschensteiner's study of Aphr's Acts citations relied (apparently) exclusively on the index of Parisot and therefore did not include an analysis of #165. Because of the significant possibility that #165 thus reflects primarily Aphr's text of Acts rather than Exod, no conclusions about his text of Exod 2:14 can be based on #165.

Exod 3:6, 14-15

#166   XVII.3(5). 334:19-335:3; 792:6-13

ܐܫܪ {A ܐܗܝܗ / B ܐܗܝܗ̇} . ܐܠ ܫܕܝ، ܘܐܕܘܢܝ

ܨܒܐܘܬ. ܒܗܠܝܢ ܫܡܗ̈ܐ ܐܬܩܪܝ،
ܐܠܗܐ.

#167 XXII.(2). 420:9-11; 993:19-22

ܘܟܕ ܐܡܪ ܡܪܝܐ ܠܡܘܫܐ ܡܢ ܣܢܝܐ
ܗܟܢܐ ܐܡܪ ܠܗ. {A ܕܐܢܐ / B ܐܢܐ} ܐܢܐ
ܐܠܗܗ ܕܐܒܪܗܡ ܘܕܐܝܣܚܩ ܘܕܝܥܩܘܒ

#168 XXII.(2). 420:13-15; 993:25-27

ܡܢ ܫܡܗܐ ܕܫܡܥ ܕܐܡܪ ܐܠܗܐ
ܠܡܘܫܐ ܕܐܢܐ ܐܢܐ ܐܠܗܗ {A ܕܐܒܪܗܡ / B ܕܐܒܪܡ}
ܘܕܐܝܣܚܩ ܘܕܝܥܩܘܒ

#166 consists of a formal quotation of God's words to Moses followed by a sentence in which Aphr alludes to three different names for God. It is not clear whether this latter sentence is intended to include names used for God in Exod ch 3, from which the formal quotation ostensibly comes, or whether this is a summarizing statement that includes divine names from other biblical passages.

The formal quotation in #166 is clearly Aphr's conflation, probably from memory, of a portion of Exod 3:15 P (ܗܘ ܫܡܝ، ܠܥܠܡ ܘܗܘ ܕܘܟܪܢܝ ܠܕܪܕܪܝܢ) and Exod 3:6 P ("I am the god of your fathers, the god of Abraham, the god of

Isaac, the god of Jacob"). This appears to present a literal
reproduction of Aphr's text of the final portion of vs 15, but
its testimony is otherwise uncertain. The clause, "I am the god
of your fathers, the god of Abraham, the god of Isaac, the god
of Jacob," is an almost exact reproduction of part of Exod 3:6 P,
differing from the latter only in the plural noun "fathers" (P
reads the singular) and in the plural pronominal suffix "your"
on "fathers" (P reads the singular suffix). Because the divine
reply in Exod 3:6 is addressed to Moses as an individual, rather
than to the Israelites, it is very difficult to think that any
text of Exod would utilize the plural pronominal suffix in vs 6,
and Aphr indeed stands alone in this reading. This creates the
strong suspicion that this clause in #166 is not a literal citation. This suspicion is reinforced by the plural form of the
noun "fathers," which, while not incompatible with the context
in Exod ch 3, is almost entirely unsupported by the other ancient
witnesses. Only a few mss of the Sam (אבתיך), two LXX mss (58
and 72), and a citation by Justin Martyr read the plural form
of the noun here. Unfortunately, Ephraem does not cite this vs.

The plural form of both the noun "fathers" and its pronominal suffix can be explained as the result of contamination
by parallel passages:

Exod 3:15   ܡܪܝܐ ܐܠܗܐ ܕܐܒܗܬܟܘܢ ...
ܐܠܗܗ ܕܐܒܪܗܡ ܐܠܗܗ ܕܐܝܣܚܩ ܘܐܠܗܗ
ܕܝܥܩܘܒ . . . .

Exod 3:16 ... ܡܪܝܐ ܐܠܗܐ ܕܐܒܗ̈ܝܟܘܢ ...
ܐܠܗܗ ܕܐܒܪܗܡ ܘܕܐܝܣܚܩ ܘܕܝܥܩܘܒ ....

Acts 7:32 ܐܢܐ ܐܢܐ ܐܠܗܐ ܕܐܒܗ̈ܝܟ
ܐܠܗܗ ܕܐܒܪܗܡ ܘܕܐܝܣܚܩ ܘܕܝܥܩܘܒ ....

The conflated form of the citation in #166 suggests <u>memoriter</u> quotation, and the opportunity for confusion of such similar vss is a <u>memoriter</u> quotation is obvious. In addition to the influence of these vss, there would also be a strong tendency in a non-literal citation to place the noun in plural form for agreement with the immediately successive list of three "fathers," Abraham, Isaac, and Jacob. These factors make it impossible to rely on #166 as a witness to Aphr's text of this portion of Exod 3:6.

The final sentence in #166 reflects the form of the divine self-disclosure in Aphr's text of Exod 3:14 (ܐܗܝܐ ܐܫܪ ܐܗܝܐ), a form that agrees with P in transliterating the MT. No textual witness is provided by the other divine names in this final sentence, however, because one cannot be certain what biblical passage is their source. Although he may be taking ܐܠ ܫܕܝ from his text of Exod 6:3, the parallel account of Exod ch 3, it is not certainly so, and the source of ܘܐܕܘܢܝ ܨܒܐܘܬ remains completely unknown, although Wright and Parisot reasonably suggest Jer 32:18.

#167 and #168 occur so close together, indeed as repetitions of the same citation, that they are to be considered one

witness. Accordingly, the only significant ms variant which
occurs within them--the difference in the name Abram/Abraham in
#168--can be evaluated by means of comparison; the longer form
of the name in ms A is to be adopted, because it occurs in both
mss in #167. The introduction of these citations as God's utter-
ance from the bush, as well as the opening words (ܐܢܐ ܐܢܐ),
point to Exod 3:6 as the intended source. It is clear, however,
that these do not present a literal reproduction of that vs.

Not only is Aphr obviously abbreviating his text in omitting "the god of your father," but also the text-form of the following series of nouns is different from that in vs 6 in P and
all other witnesses. In Aphr's citations, the more concise construction is used in which the nomen regens ("god") of the compound construct chain is given only once, in contrast to Exod 3:6
P where ܐܠܗܐ is repeated before each of the three proper
names. Since this more concise text-form is found in Exod 3:16
P and, with the same introductory construction (ܐܢܐ ܐܢܐ
. . . .ܐܠܗܐ) in Acts 7:32 P, the most reasonable judgment
is that these citations represent an inexact reproduction of
Exod 3:6, one that is heavily influenced by Exod 3:16 and Acts
7:32.

*Exod 3:14 [. . .] ܐܗܝܐ ܐܫܪ ܐܗܝܐ [. . .]

ܐܗܝܐ 2° 5b1 7a1 7h13 8a1 11l1 12b1.2 MT Sam TO
TN¹ TJ¹(היהית) TSam LXX(ὁ ὤν) Vg(qui sum)] ܐܝܗ 8a1ᶜ
10j1 11l2 →

*Exod 3:15 ܗܘܐ ܠܥܠܡ ܫܡܝ ܗܘ [. . .]

ܕܘܒܪ̈ܝ ܠܕܪ̈ܕܪ̈ܝܢ.

ܘܗܘ 7al 7h13 8al 10j1 1111.2 12b1.2 MT Sam Tgs TSam LXX Vg] omit waw 5b1

Exod 4:16; 7:1

#169 XVII.3(3). 333:11-14; 788:18-23

ܐܡܪ ܠܗ ܡܪܝܐ {A ܕܥܒܕܬܟ / B ܕܝܗܒܬܟ} ܐܠܗܐ

ܠܦܪܥܘܢ. ܘܝܗܒ ܠܗ ܟܗܢܗ ܢܒܝܐ.

ܘܐܗܪܘܢ ܠܡ ܐܚܘܟ ܢܡܠܠ ܠܟ ܥܡ

ܦܪܥܘܢ ܘܐܢܬ ܬܗܘܐ ܠܗ {A ܠܐܠܗܐ / B ܠܐܠܗ̇}.

ܘܗܘ ܢܗܘܐ ܠܟ ܬܪܓܡܢܐ.

This passage includes two different formal citations, separated by the clause, "and he made his priest a prophet." Aphr has no interest in a detailed exposition of the scripture vss that supply his quotation here; he is concerned only with the fact that Moses is called God. This supports his argument that there was a precedent already before the coming of Christ for the "honored title of divinity" being given to righteous men. (Dem XVII has as its title and theme, "On Christ, That He is the Son of God.")

It is not surprising, therefore, to discover that Aphr handles his bible text quite loosely in #169. While Exod 4:16 and 7:1 clearly lie behind this quotation, they are mixed together carelessly. In the first component of the citation ("I have made

you as God to Pharaoh"), Aphr appears to be reproducing literally his text of Exod 7:1. The situation is complicated, however, by the ms variation. Wright and Parisot both follow ms
B, but this is probably not the better reading; because it agrees
with P, it can be readily accounted for as a correction. Also,
Aphr echoes this quotation two times in the lines that immediately follow #169 (788:24-26), both times employing the verb
ܥܒܕ . It would be unusual for him to change verbs in such a
closely reasoned discourse.

Assuming that ܗܥܒܕܟ is Aphr's original reading
in #169, it nevertheless remains impossible to be certain that
this verb is present in his bible text and that it is not his
stylistic alteration of his text. On the whole, #169 is a quite
free citation, perhaps made from memory. While the MT, Sam, TSam,
and LXX all agree with P in reading a form of the verb ܢܬܢ ,
various other verbs are reflected in the TO, TJ[1], TN[1]mg, and Vg.
Ephraem does not cite this vs.

In the second component quotation in #169, despite the
mark of formal quotation (ܕܝܢ), one encounters a confused rendering of Exod 4:16. The first clause echoes primarily Exod
4:16a P ("He shall speak for you to the people"), but it has
become contaminated here by Exod 7:2 P ("and Aaron your brother
shall speak to Pharaoh"). It provides no clear witness to Aphr's
scripture text. Similarly, the general structure of the parallel passage in Exod 7:1 has contaminated the otherwise accurate

reproduction of Exod 4:16b,c. This accounts for the transposition of the clauses ("and you will be as God to him" and "and
he will be a spokesman for you"). No other witness supports this
transposition. Aphr's bible text may agree with TN[1] in reading
ܪܒܘܝܗ, against P, TO, TJ[1], and TSam, which read the
slightly different ܪܒܘܝܗܘ. The freedom that is apparent
in the citation, however, prevents complete confidence in its
literalness at this point also.

Exod 4:19

#170   XXI.(10). 405:15-16; 957:19-20

ܠܬܪܐ ܪܒܘܝ ܐܠ ܐܡܪ ܠܗ ܐܠܟ ܐܡܘܕ ܗܘ ܠܟܥܢ

ܐܢ̈ܝܐ ܪ̈ܒܝܢ ܗܘܘ ܠܢܦܫܟ .

This formal quotation occurs within a fairly long list
of parallels that Aphr draws between the life of Moses and that
of Jesus. All of the other paired references in the list are
mere allusions to biblical facts. This alone, along with its NT
counterpart, Matt 2:20, which follows it, is a direct quotation.
It is undoubtedly made from memory, as is Matt 2:20, which is
quoted somewhat freely. The quoted text agrees with P except
for the absence of ܠܒܥܘܢ before ܐܢ̈ܝܐ. It is of course
not at all impossible that this omission is a feature of Aphr's
bible text. However, among the other ancient witnesses, including Ephraem (Comm IV.3 lines 9-10), only one Greek minuscule (c)
agrees with this omission, and it could be influenced by the
Greek text of Matt 2:20. Given the fact that Aphr's quotation

of the very similar sentence in Matt 2:20 also lacks this adjective (. . . ܕܡܝܬܘ ܠܗܘܢ ܐܝܠܝܢ ܕܒܥܝܢ ܗܘܘ ܢܦܫܗ . . . .), it is not unlikely that the omission of ܟܠܗܘܢ in the Exod citation is due to the immediate influence of the Matt text. Aphr's desire to show the parallels between Moses and Jesus would incline him to maximize the resemblance between the Exod vs and its counterpart in the Gospel.

*Exod 4:19 [. . .] ܕܡܝܬܘ [ܠܗܘܢ] ܓܒܪܐ
ܕܒܥܝܢ ܗܘܘ ܢܦܫܟ.

ܠܗܘܢ LXX[c]] add ܟܠܗܘܢ P MT Sam Tgs TSam LXX Vg

Exod 4:22, 23

#171 XVI.2(5). 327:1-3; 773:19-21

ܘܠܡܨܪܝܐ ܐܡܪ ܡܪܝܐ. ܕܐܡܪ ܠܦܪܥܘܢ.
ܫܒܘܩ {ܠܒܪܝ A / ܒܪܝ B} ܘܢܦܠܚܢܝ. ܘܬܘܒ ܐܡܪ
ܒܪܝ ܒܘܟܪܝ ܐܝܣܪܝܠ.

#172 XVII.3(4). 333:19-334:2; 789:4-10

ܠܗ ܓܝܪ ܠܐܝܣܪܝܠ ܒܪܝ ܒܘܟܪܝ {ܩܪܝܗܝ A / B omits}
ܟܕ ܫܠܚ ܠܦܪܥܘܢ ܒܝܕ ܡܘܫܐ ܘܐܡܪ
ܠܗ ܒܪܝ ܒܘܟܪܝ ܐܝܣܪܝܠ. ܐܡܪܬ ܠܟ
ܕܫܒܘܩ ܠܒܪܝ ܘܢܦܠܚܢܝ. {ܘܐܠܐ B / ܘܐܢ ܠܐ A}
ܫܒܩܬ ܠܡܫܕܪܘ. ܗܐ ܩܛܠ ܐܢܐ ܠܒܪܟ

ܒܘܟܪܝ.

#173 XVII.3(4). 334:11; 789:21-22

ܐܝܟ ܐܣܪܝܠ ܒܪܝ ܒܘܟܪܝ. { B ܕܒܪܗ, / A ܕܒܪܐ }

#174 XIX.(1). 357:3-4; 845:4-6

ܘܐܡܪ ܠܗ ܕܐܡܪ ܠܦܪܥܘܢ: ܒܪܝ ܒܘܟܪܝ,
ܐܣܪܝܠ ܐܫܒܩ ܠܟ ܠܒܪܝ ܕܢܦܠܘܚܠܝ.

#171, #172, and #174 are formal quotations of portions
of Exod 4:22-23; #173 is an allusion to the final three words
of vs 22, echoing #172, which is cited a few lines earlier. None
of the three quotations reproduces the entire text of vss 22-23,
but their respective contexts suggest that this is the result
of Aphr's condensation and excerpting of his scripture text.

#172 comes close to being a complete reproduction of vss
22-23. It occurs within a series of proof-texts that are selected to buttress Aphr's argument that already in the OT the Jews
were called God's sons. He seeks here to counter the anti-Chris-
tian charge that the phenomenon of a human being (Jesus) claiming
to be the son of God is unthinkable. His interest in the text
of vss 22-23 is limited to the phrase "my first-born son Israel"
in God's statement at the end of vs 22, and he understandably
skips over the earlier part of vs 22. That Aphr bothers to proceed to quote the entire text of vs 23 also is surprising, since
it is not relevant to his point. With no contextual influences

thus coming to bear on this part of the citation, it must be taken seriously as a literal reproduction of his text of vs 23.

#171 is presented by Aphr to support his two-part argument that God's people were regarded as his sons and that the identity of sonship belongs only to those who obey God. He excerpts two portions of Exod 4:22-23, citing them separately for maximum emphasis. He first quotes the imperative clause of vs 23 ("send forth my son that he may serve me"), prefaced by the opening words of vs 22. Unquestionably, Aphr is telescoping his bible text at this point. It is difficult to know which ms preserves the original reading in #171. ,ܒܪܝ agrees with P and thus might be a correction; but the object of ܨܘܪ is often marked by a prefixed ܠ or ܒ , and the absence of ܠ here could be a mechanical error.[5] In any case, the witness of #172 and #174 makes it certain that Aphr's bible text reads ,ܒܪܝ . #171 also quotes the closing phrase of vs 22, corroborated again by #172 and #174.

In #174 Aphr cites vs 23 in condensed form. Here he is not interested in the idea of sonship, but rather in the command to "send forth my son." This text is cited within a concise sketch of the history of Israel merely to dramatize Aphr's narration of the exodus from Egypt: "The voice of the Holy One was heard by Moses. He sent him to take his people out of Egypt, out of the house of Pharaoh, the bondage of the Egyptians. . . ." #174 is followed by a citation of Deut 4:34, which is also given in condensed form.

Because of orthographic inconsistency on the part of mss A and B-B throughout the Dems, it is impossible to be entirely certain which form of the name "Israel" and of the conjunction "if not" occurs in Aphr's bible text.

*Exod 4:22 ܐܡܪ[] ܠܦܪܥܘܢ [. . .] ܒܪܝ
ܒܘܟܪܝ ܐܝܣܪܝܠ.

Aphr = P

*Exod 4:23 ܐܡܪܬ ܠܟ ܕܫܕܪ ܠܒܪܝ
ܘܢܦܠܚܢܝ [ܘܐܠܐ] ܨܒܝܬ ܠܡܫܕܪܘ
ܗܐ ܩܛܠ ܐܢܐ ܠܒܪܟ ܒܘܟܪܟ.

ܕܫܕܪ 5b1 Ephraem(Comm IV.3 lines 12-13; adds ܠܝ)[6]]
ܕܬܫܕܪ 7a1 7h13 8a1 8b1 9b1 10b2 10j1 11l2 12b1.2;
שלח MT Sam TO TN[1] TSam; פטור TJ[1]; ἐξαπόστειλον LXX;
dimitte Vg| ܘܢܦܠܚܢܝ 7a1 7h13 8a1 8b1 9b1 10b2 10j1
11l2 12b1.2] omit waw 5b1 Ephraem MT Sam Tgs Tsam|
ܨܒܝܬ] ܨܒܐ ܐܢܬ P| ܠܡܫܕܪܘ 5b1] add ܠܒܪܝ
7a1 7h13 8a1 8b1 9b1 10b2 10j1 11l2 12b1.2; לשלחו MT
Sam; לשלחותיה TO; למיפטריה TJ[I]; למשלח יתיה TN[1];
למשלחאה TSam

Exod 5:2

#175 XXIII.(55). 491:17-18; II 113:7-9

ܐܡܪ ܠܟ ܦܪܥܘܢ { A ܕܡܢܘ / B ܡܢܘ } ܐܠܗܐ.
ܘܦܠܚܬܗ، ܐܝܟ ܡܪܕܘܬܐ ܒܥܒܐ ܕܫܠܝܐ.

This very brief quotation of the first part of Pharaoh's reply in Exod 5:2 is deliberately partial, occurring within a direct address to God by Aphr in which he contrasts Pharaoh's

sarcastic question with God's subsequent destruction of him.
The textual value of such a tiny fragment of text is doubtful.
Such a passing reference, imbedded entirely within a larger sentence of Aphr's own composition, may easily deviate from the
biblical text.

The uncertainty that attaches to this passage is particularly frustrating, because its reading of ܐܠܗܐ differs from
P (ܡܪܝܐ) and most other witnesses, which attest the Tetra-
grammaton. Aphr employs ܡܪܝܐ elsewhere in the immediate context of #175. That he switches to ܐܠܗܐ here increases the
likelihood that it is a feature of his scripture text.

> *Exod 5:2   [. . .] [ܐܠܗܐ] ܒܝܕ [. . .]
>
> ܐܠܗܐ LXX[A] Ethiopic[c] Chrysostom] ܡܪܝܐ P MT Sam
> Tgs TSam Vg

Exod 8:21-22

#176 XV.4(3). 311:7-12; 737:25-740:5

ܪܚܡܝܐ }A ܫܘܬܐ{ }B ܕܒܚܝ{
B ܫܘܬܐ A ܬܘܪܝ ܕܒܚܝ
ܠܐܠܗܝܗܘܢ ܕܡܨܪܝܐ .

This passage is one of several citations made in section
(3) of the Dem to show that the Egyptians in biblical times worshipped sheep and oxen as deities. Its significance derives in
part from the explanation which precedes it (737:11-13): "But
the Egyptians did not eat the meat of sheep and oxen, for these
were their gods." The passage forms part of Aphr's larger argument that the dietary laws of the OT have nothing to do with the
essence of righteousness but were instituted merely as a practi-
cal measure to direct the Israelites away from the Egyptian idol-
atry into which they had fallen during the bondage. The most
important part of the quotation for Aphr, therefore, is Moses'
reply to Pharaoh in the final part of the last sentence.

The preceding sentence, which purports to give Pharaoh's
earlier answer to Moses' request is essentially a reflection of
Exod 8:21, but it is a loose citation in which elements from Exod
10:8 (ܐܢܬܘܢ ܐܦ ܕܒܚܝ ܦܠܚܘ ܙܠܘ) and
12:31 (ܕܒܚܝ ܦܠܚܘ ܦܠܘܚܘ ܘܙܠܘ) appear to be conflated as well. The citation is too free to afford a reliable
textual witness, but the possibility must at least be noted that
the phrase ܒܐܪܥܐ ܕܡܨܪܝܢ is an authentic feature of
Aphr's scripture text. TN[1] agrees with this reading in its
בארעא דמצרים. Given the conflated nature of the citation,

however, it is probable that this longer reading is a deviation
from Aphr's text of vs 21 under the influence of vs 20 P: . . .
‏ܕܢܐܪܥ‎ ‏ܐܘܪܐ‎ ‏ܘܒܪܬܗ‎ . In vs 21, P (‏ܒܐܪܥܐ‎)
preserves the spareness of the MT (‏באַרץ‎; so Sam, TO, TSam, LXX,
and Vg; LXX[mss] and TJ[1] read "in this land"). Ephraem (Comm VIII.3
lines 17-18) is surely being paraphrastic with ‏ܒܐܪܥܐ‎.

The citation of Exod 8:22 has telescoped the text to omit
"we sacrifice to the Lord our God from among the idols/abomina-
tions of the Egyptians." This is Aphr's own streamlining of his
scripture text as he hastens to the ‏ܐܢ‎-clause, which is his
chief interest. Given this looseness in the earlier part of the
vs, one is reluctant to believe that other deviations from P
before the ‏ܐܢ‎-clause are not also to be attributed simply to
Aphr's manner of quoting. The use of ‏ܡܬܡܨܝܢܘ‎ in contrast
to P ‏ܬܩܢ‎ (cf. MT ‏נכון‎; Tgs ‏תקין/תקן‎; LXX δυνατὸν; Vg potest)
looks like his paraphrase. So too the addition of ‏ܦܠܚܢ‎
after ‏ܗܢܐ‎, an addition that is unique among the ancient witnesses. The entire portion of the quotation of vs 22 which precedes the ‏ܐܢ‎-clause appears to be a close paraphrase of Aphr's
text, shaped to vivify the vs which now has to stand outside the
larger Exod narrative.

The final clauses of the quotation, the ‏ܐܢ‎-clause and
its apodosis, fall almost exactly into the text-form of P,[7] and
one is more inclined to see them as a literal reproduction of
Aphr's text. Here also caution is order. The only variant from

P is the noun (certainly plural, with ms A) ܚ̈ܝܘܬܐ. This reading is without support elsewhere. P reads ܕܕ̈ܚܠܬܐ; cf. MT, Sam, TSam תועבת; LXX βδελύγματα; and Vg <u>abominationes</u>. TO and TJ[1] also reflect the MT, although with exegetical expansions.[8] Ephraem intersperses citation with exposition at this point in his commentary to such an extent that it is impossible to be certain what his bible text itself reads.[9] Because Aphr's sole purpose in making this quotation is to prove that the Egyptians worshipped animals, the probability is that he has deliberately replaced the ambiguous noun of his text (ܕܕ̈ܚܠܬܐ = P) with a synonym that clarifies the meaning of the vs as a support for his theological argument. It seems entirely unlikely that his text reads ܚ̈ܝܘܬܐ in vs 22. Because of these uncertainties, #176 cannot be taken as a reliable witness to Aphr's text.

<u>Exod 10:7</u>

#177 XIV.26(42). 293:12-14; 696:17-19

{B ܘܦܪܥܘܢ / A ܘܠܦܪܥܘܢ} ܡܠܟܐ ܡ̈ܠܟܘܗܝ ܘܪ̈ܘܪܒܢܘܗܝ

ܕܐܒܕܬ ܠܗ ܡܨܪܝܢ ܒܚܛܗܝܢ. ܘܠܐ

ܥܒܕ ܡܠܟܗܘܢ ܕܥܒ̈ܕܘܗܝ

This brief allusion to Exod 10:7 is one in a lengthy series of references to biblical events by which Aphr seeks to illustrate the importance of being receptive to sound advice. The allusion is not an exact reproduction of P and is probably made from memory. The final portion of vs 7 P (ܕܐܒܕܬ ܠܗ

ܡܫܝܪܝܢ) appears to be reflected here; the addition of ܒܡܥܪ̈ܒܝ, a feature that is absent from all other witnesses, is surely Aphr's interpretative expansion of his text. A clear textual witness is not provided.

Exod 12:3, 5-7, 9, 11, 23, 46, 48

#178 XII.1(1). 217:2-16; 505:2-508:3

ܐܡܪ ܠܗ ܡܪܝܐ ܠܡܘܫܐ. ܕܢܐܡܪ ܠܟܢܘܫܬܐ
ܕܒܢ̈ܝ ܐܝܣܪܝܠ ܘܢܣܒܘܢ ܠܗܘܢ ܐܡܪܐ
ܚܕ ܒܪ ܫܢܬܗ. ܐܡܪܐ ܕܠܝܬ ܒܗ ܡܘܡܐ.
ܡܢ ܐܡܪ̈ܐ ܐܘ ܡܢ ܓܕ̈ܝܐ ܢܣܒܘܢ. ܘܢܟܣܘܢ
ܦܨܚܐ ܠܡܪܝܐ ܟܠܗܘܢ ܒ̈ܢܝ ܐܝܣܪܝܠ.
ܐܡܪ ܠܗ ܡܪܝܐ ܠܡܘܫܐ ܕܢܣܒܘܢ ܐܡܪܐ
ܡܢ ܒܥܣܪܬܐ ܒܝܪܚܐ. ܘܢܗܘܐ ܢܛܝܪ
ܠܗܘܢ ܥܕܡܐ ܠܐܪܒܥܣܪܐ ܒܗ ܒܝܪܚܐ
ܘܢܟܣܘܢܗ ܒܡܥܪ̈ܒܝ ܫܡܫܐ ܘܢܪܫܘܢ ܡܢ
ܕܡܗ ܥܠ ܬܪܥܐ ܕܒܬܝܗܘܢ ܡܢ ܡܚܒܠܢܐ.
ܕܠܐ ܢܥܘܠ ܥܠܝܗܘܢ ܟܕ ܥܒܪ ܡܚܒܠܢܐ
ܒܟܠ ܐܪܥܐ ܕܡܨܪܝܢ. ܘܢܐܟܠܘܢܗ
ܠܐܡܪܐ ܡܣܪܗܒܐܝܬ ܥܠܗ̇ ܒܦܛܝܪܬܐ.
ܘܗܟܢܐ ܠܗ ܬܐܟܠܘܢܗ. ܟܕ ܚܨ̈ܝܟܘܢ
ܐܣܝܪܝܢ. ܘܡܣܐܢܝܟܘܢ ܒܪ̈ܓܠܝܟܘܢ.
ܘܫܒ̈ܛܝܟܘܢ ܒܐܝ̈ܕܝܟܘܢ. ܘܥܒܕ ܐܝܟ
ܕܡܣܪܗܒܐܝܬ ܬܐܟܠܘܢܗ. ܘܠܐ ܠܟ
ܬܐܟܠ ܡܢܗ ܒ̇ ܢܐ. ܘܐܦ ܠܐ ܒ̇
ܡܒܫܠ ܡܒܫܠ ܒܡ̈ܝܐ. ܐܠܐ ܒ̇ ܛܘܝ

ܒܢܘܪܐ. ܘܠܐ ܢܦܘܩ ܡܢܗ ܠܒܪ ܡܢ
ܒܝܬܐ. ܓܪܡܐ ܠܐ ܢܬܒܪ ܒܗ.

#179 XII.1(2). 218:2-3; 508:8-11

ܘܢܗܪ ܐܝܟ ܟܠ ܢ̈ܡܘܣܘܗܝ, ܘܐܝܕܪ
ܠܗܘܢ. ܕܒܒܝܬܐ ܚܕ ܢܬܐܟܠ ܘܠܐ ܠܡ
ܢܦܩܘܢ ܡܢܗ ܠܒܪ ܡܢ ܒܝܬܐ.

#180 XII.4(5). 221:8-9; 516:8-10

ܐܡܪܐ ܓܝܪ ܕܕܟܪܐ ܐܝܬܘܗܝ, ܦܪܘܩܢ.
ܒܪ ܫܢܬܐ ܕܠܝܬ ܒܗ ܡܘܡܐ.

#181 XII.6(9). 224:18-20; 525:5-8

... ܟܠ ܚܕ ܐܡܪܐ ܕܦܨܚܐ. ܐܟܠܐ
ܦܫ ܟܠܗܘܢ, ܡܢܝܢܐ. ܕܒܒܝܬܐ ܚܕ
ܡܬܐܟܠ. ܘܠܐ ܒܒ̈ܬܐ ܣܓܝܐܐ.

#182 XII.6(9). 225:3-4; 525:15-17

ܘܐܡܪ ܕܠܐ ܬܐܟܠܘܢ ܡܢܗ ܟܕ ܚܝ. ܐܦܠܐ
ܟܕ ܡܒܫܠ ܡܒܫܠ ܒܡܝܐ.

#183 XII.6(9). 225:6-8; 525:20-23

ܘܐܡܪ ܕܗܟܢܐ ܬܐܟܠܘܢܗ, ܟܕ ܚܨ̈ܝܟܘܢ
ܐܣܝܪ̈ܢ. ܘܡܣܢ̈ܝܟܘܢ ܒܪ̈ܓܠܝܟܘܢ
ܘܫܒ̈ܛܝܟܘܢ ܒܐܝ̈ܕܝܟܘܢ.

#184 XII.6(9). 225:12; 528:2-3

ܘܐܡܪ ܬܘܒ ܕܓܪܡܐ ܠܐ ܢܬܬܒܪ ܒܗ.

#185 XII.6(9). 225:22; 528:15-16

ܘܕܐܡܪ ܕܐܘܟܠܘܗܝ, ܒܣܘܪܗܒܐܝܬ.

These quotations, all of which pertain to the Jewish

feast of Passover, come from a relatively limited section of material in Dem XII, "On the Passover." #178 appears to contain two formal quotations of statements by God to Moses, but both prove to be loose mixtures of elements from various biblical vss. The first citation in #178 (505:3-7) conflates portions of Exod 12:3 P (ܠܟܠܗ ܟܢܘܫܬܐ ܕܒܢܝ ܐܝܣܪܝܠ . . . ܢܣܒܘܢ ܢܦܫܝܢ ܠܗܘܢ); Num 6:14 P (ܐܡܪܐ ܚܕ ܒܪ ܫܢܬܐ ܕܠܝܬ ܒܗ ܡܘܡܐ);[10] Exod 12:5 P (ܡܢ ܐܡܪܐ ܘܡܢ ܥܙܐ ܬܣܒܘܢ); and Exod 12:48 P (ܘܢܥܒܕ ܦܨܚܐ ܠܡܪܝܐ), most of which are not reproduced exactly. Such a passage is of no value as a textual witness.

The second citation with #178 (505:8-508:3) is of no greater textual value. It is made up of a mixture of elements, many very loosely handled, from the following vss: Exod 12:3 P (ܒܥܣܪܬܐ ܒܝܪܚܐ . . . ܢܣܒܘܢ ܢܦܫܝܢ); Exod 12:6 P (ܘܢܗܘܐ ܢܛܝܪ ܠܟܘܢ ܥܕܡܐ ܠܐܪܒܥܣܪܐ ܘܢܟܣܘܢܗ . . . ܒܡܥܪܒ ܫܡܫܐ); Exod 12:7 P (ܘܢܣܒܘܢ ܡܢ ܕܡܗ); Exod 12:23 P (ܡܚܒܠܢܐ); Exod 12:11, 9, and 46 P.

Although Exod 12:9 is cited very loosely in #178, Aphr quotes it literally in #182. The omission of the last half of the vs in #182 is without question due to Aphr's deliberate excerpting. His purpose is to point out that Jesus was in all respects the ultimate paschal lamb. Inclusion of the final part

of the vs, "and its head and its knees and its internal parts,"
would not commend itself to Aphr's argument.

Similarly, #183 and #185, both of which are formal and
literal citations, supplement #178 to afford a clear reflection
of Aphr's text of Exod 12:11. Here too the text has surely been
abbreviated in the quotation, the final "because it is the Lord's
Passover" not being necessary to Aphr's discussion at #183 and
#185 and being directly unsuitable to the rehearsal of the ritual
components of the Passover in #178. Because the imperative
clause has been lifted from its context in the biblical vs, and
because Aphr characteristically uses dalath after the introductory word of a quotation, it is impossible to know from #185
whether Aphr's text reads a waw prefixed to the imperative verb
ܐܟܘܠܘܗܝ.

The final two sentences in #178 constitute a close paraphrase of Exod 12:46. This witness is supplemented by the literal citations of the same vs found in #179, #181 (only "in one
house is it to be eaten" constitutes the quotation here), and
#184. Unfortunately, it is impossible to be certain that Aphr's
bible text actually omits ܡܢ ܒܣܪܐ. All other witnesses
except the Old Latin include the phrase, and its absence here
may simply be Aphr's characteristic abbreviating tendency showing
itself. Nor can #178 and #179 be considered two independent witnesses, being separated by only a few lines. I suspect that Aphr
is merely condensing his scripture text at this point.

The second of the two sentences from Exod 12:46 is in fact not quoted from the Exod vs itself in #178 or #184. At both of these locations, John 19:36 P contaminates the citation, thus explaining the use of the third-person passive verb form in place of the second-person active. That this vs from John is on Aphr's mind at this time is clear from the fact that he quotes it directly a few lines after #184 at 528:5-6.[11]

*Exod 12:9 ܠܐ ܬܐܟܠܘܢ ܡܢܗ ܟܕ ܚܝ

ܐܠܐ ܟܕ ܛܘܐ ܒܢܘܪܐ

[. . .]

ܐܠܐ 5b1 7h13 8b1 9b1 9 1̲4.5 10b1.2 11 1̲4.5 12b1.2 TO TN⊥] ܘܐܠܐ 7al 9 1̲3.6 11 1̲1; ובשל MT Sam TSam; ולא TJ¹; οὐδὲ LXX; nec Vg.

*Exod 12:11 [] ܗܟܢܐ ܬܐܟܠܘܢܝ̈ ܟܕ

ܚܨܝ̈ܟܘܢ ܐܣܝܪ̈ܝܢ ܘܣܐܘܢ̈ܝܟܘܢ

ܒܪ̈ܓܠܝܟܘܢ ܘܚܘܛܪ̈ܝܟܘܢ ܒܐܝ̈ܕܝܟܘܢ

ܐܘܟܠܬܗ, ܒܣܪܗܝܒܘܬܐ [. . .]

Aphr = P

*Exod 12:46 ܒܒܝܬܐ ܚܕ ܬܬܐܟܠ ܘܠܐ

ܬܦܩܘܢ [ܒܣܪܐ] ܠܒܪ ܡܢ ܒܝܬܐ [. . .]

ܒܣܪܐ 5b1 7al 7h13 9b1 9 1̲3.6 10b1 12b1.2] omit 8b1; add ܡܢ ܒܣܪܐ P MT Sam Tgs TSam LXX Vg

Exod 12:33

#186 XIX.1(1). 358:19-21; 849:10-12

ܘܐܡܪܝܢ ܕܟܠܢ ܡܝܬܝܢ ܚܢܢ. ܘܐܘܚܠܬ

[Syriac text] { B̲ [Syriac] } [Syriac]

{ A omits }

[Syriac text] ·

This two-part formal citation of Exod 12:33 immediately
follows a paraphrastic allusion to part of the same vs at 849:6-10
([Syriac text]

[Syriac]). Aphr introduces these references to support his
argument that the Israelites were rebellious already in the very
beginning and would not even have left Egypt in the first place
had not the Egyptians forced them to leave. Although the first
piece of quoted material ("We are all dead") is a literal reproduction of the final part of vs 33 P, it is not possible to determine Aphr's text for the phrase that introduces it.

The second section of the passage presents a citation of
the first portion of vs 33. It differs from P in three features:
the placement of [Syriac] after [Syriac] (if ms B̲ is followed,
as the text most unlike P), the omission of [Syriac]
after [Syriac], and the addition of the pronominal suffix on
"land" ([Syriac]). This part of the citation has the appearance of a close paraphrase, and one cannot be certain that it
reflects a scripture text marked by these departures from P.

In trying to prove his contention that the Israelites
had to be forced out of Egypt, Aphr first presents the interpretative paraphrase of vs 33 already mentioned. That paraphrase
(849:6-10) is shaped to give maximum support to his argument.

206

The adverb ܣܝܪ̈ܗܒܐ is omitted; it is irrelevant to the
point being made, and its absence serves to increase the promi-
nence and force of the verb ܘܐܠܨ. Throughout section (1)
of Dem XIX prior to #186, Aphr chooses to refer to the Israelites
only by means of pronouns, which refer back to "his people"
(ܥܡܗ) in 845:2. So also in the paraphrase in 849:6-10, Aphr
omits ܥܡܗ in favor of the more concise ܐܢܘܢ. For the
sake of clarity, he gives ܠܝܣܪ̈ܠܝܐ rather than merely ܐܝܠܝܢ.

When he attempts to buttress this paraphrase with formal
citation, there can be little doubt that Aphr succeeds only partially in recalling the exact text of Exod 12:33. He correctly
remembers the presence of ܡܢ ܕ̈ܪ and ܥܡܐ, and places
them in #186. Otherwise, his recall of the vs is hampered by
the paraphrase which he has just written. He retains ܐܢܘܢ
immediately after ܕܐܠܨ instead of restoring it to its place
following ܕ ܥܠܝܗܘܢ, and he retains the pronominal suffix on
"land." None of these departures finds support among other witnesses (although one Greek minuscule does attest the suffix on
"land"). One cannot confidently accept #186 as a literal reproduction of Aphr's text for the first part of vs 33.

*Exod 12:33　　　ܠܒ[] [. . .] ܘܝܬܪ ܫܠ.
Aphr = P

Exod 12:44-45

#187 XII.1(2). 218:8-11; 508:17-21

ܘܟܠ ܥܒܕ ܕܙܒܢ ܟܣܦܐ. ܕܓܒܪܐ ܐܝܟܪ̈ܐ

ܠܐ ܢܐܟܘܠ ܡܢܗ ܦܨܚܐ. ܘܥܒܕܐ
ܙܒܝܢ ܟܣܦܐ ܕܢܡܘܣܐ ܠܗ ܗܘܐ ܕܓܙܝܪ
ܒܣܪܐ ܕܓܙܘܪܬܗ ܗܝܕܝܢ ܢܐܟܘܠ ܡܢ
ܦܨܚܐ.

#188 XII.6(9). 224:21-22; 525:9-10

ܘܐܡܪ ܬܘܒ ܕܠܐ ܢܐܟܠܘܢ ܡܢܗ ܐܓܝܪܐ
ܘܬܘܬܒܐ.

#189 XII.6(9). 225:16-17; 528:7-9

ܘܐܡܪ ܕܥܒܕܐ ܙܒܝܢ ܟܣܦܐ. ܟܕ ܗܘܐ
ܓܙܝܪ ܒܣܪܐ ܕܓܙܘܪܬܗ. ܘܗܝܕܝܢ
ܢܐܟܘܠ ܡܢ ܦܨܚܐ.

Although these three passages present themselves as formal citations of part or all of Exod 12:44-45, each proves to be paraphrastic and inexact to some extent. #187 begins with a nearly literal reproduction of vs 45, departing from P only in the addition of ܡܢ ܦܨܚܐ. This is surely not a feature of Aphr's bible text; it is added here merely to clarify the referent of ܡܢܗ, otherwise now obscured by the removal of the vs from its context in Exod ch 12. That #187 reproduces vs 45 P almost exactly necessitates the conclusion that #188, which appears to quote vs 45 also, is not a literal citation. No other witness supports the word order and plural verb form for vs 45 as reflected in #188.

Both #189 and the second half of #187 present close paraphrases of Exod 12:44. The omission of ܕܙܒܢܬܐ after ܥܒܕܐ

must also be regarded as Aphr's economizing, given the freedom that is evident in the remainder of the quotation and the agreement of all other Semitic witnesses with P. The same is true of the omission of the preceding ܘܟܠ. Nor is the addition of ܒܣܪܐ ܕܥܘܪܠܘܬܗ a feature of Aphr's bible text. Rather, he is probably quoting from memory here, and he confuses the Exod vs with Gen 17:11-14 (cf. 17:23-27), where instructions to circumcise the ܙܒܝܢ ܟܣܦܐ (among others) specifically mention ܒܣܪܐ ܕܥܘܪܠܘܬܗ. One finds no firm evidence in #189 and #187 of a text of Exod 12:44 that varies from P, but no clear reflection of the text is provided in either passage.

*Exod 12:45 ܬܘܬܒܐ ܘܐܓܝܪܐ ܠܐ ܢܐܟܘܠ ܡܢܗ.

Aphr = P

Exod 14:12

#190 XIX.1(1). 358:14-16; 849:1-5

ܐܝܟ {ܕܐܡܪܘ B / ܕܐܡܪܝܢ A} ܠܡܘܫܐ ܟܕ ܡܬܟܬܫܝܢ

ܗܘܘ ܒܗ. ܒܡܨܪܝܢ ܕܗܘ ܦܬܓܡܐ ܕܐܡܪܢ

ܠܟ ܒܡܨܪܝܢ ܕܫܒܘܩܝܢ {ܢܦܠܘܚ B / ܕܢܦܠܘܚ A}

ܠܡܨܪ̈ܝܐ ܡܛܠ ܕܛܒ ܗܘܐ ܠܢ ܒܡܨܪܝܢ.

This formal citation of Exod 14:12 reproduces most of the vs exactly as in P. Serious question about its literalness must be raised, however, especially in the final portion, where Aphr

seems to fall into the text of a parallel statement from Num 11:18
P: ܒܡܨܪܝܢ ܠܢ ܗܘܐ ܛܒ ܗܕ. That this is
due to casualness or _memoriter_ confusion in the quotation rather
than to a deviant scripture text is suggested by the omission of
the interrogative element (ܗܘܐ ܠܐ) at the beginning of the
vs. Whether or not this omission is consciously made, it certainly comes about in the interest of maximum directness and
emphasis in the quotation. P and all other witnesses begin Exod
14:12 with this interrogative construction, and it is difficult
to think that any text would lack it, given the location of the
vs at the end of a series of similar rhetorical questions in Exod
14:11.

Because of the abbreviating tendency evident in the omission of ܗܘܐ ܠܐ, one must entertain doubts about the literalness of the quotation also in its omission of ܗܘܐ after
ܕܐܡܪܝܢ. This shorter reading is supported by ms 5b1, but
could this be mere coincidence? This omission, like the earlier
one, may be simply the result of Aphr's tendency to condense his
text in the quotation. His text might contain the auxiliary verb.

The uncertainty of the witness of #190 is increased by
the disagreement of the mss concerning the presence of _dalath_
on ܢܦܠܘܚ. One might assume that ms A shows a reading that
is a later correction to the main P tradition, but mss 7a1 and
→ omit the _dalath_, and it is not certain which of the readings
would have been more familiar to a sixth century scribe.

*Exod 14:12 [ܕܐܡܪܬ] ܗܘ ܦܬܓܡܐ [. . .]
[ܢܦܠܘܚ] ܠܟ ܒܡܨܪܝܢ ܕܫܒܘܩܝܢ
[. . .] ܠܡܨܪܝܐ ܕܛܒ ܗܘܐ ܠܢ

ܗܘ 9l6] ܗܢܘ 5b1 7a1 7h13 8b1 9b1 9l5.6 10b1.2 11l4.5 12b1.2| ܕܐܡܪܬ 5b1 MT Sam Tgs TSam] add ܗܘܝܬ 7a1 7h13 9b1 9l5 10b1.2 11l4.5 12b1.2; ܗܘܝܬ ܕܐܡܪܬ 8b1 9l6| ܢܦܠܘܚ 7a1 →] pr dalath 5b1 7h13 8b1 9b1 9l5.6 10b1.2 11l4.5 12b1.2; pr waw MT Sam Tgs TSam

Exod 17:9

#191 III.8(11). 53:14-18; 121:8-13

ܟܬܝܒ ܓܝܪ ܒܢܡܘܣܐ ܡܘܫܐ. ܕܐܡܪ ܐܠܗܐ
ܠܡܘܫܐ. ܐܡܪ ܠܝܫܘܥ ܒܪ ܢܘܢ. {B ܘܢܓܒܐ / A ܢܓܒܐ}
ܠܗ ܓܒܪܐ. ܘܢܥܒܕ ܩܪܒܐ ܥܡ ܥܡܠܝܩ.
ܘܐܙܠ ܝܫܘܥ {B omits / A ܒܪ ܢܘܢ}. ܘܥܒܕ ܩܪܒܐ
ܥܡ ܥܡܠܝܩ. ܘܐܙܕܟܝ ܥܡܠܝܩ ܒܐܝܕܐ
ܕܝܫܘܥ. ܒܦܫܛ ܐܝܕܘܗܝ ܕܡܘܫܐ.

Although this passage presents itself as a formal quotation of God's command to Moses concerning Joshua, evidently Exod 17:9, it is actually a free paraphrase of the latter vs. Aphr departs from the manner of direct quotation used in P and all other witnesses for the prescribed instruction to Joshua. In place of the imperative in P, "Choose for yourself men," Aphr's quotation reads (with or without the waw on the verb), ". . . that he should choose for himself men." No certain witness to

Aphr's scripture text is provided by this passage, although ܘܓܒܐ ܠܗ ܓܒܪ̈ܐ probably echoes a text identical to P (ܓܒܝ ܠܢ ܓܒܪ̈ܐ), in which case Aphr does not provide corroboration for an ancient Syriac reading in Exod 17:9 which Vööbus identifies in B. M. Add. 14534: ܓܒܝ ܠܢ ܓܒܪ̈ܝ ܚܝܠܐ (cf. TJ[1] גוברין גיברין ותקיפין).[12]

<u>Exod 17:12</u>

#192 I.10(14). 18:17-18; 33:26-36:2

ܐܝܟ ܕܟܬܝܒ ܕܗܘܝ ܐܝ̈ܕܘܗܝ ܒܗܝܡܢܘܬܐ.
ܥܕܡܐ ܕܥܪܒ ܫܡܫܐ.

This citation of the final portion of Exod 17:12 is inserted within the list of examples of faith that composes section (14) of Dem I. Aphr cites this sentence (certainly an excerpt from the longer text of vs 12) to confirm the preceding element in the Symbol: "By faith he spread out his hands and defeated Amalek." Like the MT (אמונה), P employs a term at this point whose ambiguity invites reinterpretation. Within the context of the Exod narrative, ܒܗܝܡܢܘܬܐ certainly means "steadily." In other contexts, of course, the same noun can mean "faithfulness" or "faith," and it is this latter sense that Aphr attributes to it in this quotation.

*Exod 17:12 [. . .] []ܗܘܝ ܐܝ̈ܕܘܗܝ
ܒܗܝܡܢܘܬܐ ܥܕܡܐ ܕܥܪܒ ܫܡܫܐ.

Aphr = P

Exod 17:14

#193 III.8(11). 53:20-54:4; 121:16-23

ܗܟܢ ܐܡܪ ܡܪܝܐ ܠܡܘܫܐ. ܟܬܘܒ ܣܦܪܐ
ܕܕܘܟܪܢܐ. ܘܣܝܡ ܩܕܡ ܝܫܘܥ ܒܪ ܢܘܢ.
{ܡܛܠ B / ܡܛܠ A} ܕܡܥܛܐ ܡܥܛܐ ܐܢܐ. ܕܘܟܪܢܗ
ܕܥܡܠܩ ܡܢ ܬܚܝܬ ܫܡܝܐ. ܘܐܦܢ ܒܥܡܗܘܢ
ܪܘܚܐ ܥܡ ܥܡܠܩܝ̈ܐ. {ܕܟܬܒ B / ܕܐܟܬܒ A}
ܫܡܗܘܢ. ܕܟܬܒ {ܒܣܦܪܐ A / ܒܣܦܪܗ B} ܩܕܝܫܐ
ܕܐܠܗܐ. ܕܐܡܪ ܕܡܥܛܐ ܡܥܛܐ {B omits / A ܐܢܐ}
ܠܗܘܢ ܠܥܡܠܩܝܐ.

This passage presents a formal quotation of Exod 17:14 (121:16-19) followed by a partial and paraphrastic allusion to the same vs (121:20-23). The latter is too free to be of textual significance (the reading of ms B, surely the original, accentuates its looseness in the omission of the first-person pronoun), but the former appears to be exact. The text reflected differs from P only in the phrase ܣܦܪܐ ܕܕܘܟܪܢܐ. Aphr stands entirely alone in this reading. While one cannot dismiss the possibility that this reading is the result of memoriter error, perhaps contamination by the similar clause in Mal 3:16 P (ܟܬܘܒ ܒܣܦܪܐ ܕܕܘܟܪܢܐ[13]), the exactness with which the remainder of the vs appears to be reproduced compels one to take this element seriously as a possibly authentic feature of Aphr's bible text.

*Exod 17:14 [. . .] ܟܬܘܒ ܣܦܪܐ ܕܕܘܟܪܢܐ
ܘܣܝܡ ܩܕܡ ܝܫܘܥ ܒܪ ܢܘܢ ܕܡܛܠ
ܕܡܥܛܐ ܡܥܛܐ ܐܢܐ ܕܘܟܪܢܐ ܕܥܡܠܝܩ
ܡܢ ܬܚܝܬ ܫܡܝܐ.

ܕܘܟܪܢܐ ܗܢܐ ܒܣܦܪܐ] ܣܦܪܐ ܕܕܘܟܪܢܐ
7al 7hl3 8bl 9bl 10bl.2 11l1 12bl.2; ܗܢܐ ܕܘܟܪܢܐ
ܒܣܦܪܐ 5bl 10l1 Ephraem(Comm XVII.3 lines 26-27)
MT Sam Tgs TSam LXX Vg

Exod 19:10, 15

#194 XVIII.4(4). 349:2-4; 825:19-23

ܐܡܪ ܠܗ ܡܪܝܐ ܠܡܘܫܐ. ܕܢܚܘܬ ܠܘܬ ܥܡܐ}

ܘܢܩܕܫ ܐܢܘܢ ܬܠܬܐ ܝܘܡܝܢ {A / B omits} ܘܗܟܢܐ

ܐܡܪ ܠܗܘܢ ܡܘܫܐ ܦܫܝܩܐܝܬ ܕܠܐ
ܬܬܩܪܒܘܢ ܠܐܢܬܬܐ.

This passage includes two immediately successive formal citations, the first ostensibly of Exod 19:10, the second of part of Exod 19:15. The former is in fact a loose paraphrase of Aphr's text, echoing elements of Exod 19:11 and 14 P as well as 19:10. It is not impossible that a text of vs 10 is reflected here which reads ܢܚܘܬ rather than ܐܙܠ (so P); support for such a reading may be found in the LXX, which reads καταβὰς. "Three days," however, is certainly paraphrastic, and the literalness of the earlier part of the vs must also remain in doubt.

The second citation is an exact reproduction of the final portion of Exod 19:15 P. It is surely a deliberate excerpt from the longer vs, the earlier part of which does not contribute to Aphr's theme here--the spiritual inferiority of marriage as compared to celibacy.

The omission of the first part of the passage by ms B is an accident due to homoioteleuton. The phrase ܬܠܬܐ ܝܘ̈ܡܝܢ occurs also in the immediately preceding sentence in 825:18.

*Exod 19:15 [. . .] ܠܐ ܬܬܩܪܒܘܢ ܠܐܢܬܬܐ.

Aphr = P

Exod 20:2, 4

#195 I.8(11). 14:19-15:1; 25:13-15

ܗܘ ܕܐܡܪ ܐܦ ܒܗ ܘܐܡܪ. {B omits / A ܠܗܘܢ}

ܕܐܢܐ ܐܢܐ ܡܪܝܐ ܐܠܗܟܘܢ. ܕܐܦܩܬܟܘܢ

ܡܢ ܐܪܥܐ ܕܡܨܪܝܢ.

#196 II.7(7). 30:13-16; 61:23-26

ܒܪܫ ܟܠܗ ܢܡܘܣܐ ܗܢܐ ܟܬܒ.

ܕܐܢܐ ܐܢܐ ܡܪܝܐ ܐܠܗܟ. ܕܐܦܩܬܟ ܡܢ

ܐܪܥܐ ܕܡܨܪܝܢ. ܠܐ ܬܥܒܕ {A omits / B ܠܟ} ܟܠ

ܟܠ ܨܠܡ ܘܟܠ ܕܡܘ.

These two formal quotations appear to be intended reproductions of Exod 20:2; #196 includes 20:4 also. The saying in
#195 is identified in the immediately preceding clause as "the
first commandment," and following the quotation Aphr adds: "For
it was not possible that while worshipping Baal they could keep
the [other] nine commandments." This identification as the first
commandment in the Decalogue does not by itself make plain whether
Exod 20:2 or Deut 5:6 is in Aphr's mind (if the distinction even
occurs to him), but the use of ܢܟܐ instead of ܢܟܐ
points to the Exod passage.

In #196 too the choice of verb points to Exod ch 20 rather
than Deut ch 5, as does the introductory phrase, "at the beginning of the whole law." The phrase "whole law" is best understood as referring to the entire corpus of Pentateuchal legislation, which of course begins at Exod ch 20, rather than to the
Decalogue alone. That Aphr so easily telescopes vss 2 and 4 and
refers to them as one commandment suggests that his enumeration
of the ten commands of the Decalogue proceeds from a grouping
together of vss 1-6 as the first command.[14] The same approach
is implied in Ephraem's comments in Comm XX.1 lines 14-21 and is
reflected in some Syriac mss of Exod.[15]

In #195 the plural form of the suffixed pronouns is a
variant to P and all other witnesses. The second person singular
is used throughout Exod 20:1-17 in P and all witnesses (including
Ephraem), and it is difficult to conceive of a plural reading in

vs 2. Here Aphr is simply conforming the citation to his discussion in section (11), which concerns "the congregation of the
house of Israel," to whom he refers continually with plural forms.
Prior to #195, the discussion begins with a quotation of Hos
10:12, which is in the second person plural. Following #195, the
Hos vs is repeated and supplemented by a quotation of Isa 55:6-7
which is also in the second-person plural. The obvious strength
of this contextual influence, combined with the second person
singular forms in #196, leaves little doubt that Aphr's bible
text probably contains singular rather than plural pronominal
forms.

Because Exod 20:2-4 have been so evidently telescoped
in #196, one cannot base any textual conclusions on the absence
of the parallel clause, "and from the house of bondage," even
though it is missing in #195 also. This clause is absent in none
of the other witnesses. Aphr is probably economizing at this
point, referring to just enough of the text of vs 2 to identify
it for his reader. Perhaps this abbreviation also reflects the
influence of the numerous passages in P where the expression
"brought you/us out/up from the land of Egypt" occurs without
the additional "(and) from the house of bondage" (e.g., Exod
32:9; Lev 19:36; 26:13).

The appearance of ܒܪܐ in #196[16] and the ms variation
concerning the presence of ܘ make it impossible to determine
Aphr's text for this part of the vs. The inclusion of ܒܪܐ,

not attested in Exod 20:4 by other witnesses, probably results from contamination by Exod 20:23 P: ܠܐ ܬܥܒܕܘܢ ܠܟܘܢ ܥܡܝ ܐܠܗܐ ܕܕܗܒܐ. In the latter vs, however, the P mss themselves differ as to the presence of ܠܟܘܢ. Ms 5b1 omits it, while all the others include it. Is it Aphr's text of vs 23 or of vs 4 which is reflected at this point in #196? Does ms A preserve the authentic reading? If so, does its omission of the prepositional compound reflect quotational abbreviation of a text of vs 4 which contains ܠܟ? Or does it accurately reproduce a text of vs 4 which is unique in omitting the preposition? Or does it reflect a text of vs 23 rather than of vs 4, one which agrees with ms 5b1? There are simply not adequate data by which to reach a conclusion. Similarly, Aphr's introduction of vs 4 in #196 by means of the usual prefixed <u>dalath</u> makes it impossible to know whether or not his text of vs 4 begins with a prefixed <u>waw</u> (so ms 5b1). These uncertainties obstruct a clear view of Aphr's text of Exod 20:4.

*Exod 20:2 ܐܢܐ ܐܢܐ ܡܪܝܐ ܐܠܗܟ.

[. . .] ܕܐܣܩܬܟ ܡܢ ܐܪܥܐ ܕܡܨܪܝܢ

ܕܐܣܩܬܟ 7a1 7h13 8a1 8b1 9b1 9l1 10b1.2 11l1 12b1.2] ܕܐܦܩܬܟ 5b1 MT Sam Tgs TF TSam LXX Vg

<u>Exod 20:7//Deut 5:11</u>

#197 XXIII.(66). 505:3-4; II 144:8-10

ܠ ܗܕܐ ܗܘܪ ܫܡܥܝܢ { B ܕܬܩܘܡܘܢ / A ܕܩܘܡܘܢ } ܠܐ

218

ܟܠ ܘܠܐ ... (Syriac text)

This passage contains what purports to be a saying of
Jesus, and the first clause of the quotation itself is apparently
from Matt 5:34. It is difficult to tell whether Aphr intends
the quotation to end with ܬܐܡܘܢ (so Parisot) or to continue
on through ܒܫܪܪܐ (so Bert[17]). The latter is more likely.
Aphr appears to conflate the Matt passage and Exod 20:7//Deut
5:11. The second sentence in the quotation is a literal reproduction of the final portion of the third commandment in P, the
wording of which is identical in Exod ch 20 and Deut ch 5.

> *Exod 20:7//Deut 5:11 ܠܐ ܬܐܡܐ [. . .]
> ܕܢܐܚܕ ܫܡܗ ܒܫܪܪܐ .
>
> Aphr = P

Exod 20:9-11; 23:12; 31:15, 17; Deut 5:14; Gen 2:2-3

#198 XIII.1(1). 321:2-8; 541:3-10

(Syriac text, several lines)

#199   XIII.1(1). 321:8-11; 541:11-14

ܝܘܝܐܘ ܂ ܢܝܣܒܘ { B ܢܝܐܘܚܐܘ} ܂ ܢܐܝܟܐܘ
                        [A ܢܝܐܘܚܐܘ]

#200   XIII.2(2). 232:5-6; 544:9-10

#201   XII.4(9). 238:11-13; 560:5-8

#202   XIII.6(10). 239:16-21; 561:16-21

ܠܗܘ ܂ܡܗܝܣܝ ܝܐܡܠܒ ܛܥ { B ܚܝܬܬܟܐܘ}
                          [A ܚܝܬܟܐܘ]
ܟܝܣܣܝܬ ܟܣܐܒ ܟܐܠܟ { B ܚܝܬܬܟܝ}
                          [A ܚܝܬܟܝ]

#203   XIII.6(10). 240:3-5; 561:25-564:2

ܐܠܐ ܚܠܦ ܕܡܠܬܐ {ܗܢܐ ܗܘ B / ܗܢܘ A} ܕܫܠܡ
ܐܠܗܐ ܠܫܒܬܐ ܢܘܚ̈ܢ ܟܠܗܘܢ ܒܢ̈ܝܗܘܢ
ܘܫܠ ܒܢܡܘܣܐ ܕܫܒܬܐ. ܡܢ ܟܠܗܘܢ
ܥܒ̈ܕܝܗܘܢ ܕܒܥܝܪ.

#204 XIII.6(11). 241:4-5; 565:4-7

ܐܠܐ ܗܕܐ ܗܝܢܐ ܡܫܬܡܥܢܐ ܕܫܠ ܐܠܗܐ
ܡܢ ܟܠܗܘܢ ܒܢ̈ܝܗܘܢ ܘܐܬܢܝܚ ܐܠܗܐ
ܒܢܡܘܣܐ ܕܫܒܬܐ

#205 XIII.6(11). 241:18-19; 565:24-26

ܕܡܢܐ ܕܝܢ ܗܕܐ {ܕܐܬܬܢܝܚ B / ܕܐܬܢܝܚ A} ܐܠܗܐ
ܡܢ ܒܢ̈ܝܗܘܢ ܘܠܫ̈ܠܐ ܗܢܐ ܡܫܬܡܥܢܐ.
ܕܐܝܟ ܕܡܠܐܐ ܠܐܐ

These passages all contain citations or allusions to the sabbath commandment within the Decalogue or to a parallel vs. Looseness in the quotation and mixture of elements from related biblical passages make it extremely difficult to find certain reflections of Aphr's scripture text here.

#199, #200, and #201 may be considered separately from the others for they stand alone in referring to the actual imperative injunction of the sabbath commandment. None proves to be an exact citation. #199 purports to make two direct quotations of the words of God to Moses (see 541:1: "The Lord commanded Moses his servant . . ."). In the first, Aphr presents a form of the command that is unattested in any other witness. It seems to be an abbreviation and combination of the following elements from three vss in P:[18]

Exod 20:10 ܐܢܬ ܘܒܪܟ ܘܒܪܬܟ ܘܥܒܕܟ ܘܐܡܬܟ
ܘܒܥܝܪܟ ܘܬܘܬܒܟ ܕܒܩܘܪܝܟ

Exod 23:12 ܬܬܢܝܚ ܡܛܠ ܕܢܬܢܝܚ ܬܘܪܟ ܘܚܡܪܟ

Deut 5:14 ܐܢܬ ܘܒܪܟ ܘܒܪܬܟ ܘܥܒܕܟ ܘܐܡܬܟ
ܘܬܘܪܟ ܘܚܡܪܟ ܘܟܠܗ ܒܥܝܪܟ
ܕܢܬܬܢܝܚ ܥܒܕܟ ܘܐܡܬܟ ܐܟܘܬܟ

The second appears to be a very loose paraphrase of the same vss, but with additional influence from Lev 25:6 P (ܠܟܘܢ . . . ܘܠܥܒܕܝܟܘܢ ܘܠܐܡܗܬܟܘܢ ܘܠܐܓܝܪܝܟܘܢ ܘܠܬܘܬܒܐ ܕܥܡܪ ܥܡܟܘܢ).

#200 also presents itself as a formal citation of a part of the sabbath commandment. The reference to animals alone is excerpted intentionally to support Aphr's preceding statement (544:6), that when the sabbath was observed "it was given so that people might rest, and not that people alone might rest, but also animals." Even in this brief quotation Aphr's memory apparently fails him. What occurs in #200 is not a text-form known for any one biblical vs in any witness but rather a conflation of Exod 23:12 P (. . . ܕܢܬܢܝܚ ܬܘܪܟ ܘܚܡܪܟ . . .) and Deut 5:14 (. . . ܘܬܘܪܟ ܘܚܡܪܟ ܘܟܠܗ ܒܥܝܪܟ . . .).

#201 does not purport to be a formal citation, but an interpretative paraphrase designed to point out the ultimate purpose of the sabbath commandment. It does not reproduce any one vs, but its series of four plural nouns echoes the portion of Lev 25:6 P given above. It provides further evidence of the fact that Aphr is not able to quote accurately any one of the similar biblical vss dealing with the sabbath. His memory of the commandment is a mixture of elements from various passages within the Pentateuch. That this mixture changes from one citation to the next makes it certain that the conflation occurs within Aphr's memory and not within his scripture text; Baumstark, looking only at 541:3-14 (= #198 and #199) was not able to reach this conclusion.[19]

Other portions of the sabbath commandment are referred to in the remainder of these quotations, the longest of which is #198. #198 is a formal citation that begins Dem XIII ("On the Sabbath"). As the foundational citation to which the following treatise refers, it might be expected to be literal. The specific scripture passage which it intends to reproduce is not indicated in any way. In fact, this quotation too turns out to be a mixture (probably _memoriter_) of elements of several parallel vss; no other witness even approximates the overall form of its text. The following portions of vss in P appear to lie behind #198:

Exod 23:12   ܝܘܡܝܢ ܥܒܕ ܬܥܒܕ ܘܒܝܘܡܐ

Exod 20:9   ܝܘܡܝܢ ܟܠ ܬܥܒܕܘ ܘܬܦܠܘܚ ܥܒܕ ܫܬܐ

Exod 20:10   ܐܠܗܟ ܠܡܪܝܐ ܫܒܬܐ ܫܒܝܥܝܐ ܘܒܝܘܡܐ

Exod 31:15 ܪܘܚ ܗܝ ܩܕܝܫܐ ܠܡܪܝܐ ܫܒܬܐ

Exod 20:11 ܒܫܬܐ ܝܘܡܝܢ ܥܒܕ ܡܪܝܐ ...

Exod 31:17 ܒܫܬܐ ܝܘܡܝܢ ܥܒܕ ܡܪܝܐ ...

Gen 2:3 ܘܒܪܟ ܐܠܗܐ ܠܝܘܡܐ ܕܫܒܬܐ ...

Gen 2:2 ܘܐܬܬܢܝܚ ܡܪܝܐ ...

The conflated nature of #198 prevents it from offering a clear witness to Aphr's text of any of the passages listed. Exod 20:9-11 appears to be the dominant source for the quotation, with contamination by the other passages.[20]

Similarly, #202 presents itself as a formal citation but proves to be a mixture of elements from Exod 20:11; 31:17; and Gen 2:3. Here the text is sufficiently different from #198 to make it certain that Aphr--not his scripture text--is the source of the conflation. As in #198, Aphr utilizes the compound verb phrase ܢܝܚ ܕܐܬܬܢܝܚ, but here the context provides a possible motive for Aphr's alteration of his text of Exod 20:11. He cites #202 as a basis for his following argument that the reason for God's resting on the seventh day (cf. Gen ch 1) was not divine fatigue after the creative labor. To emphasize this, in making the scripture quotation Aphr reaches out (consciously or not) for that compound phrase in which ܐܬܬܢܝܚ is qualified. Whereas ܐܬܬܢܝܚ ("rested") may lend itself to misunderstanding, ܫܠܝ ("ceased") does not. Joining the two words in a parallel compound, as in Exod 31:17 P, tends to define ܐܬܬܢܝܚ by ܫܠܝ. To quote in this form the vs which he is about to explain gives Aphr the advantage in his argument. Note that in the question that occurs after the quotation itself in #202, he uses only the one verb: "What shall we say concerning this [saying] that God 'rested' on the seventh day?"

Aphr's manipulation of ܐܬܬܢܝܚ and ܫܠܝ to serve his exegetical purposes is evident also in #203, which occurs only a few lines after #202. #203 is not to be taken as a formal or direct quotation. Aphr himself states that this in interpretative paraphrase: "Rather the _meaning_ of the expression is this. . . ." Here he employs ܫܠܡ and ܫܠܝ, the latter in place of ܐܬܬܢܝܚ. Also in the other quotations in this group, the supplementation of ܐܬܬܢܝܚ by ܫܠܝ may be suspected to derive from a concern to avoid any scriptural reference that could be taken to mean that God was wearied after the six days of creation. In #198 and #202, ܐܬܬܢܝܚ is never used by itself

with "God" or "Lord" as the subject.

#204 also is to be understood as interpretative paraphrase

rather than direct citation. It bears a general resemblance to

Gen 2:2 P but is actually a compound clause of Aphr's own con-

struction, whose sole function is to place in parallel the verbs

ܐܬܬܢܝܚ and ܥܒܕ.

#205 makes a reference to the general text that is at

issue in all of these passages, but it too is not a formal cita-

tion (Parisot to the contrary). Neusner (with Bert[21]) is correct

in seeing this as a mere allusion: "Now similarly this matter

that God rested from his works, by fools thus is understood, as

if he were fatigued. . . ."[22]

Although the quotations in this group appear to paraphrase

and conflate various vss in P, none appears to be sufficiently

literal to afford a clear view of Aphr's scripture text.

<u>Exod 20:13, 14, 17//Deut 5:17, 18, 21</u>

#206 III.3(4). 47:19-21; 108:3-5

ܘܠܐ ܐܬܚܙܝ ܐܫܪ ܗܡܟܐ ܀ ܗܡܟܐ ܕܝܘ ܠܐ

܀ ܠܢܦܫܝܢ ܕܐܬܐ ܡܪܝܩ ܀

#207 XIII.2(2). 233:1; 545:10-11

ܦܣܩ ܠܝ ܣܗܕܐ ܣܪܝܩܐ ܒܚܒܪܗ ܘܠܐ ܬܓܢܘܒ .

#208 XIII.2(2). 233:4-5; 545:16-17

ܒܪܚܡ ܠܚܒܪܟ ܘܠܐ ܬܚܡܘܕ .

226

#209 XVIII.7(9). 354:3-5; 837:22-25

[Syriac text, 3 lines]

Each of these contains a formal citation of one or more
of the commands of the Decalogue. Although the references to
"the Law" in #207 and #209 show that Aphr there thinks of the
OT as the source of his citation, the specific biblical passage
which is actually the source of the quoted text-form is not certain. Only for the commandment against coveting is it clear that
Exod ch 20//Deut ch 5, rather than a NT vs, is the source.

The only one of the four that requires comment is #209,
and this is because of its order of the commands. #209 cannot
be taken as proof that Aphr knows a text of the Decalogue which
places the tenth commandment prior to the prohibitions against
adultery and killing.[23] The order in #209 is dictated by Aphr's
exegetical argument. Dem XVIII, "Against the Jews on Virginity
and Sanctity," makes a prolonged defense of celibacy, denouncing
along the way the evil desire which leads men astray. Aphr comes
to this latter emphasis again in section (9): "David was beloved
in his youth, but in his desire for Bathsheba. . . ." Having
identified David's lust [ܪܓܬܐ] as the foundational sin which
led him into more general law-breaking, Aphr naturally places
the tenth commandment (in deliberately abbreviated form[24]) first
in the list of laws broken by David. The spiritual primacy of

this command in the thinking of Aphr is illustrated also by his
comments following #209 at 837:26-840:4: "Amnon was excellent
in his virginity, but because of his unclean lust [ܕܐܡܘܝܒܐ
ܕܠܝ] for his sister, Absalom killed him. Solomon was worthy
and beautiful in his virginity, but in his old age through his
desire [ܕܠܝܒ] for women his heart turned away from God."

    *Exod 20:13//Deut 5:17   .ܠܐ ܬܩܛܘܠ

    Aphr = P

    *Exod 20:14//Deut 5:18   .ܠܐ ܬܓܘܪ

    Aphr = P

    *Exod 20:17//Deut 5:21   ܠܐ ܬܪܓ [...] ܠܟ
                 ܡܕܡ ܕܐܝܬ ܠܚܒܪܟ.

    Aphr = P

Exod 20:19

#210   XVIII.4(5). 349:21-350:1; 828:23-24

ܘܐܡܪܘ ܠܡܘܫܐ ܕܠܐ ܢܡܠܠ ܥܡܢ ܐܠܗܐ
ܕܠܐ ܢܡܘܬ.

    This formal citation of Exod 20:19 is intentionally par-
tial. Aphr cites only that portion of the vs which he needs to
establish his earlier assertion that the Israelites were afraid
when God spoke to Moses from Mount Sinai.

    *Exod 20:19 [...] [] ܠܐ ܢܡܠܠ ܥܡܢ ܐܠܗܐ
                           ܕܠܐ ܢܡܘܬ.

    Aphr = P

Exod 23:10-11

#211 XIII.5(9). 238:15-19; 560:11-15

ܐܡܪ ܓܝܪ ܡܘܫܐ ܟܕ ܝܗܒ ܢܡܘܣܐ ܠܥܡܐ
ܕܫܬ ܫܢܝܢ ܬܙܪܘܥ ܐܪܥܟ ܘܬܟܢܫ
ܥܠܠܬܗ̇. ܘܒܫܢܬܐ ܫܒܝܥܝܬܐ ܬܪܒܝܗ̇
ܘܬܫܒܩܝܗ̇ ܕܢܐܟܠܘܢ ܡܣܟܢܐ ܕܥܡܟ.
ܘܫܪܟܐ ܬܐܟܘܠ ܚܝܘܬ ܒܪܐ.

#212 XX.1(2). 378:14-18; 896:25-897:3

ܘܬܘܒ ܟܬܒ ܐܝܟ ܘܐܡܪ ܠܗܘܢ ܕܫܬ
{B omits / A ܠܟ} ܫܢܝܢ ܬܙܪܘܥ ܐܪܥܟ ܘܬܟܢܫ
ܥܠܠܬܗ̇. ܘܒܫܢܬܐ ܫܒܝܥܝܬܐ ܬܪܒܝܗ̇
ܘܬܫܒܩܝܗ̇ ܘܢܐܟܠܘܢ ܡܢܗ̇ ܡܣܟܢܐ
{A ܕܥܡܟ / B ܕܥܡܗ} ܘܫܪܟܐ ܬܐܟܘܠ ܚܝܘܬܐ
ܕܒܪܐ

Both of these are formal quotations of Exod 23:10-11. #211 comes at the close of a passage in which Aphr has argued that the sabbath was instituted to give rest to hard-worked servants and beasts (cf. #201 above). It is not quoted in company with other similar vss and, although perhaps from memory, has the better claim of the two to be a faithful reproduction of Aphr's bible text. #212 also has the appearance of a careful citation, but it varies from #211 at four points.

#212 differs from #211 and P (and all witnesses) in

reading ܕܒܩܘܡܗ instead of ܕܒܥܝ. The reading of #211
is probably the original; in #212 Aphr has departed from his bible
text under the influence of other nearby quotations. In the first
two sections of Dem XX, there are eleven different scripture quotations, among which #212 is the ninth. All deal somehow with
the subject of care for the poor. At 896:8-12 Aphr cites Deut
24:20-21, which is similar in theme to Exod 23:10-11 and which
ends with ܠܡܣܟܢܐ ܕܒܩܘܡܟ.[25] Similarly, at 896:24 there
is a citation of Deut 15:11 which contains the phrase ܡܣܟܢܐ
ܒܓܘܟ. This phrase ("the poor in its/your midst") has accidentally been included in #212 under the influence of these other
citations.

The addition of ܒܩܘܡܗ in #212 looks like a clarifying
addition made by Aphr himself. It is attested by no other witness and is not present in any parallel vs in P. If one can
assume that either #211 or #212 contains an alteration by Aphr
at this point, it is probable that #212 has the secondary reading, inasmuch as the addition of ܒܩܘܡܗ makes for a smoother and
more complete sentence than is in #211.

Two other differences between #211 and #212 are more difficult to assess--the form of the genitive phrase "beast of the
field," on the one hand, and the variation between waw and dalath
prefixed to ܬܐܟܘܠ on the other. In neither case is certainty possible concerning the reading of Aphr's bible text. It
may be significant for evaluating the former to note that on the

two other occasions when Aphr himself employs the phrase "beast of the field" (outside formal quotations), he chooses the construction with the <u>nomen regens</u> in the emphatic state and <u>dalath</u> prefixed to the <u>nomen</u> rectum: ܚܝܘܬܐ ܕܒܪܐ (897:3), and ܚܝܘܬܐ ܕܕܒܪܐ (II 113:2-3). If this small bit of evidence may be taken as an indication of Aphr's personal stylistic tendency, then one might argue that the similar construction in #212 is the most likely to represent Aphr's stylistic alteration and that #211 preserves the reading of his bible text.

If this can be granted, then a pattern emerges of stylistic alterations in #212 and comparative literalness in #211. This alone can provide a reason for choosing the prefixed <u>dalath</u> on ܐܪܥܟ in #211 as the reading of Aphr's text. Otherwise, one is left completely without a basis for deciding between the two readings. The brackets below indicate the tentativeness of both of these last two decisions.

The contexts of both #211 and #212 are such as to make irrelevant the final clause of vs 11. Its absence from the citations is surely the result of Aphr's exegetical concerns and is not a feature of his text. All other witnesses include the final clause of P.

*Exod 23:10   ܘܫܬ ܫܢܝܢ ܬܙܪܥ ܐܪܥܟ ܘܬܟܢܫ ܥܠܠܬܗ.

ܬܙܪܥ 5b1 7a1 7h13 8a1 8b1 9b1 10b1.2 MT Sam Tgs TSam] ܬܙܪܘܥ 12a1fam

*Exod 23:11   ܘܒܫܒܝܥܝܬܐ ܬܫܒܩܝܗ ܘܬܫܒܩܝܗ

[Syriac text] [Syriac text] [Syriac text] [Syriac text]
[...] [Syriac text] [Syriac text] [Syriac text]

[Syriac] [Syriac] TN¹ LXXᵐˢˢ Vg]
[Syriac] 5b1 7a1 7h13 TSam LXX($\tau\omega$ $\delta\epsilon$ ἑβδόμω);
[Syriac] 8a1* 8b1 9b1 10b1.2 12a1 12b1.2 → MT
Sam TO TJ¹] [Syriac] 5b1 7a1 7h13 8a1 10b1.2
12b1.2 MT Sam Tgs TSam LXX Vg] omit 9b1] [Syriac]
Vg(ut comedant)] [Syriac] P MT Sam Tgs TSam LXX($\kappa\alpha\iota$
εδονται)] [Syriac] TN¹ LXX Vg] [Syriac] P MT
Sam TO TJ¹ TSam LXXᵐˢˢ] [Syriac] MT(חית השדה)
Sam Tgs] [Syriac] P

Exod 23:20, 23

#213   III.10(14). 57:15-16; 132:5-7

[Syriac text block]
{ B [Syriac]
{ A [Syriac] }
[Syriac] מצרים.

Although this presents itself as a formal quotation, it
is not a literal reproduction of any known vs. It appears instead
to be a loose mixture of elements from Exod 23:20 and 23 P (cf.
Exod 33:2 also). No such text is attested by any witness for
either vs. No textual witness is afforded by this passage.

Exod 23:26

#214   XVIII.1(1). 346:2-3; 820:2-3

[Syriac text]
[Syriac text]

This formal quotation of the first portion of Exod 23:26
is one of several proof-texts which Aphr places on the lips of

232

his Jewish opponents who maintain (in response to Aphr's urging
of celibacy) that God's will for the Hebrew people was always
fertility and reproduction. The final part of the vs, "I will
fulfil the number of your days," attested in P and all witnesses,
is surely omitted here merely because of its irrelevance to the
argument at hand.

*Exod 23:26 ܐܠ[] ܗܘܬܐ ܕܝܘܠܐ ܠܐ ܘܕܠܒܝܪܐ
[. . .] ܐܪܝܬܝܫܢ

Aphr = P

Exod 32:1

#215 VIII.3(9). 162:11-12; 380:14-16

Aphr makes this formal citation of the final portion of
Exod 32:1 to illustrate the high regard for Moses that was displayed by the Israelites. Obviously, the first part of the vs,
lacking in none of the witnesses, is omitted purely because it
does not serve Aphr's argument; it is not missing from his bible
text. Wright and Parisot are correct in following the shorter
text of ms B; the addition of ܗܒܪܐ in ms A will probably
have been a correction to the dominant P text. Here, as

elsewhere in the Dems, it is not possible to know whether Aphr's text uses the independent or the enclitic first-person plural pronoun with the participle of ܝܕܥ; the scribes appear to have freely interchanged such forms in mss A and B-B. The use of the verb ܕܐܣܩܢ alone justifies the assumption that Aphr here reproduces his text of Exod 32:1 rather than that of Acts 7:40 (... ܡܛܠ ܕܗܢܐ ܡܘܫܐ ܕܐܣܩܢ ܡܢ ܐܪܥܐ (ܕܡܨܪܝܢ) ܠܐ ܝܕܥܝܢ ܚܢ ܡܢܐ ܗܘܐ ܠܗ.

*Exod 32:1 [. . .] ܕ[ܗ]ܢܐ ܡܘܫܐ ܕܐܣܩܢ ܡܢ ܐܪܥܐ ܕܡܨܪܝܢ ܠܐ [ܝܕܥܝܢ] ܚܢܢ ܡܢܐ ܗܘܐ ܠܗ.

ܕܗܢܐ 12b1] add ܓܒܪܐ 5b1 7a1 7h13 8a1 8b1 9b1 10b1.2 11b1 12a1 12b2 MT Sam Tgs TSam LXX Vg

Exod 32:10

#216 XVI.2(4). 326:1-3; 772:18-20

ܐܡܪ ܠܗ ܡܪܝܐ ܠܡܘܫܐ ܕܫܒܘܩ ܐܚܪܒܝܘܗܝ ܠܥܡܐ ܗܢܐ ܘܐܥܒܕܟ ܠܥܡܐ ܕܪܒ ܘܥܫܝܢ ܡܢܗܘܢ.

This formal quotation is difficult to assess, because it bears strong resemblance to three similar vss in P while at the same time differing from each:

Exod 32:10 (ܘ)ܗܫܐ ܫܒܘܩ ܘܢܬܚܡܐ ܪܘܓܙܝ ܒܗܘܢ ܘܐܚܪܒ ܐܢܘܢ ܘܐܥܒܕܟ ܠܥܡܐ ܪܒܐ.

Num 14:12 ܐܡܚܐ ܐܢܘܢ ܒܡܘܬܢܐ ܘܐܘܒܕ ܐܢܘܢ ܘܐܥܒܕܟ ܠܥܡܐ ܕܪܒ ܘܥܫܝܢ ܡܢܗܘܢ.

Deut 9:14 ܗܫܐ ܫܒܘܩܝܢܝ ܐܒܘܕ ܐܢܘܢ ܘܐܥܛܐ
ܫܡܗܘܢ ܡܢ ܬܚܝܬ ܫܡܝܐ ܘܐܥܒܕܟ
ܠܥܡܐ ܕܪܒ ܘܥܫܝܢ ܡܢܗܘܢ.

It cannot be finally ruled out, of course, that Aphr knows and is quoting literally a text of Exod 32:10 or Deut 9:14 that differs drastically from P and other witnesses. The more likely explanation, however, is that Aphr here mixes together elements from all three vss, with additional influence perhaps from Exod 32:32.

The first clause of the quotation appears to be an abbreviation of the corresponding clause in Deut 9:14, with some contamination by Exod 32:10. "I will wipe out this people" is a conflation of Deut 9:13 and 14 (cf. Exod 32:9-10). ܥܡܐ ܗܢܐ occurs in Deut 9:13 (and Exod 32:9). The ease with which one could confuse Exod 32:10 and 32:32 is illustrated by a remark of Ephraem, which is actually a reference primarily to Exod 32:32 (Comm XXXII.6 lines 30-31): ܘܗܝ ܕܐܡܪ ܠܗ ܕܫܒܘܩܝܢܝ ܕܐܥܛܝܘܗܝ، ܚܠܦ ܕܐܡܪ ܠܗ ܕܐܘܒܕܢ ܕܠܐ ܐܥܛܝܘܗܝ.

The course of Aphr's argument in this section of Dem XVI also would increase his tendency to produce a form of the quoted vs which employs the verb ܥܛܐ. His theme is that scripture proves that Israel was destined from the earliest period to be blotted out of God's salvation. Therefore, at 772:1 he cites Ps 69:28 (ܕܢܬܥܛܘܢ); at 772:9, Exod 32:31 and 33 (ܥܛܝܢ

and ‏,‏ܡܛܠܝܐ‏‏); at 772:11, Ps 69:28 again (‏ܬܛܠܝ‏).
That the first clause of the vs in quoted in abbreviated form
is itself not surprising in view of the fact that Aphr's major
purpose for the quotation is to prove, not simply that Israel
was early destined to be blotted out of God's economy, but also
that God had in mind to replace them with another people.

As it stands, the final portion of the quotation appears
to be a conflation of Exod 32:10 and a text of the final comparative phrase of Num 14:12 or Deut 9:14 that reads ‏ܡܝܬܪ‏ instead
of ‏ܪܒ‏ or ‏,‏ܥܫܝܢ‏. That Aphr's argument at this point provides sufficient cause for him to quote the final comparative
clause is evident, but the significance of ‏ܡܝܬܪ‏ is not certain. Aphr may know a variant text of this portion of the Num
or Deut vs. Or indeed he may know an expanded text of Exod 32:10
itself which employs the adjective. Such an expansionary text
could have affinities with TN[1] at Exod 32:10, which concludes:
‏יכלה קדמיי לממנייה [יתך לאומה] רבה ותקיפא מנהון.‏

It is important to note, however, that ‏ܡܝܬܪ‏ does not
normally express quantitative, but rather qualitative, superiority. Thus Payne-Smith defines the Pa'el participle, "good,
excellent, especial, best,"[26] and Aphr himself uses ‏ܡܝܬܪ‏
thirty-one other times, almost always to designate moral or religious superiority. Aphr's form of this final phrase, therefore,
is not a simple parallel to Num 14:12 and Deut 9:14 P; it constitutes a significant theological variant: "greater and more

worthy than they" (so Neusner[27]). One suspects that this reading, so directly supportive of Christian theology, is the result
of Aphr's interpretative paraphrase of his scripture text rather
than of his literal reproduction of it. In any case, no evidence
is available by which to remove analysis of this portion of #216
from the realm of pure speculation. It is not possible to find
here a certain reflection of Aphr's text.

Exod 32:32-33

#217 X.2(2). 192:17-19; 445:27-448:3

#218 XVI.2(4). 325:13-15; 772:6-9

These two formal quotations present interesting and difficult variants to P. Both reproduce the entire text of Exod
32:32, and #218 adds vs 33. The two quotations differ somewhat
from one another, as well as from P, and it appears that in both
cases Aphr is quoting with some freedom. The most interesting
feature of these citations is the treatment of the conditional

clause which almost certainly is part of Aphr's text of vs 32.
All P mss, like the other ancient witnesses, translate literally
the conditional conjunctions of the MT (ואם-ואין . . . אם):
‎ܪ‎ ‎ܪ‎ . . . ‎ܪ‎. Unlike the LXX, Sam, and TSam, which
add, respectively, ἄφες, אש, and הלי after the first clause, P
retains the aposiopesis of the Hebrew: "Now if you will forgive
their sins--but if not, blot me out of your book which you have
written." It would be surprising if Aphr were to retain such
cumbersome syntax in passing citations like #217 and #218, and,
indeed, in both places he substitutes interpretative paraphrase:
"<u>Either</u> forgive . . . <u>or</u> blot me out. . . ."[28]

   The other differences from P also serve to lend directness and clarity to the vs, and, therefore, it is most reasonable
to assume that they are Aphr's modifications of his text, made
to maximize its effectiveness outside its original setting in
ch 32 of Exod. Thus the verbal construction of participle plus
independent personal pronoun in vs 32 P (ܐܢ ‎ ‎ܫܒܘܩ‎) is here
condensed into the simple imperative (‎ܫܒܘܩ‎). The subject
of Moses' petition, indicated in P only by the pronominal suffix
("<u>their</u> sins") which refers back to ‎ܥܡܐ ܗܢܐ‎ in vs 31, is
made more plain in the quotations by the addition of ‎ܠܥܡܐ‎
‎ܗܢܐ‎ in #218 and ‎ܠܥܡܐ‎ in #217. It is impossible to know
whether the omission of initial ‎ܘܗܫܐ‎ in the quotation is also
the result of economizing or is perhaps an accurate reflection
of Aphr's text, which would then agree with ms 5b1. Although

the occurrence of ܚܛܗ̈ܝܗܘܢ in both P and #217 leaves little room for doubt that this is the reading of Aphr's text and that #218 is paraphrastic, nevertheless the two quotations are too inexact to provide a clear textual witness except for the final clause of vs 32 and for the main sentence (minus the introductory clause) in vs 33. (See also my discussion of Vööbus's treatment of a distant allusion to Exod 32:32 above in Chapter I.)

*Exod 32:32 [. . .] ܥܛܝܢܝ ܡܢ ܣܦܪܟ ܕܟܬܒܬ.

Aphr = P

*Exod 32:33 [. . .] ܡܢ ܕܚܛܐ ܠܝ ܐܥܛܝܘܗܝ ܡܢ ܣܦܪܝ.

Aphr = P

Exod 33:11

#219 VI.5(5). 112:7-10; 261:18-22

ܐܠܐ ܗܟܢܐ ܟܬܝܒ ܕܝܫܘܥ ܒܪ ܢܘܢ ܡܫܡܫܢܗ
ܕܡܘܫܐ ܡܢ ܛܠܝܘܬܗ. ܘܥܠ ܝܫܘܥ ܬܘܒ
ܗܟܢܐ ܟܬܝܒ ܥܠܘܗܝ. ܕܡܢ ܡܫܟܢܐ ܠܐ
ܥܢܕ ܗܘܐ.

Although this passage, viewed by itself, appears to include two formal citations, the preceding lines create a different impression. #219 is actually the final portion of a unit of thought that begins at 261:15: "For thus it is written, beloved, concerning Moses, that from the time that the Holy One was revealed to him he loved holiness, and from the time that he was sanctified, his wife did not serve him. . . ." These earlier

lines obviously present interpretative paraphrase of scripture,
but not direct quotation. And it may well be that in the parallel sentences in #219 also Aphr intends merely allusion rather
than direct quotation.

There is no doubt that the two biblical references in
#219 are paraphrastic. The first not only rearranges the word
order of P and all witnesses, but it also interprets ‮ܐܪܠ‬
as "from his youth" in order to buttress Aphr's theological argument. The word order has been changed no doubt to give special
emphasis to "Joshua son of Nun," which Aphr here sets in contrast
to Moses' wife. The second reference to Exod 33:11 also offers
a condensed and rearranged text, one which is entirely unsupported
by other witnesses and which looks like Aphr's alteration. While
P may lie behind these two references, it is not possible to find
in them a clear testimony to Aphr's bible text.

Exod 34:14

#220   III.3(5). 48:4-5; 108:11-13

‮ܠܐ {A ,ܐܣܓܕܬ B ,ܣܓܕܬ} ܣܪܟ ܪܒܗܕ ܒ ܓܝܪ‬

‮ܗܘܐ ܐܠܗܐ . ܕܒܗ ܪܓܘܬܐ, ܣܡܗ ܬܒܥ ܕܠܐ ܗܘ ܬܒܘܥܐ‬

‮ܐܠܗܐ {A ܐܫܝܪ B ܐܫܝܪ}.‬

#221   XVII.1(1). 332:7-8; 785:9-10

‮ܐܠܗܐ ܬܒܘܥܐ ܕܠܐ ܐܫܝܪ ܡܛܠ‬

240

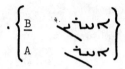

#220 provides a clear example of Aphr's tendency to conflate similar vss. The introduction of the commandment in #220 shows that Aphr has in mind the first of the Ten Commandments, but it is impossible to locate this text within either Exod ch 20 or Deut ch 5 in P or any other witness. The exact conformity of the quoted text to Exod 34:14 P leaves little doubt that this vs is the source of the text in both citations.

Aphr's error is easily explainable. In the text of the first commandment in Deut ch 5, the words ܐܫܪܐ ܐܠܗܐ occur in vs 7, and ܐܠܐ ܬܣܓܘܕ occur in vs 9. It may be that Aphr here intends to provide only a summary of the first command instead of a literal quotation, but even if this is his intention, in #220 he has fallen into the text of Exod 34:14. The fact that the quoted text in #220 is identical to that in #221 makes it certain that some passage of his bible text is manifesting itself. It is not probable that Aphr would reproduce the text of Exod 34:14 P on two separate occasions unless this same text were known to him in his own bible.

    *Exod 34:14   ܐܫܪܐ ܐܠܗܐ ܬܣܓܘܕ ܐܠܐ[ ]

                                  [. . .]

    ܐܠܗܐ
    ܐܠܗܐ 5b1 7a1 7h13 8a1 8b1 10b1.2 11b1 12b1.2]
             9͟16

CHAPTER IV

CONCLUSION

A. The Citations of Aphr as Textual Witnesses

The preceding analyses of the quotations from Gen-Exod
have demonstrated the validity of earlier warnings about the reliability of Aphr's citations as textual witnesses. Of the 221
passages examined, only about 25 are immediately recognizable
as being literal, and many of these do not reproduce an entire
vs. The looseness of so many of the citations suggests indeed
a general pattern of memoriter rather than transcriptional quotation; I found no quotation which I can be sure was made by consulting a ms.

One of the most frequent memoriter errors proves to be
accidental conflation of similar vss. The passages studied contain about 40 cases of such mixture of related texts. This large
number, coupled with the fact that most of Aphr's other citations
reflect a text firmly within the P tradition, leaves little doubt
that error on Aphr's part is involved. Baumstark's hypothesis
of a primitive Pentateuch text expanded in many places by doublet
readings does not find support here.

Other errors and alterations in the quotations are those
known from other patristic literature and already mentioned in

Chapter I: economizing condensation of a text, replacement of
initial particles by prefixed dalath, addition of words for emphasis or clarity, alteration of grammar and syntax for emphasis,
accommodation of grammar to the immediate context. One sees a
certain casualness in Aphr's manner of handling his text, which
is the chief reason why the line between quotation and allusion
is often so difficult to draw within the Dems. Despite his high
view of scripture, he usually feels free from an obligation to
quote with mechanical precision, and one doubts that he expects
his reader actually to look up the various vss to which he refers.
His concern is not with the biblical text itself, but with the
ideas which he advances; he writes, not a bible commentary, but
theological essays, "Demonstrations." All of this confirms the
principle discussed above in Chapter I, that no citation by Aphr
can be taken prima facie as an exact reproduction of his text.

On the other hand, it is equally clear that Aphr's citations are not worthless as textual witnesses. Aphr's memory of
scripture is good; his mind is stored with the clauses and sentences of his bible. He can usually repeat these without error,
a tendency to combine similar vss being the chief problem. Close
examination of the context in which it occurs, comparison with
other citations of the same passage, and watchfulness for accidental conflation frequently make it possible to discern the bible
text that underlies a given quotation. Uncertainties cannot
always be removed, of course, especially when a shorter text-form

makes it difficult to know whether or not omission of a portion of the source-text has occurred. Comparison of the citation with extant bible texts, especially Syriac mss, is extremely important in determining its textual value. Inevitably, therefore, Aphr's citations carry the greatest weight as corroborative textual witnesses; unique readings, while not to be dismissed, usually involve a much greater degree of uncertainty.

B. Aphr's Text of Genesis

The citations of Gen yield a total of 102 vss in which all or part of the text is clearly attested. Of those 102, 77 (75%) reflect a text that agrees with all P mss (including 8 in which the substance of a numeral, but not its exact text-form, agrees with P). The remaining vss can be grouped into 3 categories: those which contain variants that are entirely unsupported by any P ms, those which are supported by only a few P mss, and those which are supported by a majority of P mss (= Koster's "TR") but which differ from at least one P ms.

The first group might be expected to reveal most clearly the direction of any drastic departures of Aphr's text from the main P tradition. If the text reflected is either considerably more literal to the Hebrew (so Pinkerton) or considerably more "targumic" (so Baumstark, Vööbus), this should show up most vividly in the readings which depart from all P mss. In fact, the evidence is ambiguous. There are 18 variants, contained in 13 vss, in this group. Only one of these agrees with MT. Of

the others, which do not agree with MT, 3 are supported by one or
more targums only, one agrees with LXX (ms D) only, 2 agree with
Vg only, one agrees with LXX and Vg, and 10 are not supported by
any non-Syriac version. The latter include: addition of prefixed
dalath (15:5), omission of a phrase (15:9), use of ܪܒ instead
of prefixed dalath (17:10), addition of a copulative particle
(18:27), insertion of a proper name (27:40), two additions of
ܗܘܐ as an auxiliary verb (43:32), omission of a phrase (49:3),
omission of a preposition (49:5), and a change in word-order
involving also a lexical substitution (49:10).

The second group consists of 8 readings, contained in 5
vss, which are unsupported by the majority of P mss but which
agree with at least one. Here too the evidence is ambiguous.
Of these readings, one is supported by MT, one is supported by
a combination of targums only, 2 agree with LXX or LXX mss only,
and 2 have no support among non-Syriac versions. There is thus
neither a pronounced tendency toward literalness to MT, nor
toward the targums, nor to any one of the other versions. The
one targumic reading is striking (the addition of "kingdom" in
49:10), but this is counterbalanced by the agreement with MT,
which is also significant (the numeral in 11:26). The agreements
with P mss by these readings are as follows:

6:7	8/5b1 915 11/9b1^{mg} 1114.5 →
11:26	10/5b1
19:24	7a1 911 12b2 →

31:38   5b1 (two readings)

49:10   915^{mg} 1114.5 12b2 →

The third group consists of 10 readings, contained in 9 vss, which are supported by a majority of P mss. Here, not surprisingly, a clearer affinity with MT is evident. Seven of the readings agree with MT, one agrees with Vg only, and 2 are unsupported by non-Syriac versions.

C. Aphr's Text of Exodus

The citations of Exod yield a total of 27 vss in which all or part of the text is clearly attested. Of these, 13 agree with all P mss, a smaller proportion (48%) than in Gen.

In 4 vss, 7 readings occur which are unsupported by any P ms. One of these agrees with MT, 2 with a combination of a targum, LXX, and Vg, 2 with LXX mss only, one with Vg only, and one is unsupported by non-Syriac versions. The latter (17:14) consists of an alteration in word order with the addition of a pronoun as well. As with the Gen citations, this evidence is ambiguous. Literalness to MT is evidenced once, while departures from MT (and P) are more numerous. However, these departures do not align themselves with any one of the other witnesses. The one entirely unique reading, in 17:14, occurs at a point where there is significant disagreement among the P mss themselves, and it does not provide evidence of a distinctive pre-P tradition.

In 3 vss there are 6 readings which differ from the majority of P mss but agree with at least one. Two of the readings

agrees with MT, and the other 4 are unsupported by non-Syriac
witnesses. The latter include 2 omissions of a noun, one omission of prefixed _dalath_, and one inner-Syriac contraction. The
agreements with P mss by these by these readings are as follows:

4:23	5b1 (two readings)
14:12	9l6
14:12	5b1
14:12	7a1 →
32:1	12b1

The third group of readings includes 10, contained in
10 vss, which agree with a majority of P mss. Here again, pre-
dictably, a greater affinity with the Hebrew is in evidence.
Four of the readings agree with MT, one agrees with a combination of targums only, and 5 are not supported by non-Syriac versions.

Generalizations about the type of text known to Aphr can
be ventured only with extreme caution. It must be recalled that
his citations, despite their considerable number, do not reflect
the text of more than a small fraction of the total text of Gen
and Exod. Gen has 1534 vss, of which Aphr's citations constitute
no more than 8%; Exod has 1209 vss, of which the citations constitute no more than 2%. Furthermore, there remains the ines-
capable margin of uncertainty in determing the text witnessed
by each citation. Very important too is the fact that the above
tabulations of affinities do not yield clear results.

The only positive general conclusion that one can safely draw is that Aphr's text falls securely within the P textual tradition as already known from the mss. For both books, but for Gen especially, the heavy majority of Aphr's readings agree with the majority of P mss, many of them with all the P mss. Otherwise the data are mixed, and only negative conclusions can be safely drawn. While there are in both books some agreements with MT in the readings that depart from the majority of P mss, these are not numerous enough to characterize Aphr's text firmly as more literal to the Hebrew than the later P tradition. At the same time, there are unique readings and readings that agree with targums, LXX, or Vg against the MT, although these in turn fall short of a pattern that would indicate a wildly divergent text-type.

To say even this much is to validate the earlier provisional assessments of Wright, Nöldeke, Gwynn, Burkitt, and others, that Aphr quotes basically the text of P. It is also to contradict, at least for Gen and Exod, the view of Vööbus and especially Baumstark, that clear evidence of a dramatically deviant, primitive Pentateuch text can be found preserved in the Dems. The relatively few uniquely targumic readings noted (which are sometimes with only one of the targums and not always with the same one) are simply not sufficient basis for placing before Aphr a Pentateuch that is essentially a targum or composite of targums. It is impossible, however, to go further and claim that Aphr's

text clearly evidences an early stage of the P tradition which
is more literal than the later stages. To do so would require
finding in the citations a heavier preponderance of more literal
readings than is the case.

These findings do not necessarily contradict the quite
well established conclusion of Koster that the P mss of Exod indicate a continuous process of development in the textual tradition
from an original translation of the Hebrew text to a later less
literal Syriac vulgate text. At each stage in this process a
given ms could stand more or less close to the "center" of the
textual tradition. It may simply be that the exemplar of Gen
and Exod known to Aphr was not a very pure representative of the
main P Pentateuch text in the fourth century.

NOTES

Chapter I

[1]P. A. H. de Boer and W. Baars, General Preface, The Old Testament in Syriac According to the Peshitta Version (Leiden: Brill, 1972) vi.

[2]P. A. H. de Boer in The Old Testament in Syriac According to the Peshitta Version, I/1: Preface, Genesis-Exodus (Leiden: Brill, 1977) vii.

[3]Text and Language in Bible and Qumran (Jerusalem/Tel Aviv: Orient, 1960) 199 n. 169: "I would like to express the hope that students of that particular field [i.e., Syriac patristics] . . . will direct their attention to this problem and will make further material available."

[4]Pp. ix-lxxx.

[5]Pp. 1-10, 282-301 deal with the introductory matters. In his review (Orientalia Christiana Periodica 44 [1978] 523) Robert Murray calls Baarda's work "one of the most valuable contributions yet made to the study both of Aphrahat and of the problems of the early Syriac gospel traditions," and he terms the pages designated above "one of the best shorter introductions to the subject." The more important general discussions of the Dems and their author are: Georg G. Blum, "Afrahat," TRE 1.625-635; Arthur Vööbus, "Nachträge zum Reallexikon für Antike und Christentum: 'Aphrahat,'" JAC 3 (1960) 152-155; Wright, 1-18; John Gwynn, "Selections Translated into English from the Hymns and Homilies of Ephraim the Syrian and from the Demonstrations of Aphrahat the Persian Sage," NPNF Second Series 13/2.152-164; Bert, vii-xxxvi; Carl J. F. Sasse, Prolegomena in Aphraatis sapientis persae sermones homileticos (Leipzig: Kreysignii, 1878) 5-40. A virtually complete bibliography on Aphr through 1964 is found in Ignatius Ortiz de Urbina, Patrologia syriaca (Rome: Pontificium Institutum Orientalium Studiorum, 1965) 46-51.

[6]See Ortiz de Urbina, Patrologia syriaca, 13-16: Anton Baumstark, Geschichte der syrischen Literatur (Bonn: Marcus & Webers, 1922) 9-30; and William Wright, A Short History of Syriac Literature (London: Black, 1894) 1-39.

[7]Convenience and convention dictate use of the name

"Aphrahat" for the author of the Dems. Whether this was his name, and his only name, is fully discussed by Parisot, ix-xiv. Cf. Baarda, 4-6.

[8]Throughout this study references to passages in the Dems are given according to the column and line numbers in Parisot.

[9]193:22-25: "From the time that the two horns of the ram were broken until this time are 648 years."

[10]724:24-725:1: "I have written this letter in the month Shebat of the year 655 of the reign of Alexander son of Philip the Macedonian." Cf. Dem XXI (941:15-21): "Thus the entire calculation of years from the overthrow of Sodom until the year 655 of the reign of Alexander son of Philip the Macedonian [= A.D. 343/344] is 2276 years."

[11]The colophon, which appears on folio 115b at the end of Exod, does not add the expected "of the Greeks," though that is certainly to be understood. See further Preface, Genesis-Exodus, vi-vii; M. D. Koster, The Peshiṭta of Exodus, The Development of its Text in the Course of Fifteen Centuries (Assen/Amsterdam: Van Gorcum, 1977) 10-11; and P. Wernberg-Møller, "Some Scribal and Linguistic Features of the Genesis Part of the Oldest Peshitta Manuscript (B.M. Add. 14425)," JSS 13 (1968) 138-161.

[12]Paul E. Kahle, The Cairo Geniza (Oxford: Blackwell, 1959) 272: "We can take it for granted that at least parts of a Syriac Old Testament, and in the first instance the Torah were introduced into Adiabene during the time of its Jewish kings, i.e. in the middle of the first century B.C." (The addition of "B.C." in the 1959 edition is surely an error. It is not present in the original 1941 edition [186] and is incompatible with Kahle's whole argument, which is based on the conversion of the Adiabene royalty around A.D. 40.) But cf. Arthur Vööbus, "Syriac Versions," IDBSup 848-849: "However it is equally possible that the Old Syr. originated with the beginnings of Christianity in Mesopotamia." "The literary and historical problems of the Peshitta are extremely intricate. Its date and the identity of the revisers and translators are unknown."

[13]In the Syriac and Armenian mss, Dem I is preceded by a brief letter from an enquirer about spiritual matters, whom Aphr addresses in his Dems. It is impossible to know whether this letter is authentic or merely a literary device. This uncertainty is not significant for my purposes here; the letter includes no biblical quotations and only a few allusions, none of which is textually important.

[14]464:24-465:2: "These ten little books that I have
written for you borrow from one another and depend on one
another. Do not separate them from one another. From alaph
to yud I have written for you, each letter after its fellow."

[15]The Armenian version was first printed, accompanied
by a Latin translation, in an edition prepared by Nicolaus
Antonelli, Sancti patris nostri Iacobi, episcopi Nisibeni sermones, cum praefatione, notis et dissertatione de ascetis, quae
omnia nunc primum in lucem pro deunt (Rome: Sacra Congregatio
de Propaganda Fide, 1756). It was based on a transcription made
in 1719 for the Vatican library, of an ancient ms in the Armenian
monastery in Venice. Gwynn ("Aphrahat the Persian Sage," 154)
reports: "Armenian scholars seem to agree in the belief that
it was made in the fifth century. . . ." See also Parisot, xxxvi
(" . . . unde colligimus ad initium aureae illius aetatis lit-
terarum armeniacarum, seu medium, saeculi quinti, translationem
adsignandam esse. . . .") and Sasse, Prolegomena, 25. A new
edition of the Armenian text of some of the Dems is now available
in G. Lafontaine, ed, La version arménienne des oeuvres d'Aphraate
le Syrien, 2: Texte (CSCO 405, scriptores armeni 9; Louvain:
CSCO, 1979).

[16]Parisot (xxviii-xxxiv) cites his comments concerning
"Iacobus, cognomento Sapiens" which appear in his expansions of
Jerome's De scriptoribus ecclesiasticis. Despite the twenty-three
titles in his list, Gennadius affirms: "Comprehendit autem omne
opus suum in viginti sex libris. . . ."

[17]"Notule de littérature syriaque, La démonstration XIV
d'Aphraate," Muséon 81 (1968) 499-454.

[18]"La démonstration XIV d'Aphraate," 454: " . . .
pourrait-on aller encore plus loin et déclarer que le Lettre
XIV n'est pas d'Aphraate? . . . Ceci est possible; seul une
comparaison des styles et du vocabulaire des deux tomes des
Démonstrations avec ceux de la 'quatorzième' pourrait donner
la réponse."

[19]Gwynn, "Aphrahat the Persian Sage," 158.

[20]"La démonstration XIV d'Aphraate," 450: "Ceci nous
amène à poser la question: Pour quoi est garanti l'ordre actuel
des lettres, si ancien qu'il soit?" Fiey does not make entirely
clear whether or not he regards the acrostic pattern as secondary. On the one hand, he readily assumes early variation in the
order of the Dems in Book II, which is hardly compatible with an
original acrostic structure. On the other hand, in proposing to
"restore" Dem XXIII to its original place in Book II, he speaks
of having "changer le premier mot de l'epître pour lui donner

une initiale que convienne à son nouveau rang" (452 n. 21).

[21]See Parisot, xxx; Sasse, Prolegomena, 25; and Gwynn, "Aphrahat the Persian Sage," 154.

[22]Parisot (xxxiii-xxxiv) conveniently gives a table comparing the titles (in order) of the Dems in Gennadius, the Armenian version, and the Syriac mss.

[23]Syriac and Armenian are not cognate languages. The Armenian alphabet, having 38 characters, does not correspond to the 22-character Syriac alphabet.

[24]"La démonstration XIV d'Aphraate," 451.

[25]It was the first of the Aphr materials to be received from the Nitrian collection.

[26]Complete and authoritative descriptions of all four mss are given in William Wright, Catalogue of Syriac Manuscripts in the British Museum, Acquired Since the Year 1838 (London: British Museum, 1871) 2.401-405, 890-901. See also Parisot, lxvii-lxxx.

[27]Catalogue, 2.403.

[28]Despite the potential for confusion and error in two such similar symbols (B and B), their use, initiated by Wright, is now convention.

[29]Wright, Catalogue, 2.404.

[30]P. 287.

[31]Aphrahat and Judaism, The Christian-Jewish Argument in Fourth-Century Iran (SPB 19; Leiden: Brill, 1971) 10.

[32]"It is possible that his observation is wholly justified, but during the time I was engaged in reading Aphrahat I did not come across such evident distortions of the text" (286). Given this striking lack of corroboration for Neusner's low opinion of the mss, one is inclined to pay special attention to a statement in his preface: "My knowledge of Syriac . . . is elementary and by no means sufficient to the task" (xii). Cf. G. Quispel in his review of Aphrahat and Judaism (BO 29 [1972] 230): "This book is too superficial, written too quickly. We may expect from the very competent author that he will give us a more scholarly treatment of the same subject."

[33]B. F. Westcott and F. J. Hort, The New Testament

in the Original Greek (London: Macmillan, 1882) 1.202-203.

[34]Strangely, Baarda's discussion of "The Reliability of the Manuscripts" comes at the end of his study (286-289).

[35]P. 287.

[36]P. 287.

[37]See Arthur Vööbus, "In Pursuit of Syriac Manuscripts," JNES 37 (1978) 187-193, where he describes chancing upon, in recent years, "entire collections about whose existence there had never been a word published" (189) and points out that "documents about whose existence we had no inkling, have emerged" (193).

[38]Gwynn ("Aphrahat the Persian Sage," 159-160) acknowledges this possibility.

[39]Gwynn, "Aphrahat the Persian Sage," 159.

[40]Baarda, 287.

[41]Cf. Bruce M. Metzger, The Text of the New Testament, Its Transmission, Corruption, and Restoration (New York: Oxford University, 1968) 87: "When the manuscripts of a Father differ in a given passage, it is usually safest to adopt the one which diverges from the later ecclesiastical text. . . ."

[42]"It is possible to make too much of this aspect of the problem. While modern standards of reproduction were not in effect in the manuscript period, it would be untrue to say that verbal accuracy was not an aim of the ancient scribe-- particularly of the trained copyist" (M. J. Suggs, "The Use of Patristic Evidence in the Search for a Primitive New Testament Text," NTS 4 [1957-1958] 140).

[43]A word of caution must be added here concerning the editions of Wright and Parisot. Both editors have a definite tendency in treating manuscript variations that occur within Aphr's bible quotations to follow the opposite approach from my own: they often print in their main text that reading which most closely approaches P, relegating the more deviant reading to the bottom margin. For the student of any aspect of Aphr's biblical quotations it can be disastrous to follow uncritically the printed text of these editions without regard for the variants. Apparently some students of the gospel quotations have stumbled at this point; cf. Baarda, 285.

[44]Contrast Baarda, 284: "I must admit that one of the weaknesses of my investigation is that I did not look up the

quotations in the manuscripts that have been preserved." Note
the curiously erroneous statement in Robert Murray's review (525)
that Baarda "presents an evaluation of the eclectic editions of
Wright and Parisot in the light of a new examination of the MSS"
(emphasis added).

[45]Leo Haefeli, Stilmittel bei Afrahat dem persischen
Weisen (Leipziger Semitische Studien 4; Leipzig: Heinrichs, 1932)
128.

[46]"Aphraates and the Jews," Journal of the Society of
Oriental Research 7 (1923) 127.

[47]Whereas Wright and Parisot list, respectively, a total
of 131 and 200 quotations and allusions from Gen and Exod, I have
identified 221 such references that merit examination. Similarly,
Baarda treats 133 citations from John, whereas Parisot lists only
108 Johannine references and Wright, 71.

[48]The subject of the verb in these formulae is almost
never impersonal "it" referring to scripture itself; the subject
is normally God or a person from within the biblical passage
being cited.

[49]Cf. Theodor Nöldeke, Compendious Syriac Grammar (tr.
James Crichton; London: Williams & Norgate, 1904) par. 367: "In
all cases, in fact, ܘ may be used to introduce direct speech,
but it is not absolutely necessary. When however, ܘ is so used,
it is very often impossible to determine whether the oratio is
directa or indirecta. . . ."

[50]Preface, Genesis-Exodus (see above, n. 2).

[51]Antonio Maria Ceriani, Translatio syra pescitto veteris
testamenti ex codice ambrosiano sec. fere VI photolithographice
edita (London: Williams & Norgate, 1876-1883). Cf. Preface,Gen-
esis-Exodus, viii: "Although the value of Codex Ambrosianus must
not be underestimated . . . it seems certain that the Ambrosian
manuscript cannot be considered the most important witness. . . ."

[52]Vetus testamentum syriace (London: British and Foreign
Bible Society, 1823); a slightly altered edition was published in
1824. On the defects of Lee's work, see Joshua Bloch, "The
Printed Texts of the Peshitta Old Testament," AJSL 37 (1920-1921)
139. Although Barnes's revision of the Pentateuch portion of
Lee's edition was a significant improvement, it presents an eclectic text without critical apparatus and falls short of providing
an adequate critical edition; see W. Emery Barnes, "A New Edition
of the Pentateuch in Syriac," JTS 15 (1913-1914) 41-44.

⁵³M. G. Michel Le Jay, ed., <u>Biblia polyglotta parisien-</u>
<u>sia</u> (Paris: Vitré, 1629-1645); Brian Walton, ed., <u>Biblia sacra</u>
<u>polyglotta londinensia</u> (London: Roycroft, 1653-1657); <u>Vetus</u>
<u>testamentum syriace et neo-syriace</u> (Urmia: n.p., 1852); <u>Biblia</u>
<u>sacra iuxta versionem simplicem, quae dicitur pschitta</u> (Mosul:
Fratrum Praedicatorum, 1881-1887). A convenient and reliable
analysis of these editions is presented by Bloch, "Printed Text."
See also the evaluations by Goshen-Gottstein, "Prolegomena."

⁵⁴<u>The Peshiṭta of Exodus</u> (see above, n. 11).

⁵⁵<u>Preface, Genesis-Exodus</u>, v (speaking of Koster's study
of the Exod mss): "For those MSS which also present a text of
Genesis, similar conclusions hold good."

⁵⁶In my view it is a weakness of Baarda's work that he
provides only the bible text which he reconstructs from a given
citation and does not reproduce the text of the citation itself.
This makes it more difficult for the reader to assess his evaluation and reconstruction.

⁵⁷P. xxxv.

⁵⁸Suggs, "The Use of Patristic Evidence," 140.

⁵⁹A sampling of ancient requirements for scripture mem-
orization by candidates for church office is presented in
Metzger, <u>The Text of the New Testament</u>, 87 n. 1. They range in
extent from knowing only the Gospel of John to knowing twenty-
five Psalms, two epistles of Paul, part of a Gospel, and parts
of Deuteronomy, Proverbs, and Isaiah.

⁶⁰P. 289.

⁶¹Aphr is not unique among patristic authors in this
respect. Suggs ("The Use of Patristic Evidence," 142) describes
the most common patristic quotation as "the six words here, the
ten words there, the fifteen in another place, which offer no
evidence in themselves as to whether they are allusive or <u>memo-</u>
<u>riter</u> or transcriptional citations and whose contexts are equally
obscure in this respect. . . . Therefore above all else a knowledge of the Father whose text is being studied is required."

⁶²Bruce Metzger, "Patristic Evidence and the Textual
Criticism of the New Testament," <u>NTS</u> 18 (1971) 395.

⁶³"Patristic Evidence," 391.

⁶⁴<u>Genesis</u>, 29.

[65]I have relied upon the critical apparatus of BHS for
the readings of the Nash Papyrus and, for the Dead Sea Scrolls,
upon the "Index of Biblical Passages" in Joseph A. Fitzmyer, The
Dead Sea Scrolls, Major Publications and Tools for Study (SBLSBS
8; Missoula: Scholars Press, 1977) 152-154. For the Mishna I
have used the index and text of Philip Blackman, ed., Mishnayoth
(7 vols.; London: Mishna Press, 1951).

[66]The lack of a reliable critical edition of TSam and
TF is regrettable; the new edition of the latter by M. L. Klein
(The Fragment-Targums of the Pentateuch [AnBib 76; Rome: Pontifical Biblical Institute]) is still in press. The inadequacies of
the editions utilized (see Abbreviations) are recognized.

[67]Ephraem was Aphr's contemporary, being born (according
to the Syriac "Life of Ephraem") about A.D. 306 and dying in 373.
Cf. Ortiz de Urbina, Patrologia syriaca, 58-59. Because Ephraem's
earliest writing that can be firmly dated (the first Nisibene
hymn) belongs to A.D. 350, a little later than the Dems, it is
usually assumed that Ephraem was younger than Aphr. The tenuous-
ness of this assumption is discussed by Gwynn ("Aphrahat the
Persian Sage," 161-162).

[68]Sten Hidal, Interpretatio Syriaca, Die Kommentare des
Heiligen Ephräm des Syrers zu Genesis und Exodus mit besonderer
Berucksichtigung ihrer Auslegungsgeschichtlichen Stellung (ConBOT
6; Lund: Gleerup, 1974) 12.

[69]Wright, 16.

[70]Göttingische gelehrte Anzeigen 39 (1869) 1526-1527.

[71]Review of Ceriani, Translatio syra pescitto vetus
testamenti ex codice ambrosiano, Literarisches Centralblatt für
Deutschland 39 (1876) 1290.

[72]Frankl, Jahrbücher für die Protestantischer Theologie
5 (1879) 758, and Baethgen, Jahrbücher für Protestantischer
Theologie 8 (1882) 444. Unfortunately, I have not been able to
see either of these studies; both are cited in Leo Haefeli, Die
Peschitta des Alten Testaments (Alttestamentliche Abhandlungen
11/1; Münster: Aschendorff, 1927) 88-89.

[73]"Die Verwendbarkeit der Pešita zum Buche Ijob für die
Textkritik," ZAW 18 (1898) 329-330.

[74]Prolegomena, 34.

[75]P. xliii.

[76]"Aphrahat the Persian Sage," 162.

[77]Baarda, 12.

[78]See the thorough survey of scholarship in Baarda, 11-54.

[79]W. E. Barnes, The Peshitta Psalter According to the West-Syrian Text (Cambridge: Cambridge University, 1904); G. Diettrich, Ein Apparatus Criticus zur Pešitto zum Propheten Jesaia (BZAW 8; Giessen: Topelmann, 1905); C. Moss, "The Peshiṭta Version of Ezra," Muséon 46 (1933) 55-110; J. A. Emerton, The Peshitta of the Wisdom of Solomon (SPB 2; Leiden: Brill, 1959); Bertil Albrektson, Studies in the Text and Theology of the Book of Lamentations, with a Critical Edition of the Peshitta Text (Studia Theologica Lundensia 21; Lund: Gleerup, 1963); Leona G. Running, "An Investigation of the Syriac Version of Isaiah," AUSS 3 (1965) 138-157; 4 (1966) 37-64, 135-148; P. B. Dirksen, The Transmission of the Text in the Peshiṭta Manuscripts of the Book of Judges (Monographs of the Peshiṭta Institute 1; Leiden: Brill, 1972).

[80]JTS 6 (1905) 287.

[81]"Investigation," 143 n. 30.

[82]JTS 15 (1913-1914) 14-41.

[83]"Origin and Early History," 34.

[84]"Origin and Early History," 35.

[85]The Peshiṭta of Exodus, 178.

[86]"Ps.-Jonathan zu Dtn 34:6 und die Pentateuchzitate Afrahaṭs," ZAW N.F. 18 (1942-1943) 99-111.

[87]The works by J. Perles (Meletemata peschittoniana [Breslau, 1859]) and J. Prager (De veteris testamenti versione quam peschittho vocant quaestiones criticae [Göttingen, 1875]) have not been accessible to me; they are cited in Koster, The Peshiṭta of Exodus, 198, and Running, "Investigation," 139.

[88]"Ps.-Jonathan," 101-102. Baumstark's view, first mentioned in his Geschichte der syrischen Literatur (18), had been fully developed in four articles: "Peschitta und palästinensisches Targum," BZ 19 (1931) 257-270; "Das Problem der Bibelzitate in der syrischen Übersetzung-Literatur," OrChr 8 (1933) 208-255; "Neue orientalistische Probleme biblischer Testgeschichte," ZDMG 89 (1935) 89-118 (A passing reference to the

value of Aphr's citations is made on p. 74); and "Das Problem des christlich-palästinensischen Pentateuchtextes," OrChr 10 (1935) 201-224. On the entire debate over the possible targumic origin of the Syriac Pentateuch see Koster, The Peshiṭta of Exodus, 177-212; J. Van der Ploeg, "Recente Pešiṭta-Studies (sinds 1927)," JEOL 10 (1945-1948) 392-399; and J. H. Hospers, "The Present-day State of Research on the Pešiṭta (since 1948)," Verbum, Essays on Some Aspects of the Religious Functions of Words (Studia Theologica Rheno-Traiectina 6; Utrecht: Kemink, 1964) 148-157.

[89]"Ps.-Jonathan," 103.

[90]"Ps.-Jonathan," 103-104.

[91](Cardiff: University of Wales, 1951) 224-225.

[92](Papers of the Estonian Theological Society in Exile 9; Stockholm: Estonian Theological Society in Exile, 1958).

[93]Peschitta und Targumim, 107.

[94]Peschitta und Targumim, 16-17. Cf. Haefeli, Die Peschitta des Alten Testaments, 87-88: "Es wird aber dabei bleiben, dass die Lesart eines Kirchenschriftstellers für sich allein unter gewöhnlichen Umstanden nicht viel Wert hat, sondern erst bedeutungsvoll wird, wenn andere gewichtige Lesarten bestätigend hinzutreten." And more specifically: "Schwerlich, ja fast unmöglich wird sich der den Aphraates-Schriften zugrunde liegende Peschittatext festlegen lassen, weil Aphraates nach dem Gedächtnis zitiert und dieselbe Stelle wohl in wechselnder Gestalt aufführt" (107).

[95]The Peshiṭta of Exodus, 199-210. Koster found Vööbus's conclusions entirely unsupported.

[96]Review of Peschitta und Targumim, JSS 6 (1961) 269. Goshen-Gottstein's overall evaluation of Vööbus's book was only slightly less negative than that of Koster.

[97]I have found six citations of Gen 49:10 (see #155-#160 below); Vööbus (Peschitta und Targumim, 26) mentioned only one, #160.

[98]Peschitta und Targumim, 22.

Chapter II

[1]So Edward J. Duncan, Baptism in the Demonstrations of
Aphraates the Persian Sage (Studies in Christian Antiquity 8;
Washington, D.C.: Catholic University of America, 1945) 123-124.
He cites additional evidence for such a prayer and notes that
Tertullian's description of the invocation and descent of the
Spirit at baptism agrees with Aphr's "almost word for word." Cf.
Robert Murray, Symbols of Church and Kingdom, A Study in Early
Syriac Tradition (London: Cambridge University, 1975) 21-22, 143,
313-314.

[2]On the practice of prefixing alaph to words with initial
resh, see Nöldeke, Grammar, par. 51.

[3]If Parisot's concordance is correct at this point, Aphr
never uses any form of the verb ܟܠܐ. No reason suggests
itself for his avoiding this term; its absence from the Dems may
be accidental.

[4]"Ps.-Jonathan," 107.

[5]So Bert, 261: ". . . und wie Kraut soll es von dir
gehalten werden."

[6]Aphrahat and Judaism, 53.

[7]Nöldeke, Grammar, par. 50B: "Conversely ܢ, which one
was in the habit of so often writing,--apparently without cause,
--was in some cases attached parasitically to words ending in a
consonant. . . ."

[8]Salomon Funk (Die Haggadischen Elemente in den Homilien
des Aphraates, des persischen Weisen [Vienna: Knöpflmacher, 1891]
19-20) cites #104 as one of the indications of Aphr's dependence
on Jewish hermeneutical tradition. This is curious, since Funk
himself admits, "Die Erklärung des Aphraates ist jedoch unter
den verschiedenen Erklärungen in Gen. rab. und Parallelstellen
nicht zu finden."

[9]It is worth noting that Aphr's text of vs 16 lacks the
reading of B.M. Add. 12,174 (ܟܠܝܟܗ ܟܗܟܗ ܠܡܠܟ ܟܡ),
which, comparing TO and TJ[1] in vs 17, Vööbus (Peschitta und Targumim, 34) identifies as a reading of the primitive Syriac Pentateuch text.

[10]See Murray, Symbols, 142-150, 154-158, for a judicious
discussion of Aphr's views about marriage within the larger context of early Syrian theology.

[11]TN[1] and TF also add the conditional element to the text of vs 15, which is quoted here from TJ[1].

[12]Dating the haggadic material in the targums is diffi-cult, because both early and late elements have been taken up into the present text. Roger Le Déaut and Jacques Robert (Tar-gum du Pentateuque, 1: Genèse [SC 245; Paris: Cerf, 1978] 36) comment on TJ[1] itself: "Le contenu lui-même montre que nous sommes in présence d'un texte composite et au terme d'une longue évolution. On y trouve à la fois les traditions targumique les plus anciennes et les ajouts les plus récents. . . ."

[13]Funk (Haggadische Elemente) and Neusner (Aphrahat and Judaism) do not include these two passages among their parallels. Gavin ("Aphraates and the Jews," 137-138) does list them among his "concrete instances of Aphraates' dependence upon Jewish thought," but correctly notes that the closest parallel is in Gen. Rab. 20:5: "When the Holy One, blessed be He, said to him, 'Upon your belly you shall go,' ministering angels descended and cut off his hands and feet, and his cries resounded from one end of the world to the other. . . . 'I made you that you should go upright like man, but you would not; I made you that you should eat the food of man, but you would not. . . .'" Other occurrences of similar haggadah are listed in Etan Levine, "The Aggadah in Targum Jonathan ben Uzziel and Neofiti 1 to Genesis: Parallel References," Neophyti I. Targum palestinense MS de la bibliotheca vaticana, 2: Éxodo (ed. Alejandro Díez Macho; Madrid/Barcelona: Consejo Superior de Investigaciones Científicas, 1970) 562-563.

[14]Murray, Symbols, 8: "Whatever is the truth about Chris-tian origins elsewhere in the Syriac-speaking area, the Christian-ity of Aphrahat and Ephrem is best accountable for as a breakaway movement among the Jewish community in Adiabene." "If this inter-pretation is correct, we have an entirely plausible context for the fact that the Christian Fathers frequently echo midrashic traditions which by the fourth century they could not have received directly from Jewish teachers" (18).

[15]See the discussion between R. H. Connolly ("The Early Syriac Creed," ZNW 7 [1906] 202-223, and "On Aphraates Hom. I sect. 19," JTS 9 [1908] 572-576) and H. Leonard Pass ("The Creed of Aphraates," JTS 9 [1908] 267-284) and the literature they cite. Also more recently, Arthur Vööbus, "Methodologisches zum Studium der Anweisungen Aphrahats," OrChr 46 (1962) 28-29.

[16]So John Bowker, The Targums and Rabbinic Literature (Cambridge: Cambridge University, 1969) 133, and Le Déaut and Robert, Genèse, 105.

[17]Génesis, 24.

[18]Genèse, 104: "Qui que ce soit qui tue Caïn, (le juge-
ment) demeurera suspendu pour sept générations."

[19]This is Martin McNamara's English translation (Génesis,
507) of Díez Macho's original Spanish translation (Génesis, 24):
"Cualquiera que sea quien mate a Caín (el juico) le será sus-
pendido por siete generaciones."

[20]The understanding of the numeral in vs 15 as signify-
ing seven periods of time is shared by Gen. Rab. 23:4. Cf. σ'
non sic sed omnis qui occiderit cain ebdomatos sive septimus
vindicabitur (Hi Ep XXXVI); σ' ἑβδόμως ἐκδύκησιν δώσει (Procop
245: Syh; Ish 101); θ' per hebdomadem ulciscetur (+ is quem
genuerit generatio septima vindictam dabit Syh)(Ish 101; Hi 7).
As already noted, Ephraem quotes his bible text, one essentially
identical to P, and then goes ahead to speak of "seven generations" as his understanding of the meaning of ܫܒܥ ܕܪܝܢ.

[21]P. 397.

[22]Cf. Nöldeke, Grammar, par. 364C, who gives "suitably
to that which" as the proper meaning of ܐܝܟ ܡܕܡ ܕܩ.

[23]Although one must admit the possibility that Aphr's
text of the Gen ch 5 genealogy might read "and the total of all
the years of N was . . ." instead of "all the days of N were
. . " (so P and all witnesses), the term ܟܠܐ ("total") is
used freely by Aphr elsewhere, and it seems most likely that
the expression "the total of the years of" is of Aphr's own composition here.

[24]Cf. Kitab alMajal 107a: "God took him [i.e., Enoch]
back to the land of life, and made him live in Paradise in the
land where there is no death," cited by Bowker, Targums, 149.
Wright and Parisot appear to be correct in following ms B
("place") rather than mss A and C ("generation") in #053. The
repetition of "generation" is awkward and looks like accidental
dittography.

[25]"Ps.-Jonathan," 104.

[26]There is little to go on in deciding between the readings of mss A and B in #064. Tentatively, one can agree with
Wright and Parisot in following ms B; the addition of "to Noah"
is not necessary, given the occurrence of the proper name in the
preceding lines. Ms A seems to have a tendency to correct the
text generally in the direction of explicitness and grammatical
regularity. The dalath on ܠ in ms B conforms to the practice

in the other citations here as shown in both mss.

[27]This is Neusner's translation (<u>Aphrahat and Judaism</u>, 43-44) of 549:8-16, 18-19, 22-23.

[28]"Ps.-Jonathan," 104 n. 4.

[29]"The Creed of Aphraates," 272.

[30]Robert Murray, "Some Rhetorical Patterns in Early Syriac Literature," <u>A Tribute to Arthur Vööbus, Studies in Early Christian Literature and Its Environment, Primarily in the Syrian East</u> (ed. Robert Fischer; Chicago: Lutheran School of Theology, 1977) 119.

[31]It is evident that Aphr understands his text (which agrees with P) to say: "And Babylon was the head of his kingdom." This, of course, is contrary to the MT, and it is difficult to anticipate how Aphr then reads the second half of the vs. Ephraem seems to understand the vs quite differently, making Nimrod the subject of the verb: "Now he [Nimrod] ruled in Arak, which is Edessa, and in Akar, which is Nisibis, and Calyah Ctesiphon . . ." (Comm VIII.2 lines 24-25).

[32]The beginning of section (40) is an exception. See #090 below.

[33]Actually, P begins the table in Gen ch 11 with the inverted pattern . . . ܚܝܘ ܐܘܠܕ/. . . ܠܕ ܘܚܝܐ (cf. vss 10-11, 12-13), but it then switches to the consistent use of ܠܕ ܘܚܝܐ in vss 16-17 (and vss 14-15 in the earlier mss). Aphr begins his table according to P in vss 10-13 and maintains that pattern instead of switching.

[34]TJ[1], TN[1], and TF all follow their translation of vs 1 with a lengthy addition explaining why it was necessary for God to tell Abraham not to be afraid. Their expansions cannot be linked to Aphr's addition.

[35]Ms 1115 cannot be considered the best of witnesses inasmuch as it contains 89 uncorrected errors within a relatively small number of passages from Gen and Exod.

[36]On Aphr's overall exegetical approach in Dem XI see Murray, <u>Symbols</u>, 44-46.

[37]Parisot wrongly divides the clauses of the sentence which introduces this quotation: ". . . et signaculum circumcisio; data est enim in foedus Abrahae. . . ." Wright correctly observes the punctuation of ms A: ". . . and circumcision was

given to Abraham as a covenant and sign. . . ." So also Bert
(167) and Neusner (<u>Aphrahat and Judaism</u>, 21).

^{38}Parisot uses italics to designate the first portion
of #115 as a scripture citation, but he fails to note the source.
Wright does not identify this passage as a citation.

^{39}Both רֲחְבֵ and רֲחְמֲ are used in Syriac to
denote "fine meal"; cf. 2 Ki 7:1 and 1 Sam 1:24 P.

^{40}Even more distant and textually insignificant allusions
to this promise are found at 52:24-25; 56:7-8; and 144:20-21.

^{41}The meaning of this phrase (MT כעת חיה) has been much
disputed. Akkadian and Ugaritic parallels have now been identified which tend to confirm "next year, a year from now" as the
correct meaning. See O. Loretz, "k't ḥyh--'wie jetzt ums Jahr'
Gen 18,10," <u>Bib</u> 43 (1962) 75-78, and Reuben Yaron, "KA'ETH HAYYAH
and KOH LEHAY," <u>VT</u> 12 (1962) 500-501.

^{42}Cf. Nöldeke, <u>Grammar</u>, pars. 311-313.

^{43}The Hebrew verb שלח in Pi'el may in some contexts properly be translated "let go, set free"; so <u>BDB</u>, 1019a.

^{44}<u>Aphrahat and Judaism</u>, 53: "'When the time came to
recline,' it is written, 'they. . . .'"

^{45}Bert, 262.

^{46}Parisot (147:7-8: "catulus leonis Iuda") and Gustav
Bickell (<u>Ausgewählte Schriften der syrischen Kirchenväter
Aphraates, Rabulas und Isaak von Ninive, zum ersten Male aus dem
Syrischen übersetzt, Ausgewählte Abhandlungen des Bischofs Jakob
Aphraates von Mar Matthäus</u> [Bibliothek der Kirchenväter 102;
Kempten: Kösel, 1874] 70: "den jungen Löwen Juda") both present
the expected translation of this phrase. However, without expla-
nation, Bert (56) translates: "der Embryo [sic] des Löwen Juda."
Such a meaning for רֲ יֲאֲ is unattested elsewhere, and Ephraem
(Comm XLII.5 lines 8-10), who discusses the vs but does not cite
it formally, clearly understands the phrase as denoting a whelp
or pup: "Not like an old lion, but rather like a 'whelp of a
lion' (רֲ יֲאֲרֲ רֲ יֲאֲ)."

^{47}The absence of רֲoֲaֲlֲzֲ in #157 is misleading. As
both Baarda (295-296) and Murray (<u>Symbols</u>, 283 n. 7) have noticed,
this noun occurs in the immediately preceding lines and is the
referent of ,ֲmֲ.

^{48}Vööbus (<u>Peschitta und Targumim</u>, 26) cites Babai of Izla,

Catholicos Timotheos, and Dionysios bar Salibi as attesting this
addition: "Diese unsere Lesart ist eine der man fast überall
auf dem syrischen Boden begegnet."

[49]Peschitta und Targumim, 25-26, 107.

Chapter III

[1]Koster (The Peshitta of Exodus, 136) assesses ms 8b1
as follows: "The few agreements of 8b1's peculiar readings with
MT can serve as a proof--if at least they are not all of a sec-
onday origin--that the readings peculiar to 8b1 were not brought
about by a single careless copyist, but that they definitely stem
from a longer pre-history which ran parallel with the development
of BTR as a whole."

[2]One must recall the condition attached to Koster's evaluation of ms 8b1 in regard to its peculiar readings (see n. 1
above): ". . . if at least they are not all of a secondary origin. . . ."

[3]J. Kerschensteiner, "Beobachtungen zum alt-syrischen
Actatext," Bib 45 (1964) 63-74. He evaluates the previous work
by Theodor Zahn and Arthur Vööbus in addition to analyzing the
Acts citations of Aphr ("etwa 8 Stellen"), Ephraem, and Liber
Graduum.

[4]"The Syriac New Testament in Early Patristic Tradition,"
La Bible et les pères. Colloque de Strasbourg (1er-3 octobre 1969)
(Paris: Presses Universitaires de France, 1971) 268.

[5]It must be acknowledged that Aphr need not be assumed
to be rigidly consistent. Like others, he does not always mark
a definite object of the verb with ܠ. Nöldeke (Grammar, par.
288B) notices a clause ("they have profaned my sabbath") which
Aphr uses three different times, once prefixing ܠ to the noun
and twice not.

[6]Caution is in order in relying upon Ephraem here. He
seems to be quoting loosely, certainly only partially.

[7]Wright and Parisot unnecessarily correct the reading
of mss A and B (ܩܘܕܡܝܗ) to ܩܘܕܡܝܗܘܢ . Although
the latter is the regular plural form of the noun, when the plural
of this noun takes on prefixed ܠ to form the prepositional compound meaning "before, in front of," the contracted form ܠܩܘܕܡ
is often used, as here and in vs 22 in ms 7a1. See Robert Payne
Smith, Thesaurus Syriacus (2 vols.; Oxford: Clarendon, 1879-1901)
2. cols. 2868-2869.

8TO ‏ליה‏ ‏דחלין‏ ‏דמצראי‏ ‏בעירא‏ ‏ארי‏; TJ[1] ‏דהינון‏ ‏אימריא‏ ‏ארום‏
‏דמצראי‏ ‏טעוותהון‏. TN[1] reads similarly (‏טעוותיהן‏ ‏אינון‏ ‏מרחקא‏ ‏ארום‏
‏דמצריי‏), although there is disagreement as to the precise translation. Díez Macho (Éxodo, 46 n. 14) thinks that the text is
defective and that the noun ‏אימריא‏ (a marginal gloss) must be
supplied in order to read: ". . . because [lambs] are an abomination; they are the idols of the Egyptians." Le Déaut and Robert
(Targum du Pentateuch, 2: Exode et Lévitique [SC 256; Paris: Cerf,
1979] 62), however, are probably correct in viewing the text as
grammatical in its present form, reading: ". . . car les idoles
des Égyptiens sont une abomination. . . ."

9Comm VIII.3 lines 17-18:

[Syriac text]

10Again at this point Aphr demonstrates his tendency to
combine similar and parallel vss in his quotations. Not only
does the text of Num 6:14 P intrude itself here in a reference
to Exod ch 12 (vs 5), but also in #180 the expected quotation
of Exod 12:5 turns out to be the text of Lev 23:12 P.

11Baarda (251-254) gives careful treatment to the citation at 528:5-6, without recognizing that #184 also preserves
the text of John 19:36.

12Baumstark ("Ps.-Jonathan," 108) mentions #191 in passing as one of several passages in the Dems where one cannot be
certain whether or not free citation is involved. "Solche Dinge
noch als blosses Ergebnis gedächtnismässig freier Zitation zu
begreifen oder daran zu glauben, dass sie in einem vormasoret-
ischen Pentateuchtext oder auch nur selbst in einem paraphras-
tischsten Targum wirklich gestanden hätten, fällt allerdings
gleich schwer, und doch ist eine dritte Möglichkeit eben nicht
gegeben." That he does not venture to discuss it in detail may
perhaps be taken as an indication that Baumstark is inclined to
regard #191 as a case of memoriter carelessness in quoting. Cf.
Vööbus, Peschitta und Targumim, 27.

13The concept of the "book of memorials" was of course
important already in early Jewish hermeneutical traditions; see
"Excursus I. Le 'livre des memoriaux'" in Roger Le Déaut, La
nuit pascale (AnBib 22; Rome: Pontifical Biblical Institute, 1963)
66-71.

14Exod 20:4 is echoed sufficiently clearly at 64:1
(. . . . [Syriac text])
to make it certain that Aphr does know vs 4, although one cannot
reconstruct his text from this reference.

266

[15]M. D. Koster, "The Numbering of the Ten Commandments in Some Peshitta Manuscripts," VT 30 (1980) 468-473.

[16]This word must be understood, with Parisot ("mecum"), as a preposition with suffix, not as a vocative of the noun ("my people"), which is the translation offered by Frank H. Hallock, "De caritate, Translated from the Syriac of Aphraates," Journal of the Society of Oriental Research 14 (1930) 22. This is confirmed by the parallel use of ܥܡܝ in the line following #196 (quoted above in n. 14) and by Exod 20:23 P, which translates Hebrew אִתִּי by ܥܡܝ.

[17]P. 415.

[18]The plural form of the noun ܡܘܗ̈ܒܬܐ in #199 defies explanation. It sits awkwardly alongside the singular form ܘܫܒܝܐ, which is not naturally a collective. One suspects here a mechanical error in which an original ܡܘܗܒܬܐ was misread as ܡܘܗ̈ܒܬܐ (so ms A), which in turn was supplied with seyame (so ms B). #200 makes it virtually certain that Aphr's bible text does not read ܡܘܗ̈ܒܬܐ, whether Exod 23:12 or Deut 5:14.

[19]Confronted with the two alternate explanations of memoriter error or a wildly variant scripture text, Baumstark comments in connection with 541:3-14: "Eigenartigsten textlichen Mosaiken gegenüber, die manche Zitate Afrahaṭs darstellen, wird es allerdings eines feinsten Fingerspitzengefühls bedürfen, um sich für die eine oder die andere der beiden theoretisch möglichen Erklärungen des Befundes zu entscheiden" ("Ps.-Jonathan," 104).

[20]It is interesting to note that TN[1] employs the compound expression היה שבא ונייח in all three passages, Gen 2:2; Exod 20:11; and Exod 31:17, whereas P, following MT, employs the corresponding compound (ܘܐܬܬܢܝܚ ܫܒܬ) only in Exod 31:17, elsewhere reading ܘܐܬܬܢܝܚ by itself. #198 might reflect a text of Exod 20:11 that reads both verbs. Since other aspects of the quotation reflect memoriter contamination, however, and since Exod 31:17 P is so nearly identical to Exod 20:11, the most reasonable conclusion is that the compound expression in #198 results from a combination of Aphr's text of Exod 31:17 and 20:11.

[21]P. 204.

[22]Aphrahat and Judaism, 48.

[23]On the varying order of the sixth and seventh commandments of the Decalogue in the ancient versions, see David Flusser, "'Do Not Commit Adultery,' 'Do Not Murder,'" Textus 4 (1964) 220-224.

24In #206 Aphr has telescoped his text of the commandment against coveting to sharpen its application to Ahab's theft
of Naboth's vineyard, which is referred to in the preceding lines.
"Vineyard" is not one of the neighbor's possessions that is mentioned explicitly in the text of the commandment.

25Actually, neither Deut 24:20 nor 21 P ends with this
phrase. Aphr is handling his text with some freedom in this
quotation; his quotation in 896:8-12 appears to be contaminated
by Deut 26:11 or 28:43 P, both of which end with ܟ݁ܐ܃ܐܘܬܒܐ
ܢܩܘܕܒ.

26J. Payne Smith, A Compendious Syriac Dictionary (Oxford:
Clarendon, 1903), 200a.

27Aphrahat and Judaism, 64. Cf. Parisot "clariorem" and
Bert (274) "erhabener."

28Wright and Parisot to the contrary, the reading of ms
B (ܘܐܪ) is to be rejected in #217. #218 shows clearly that
Aphr understands vs 32 as containing disjunctive conditional
clauses, "either . . . or. . . ." There is, however, no evidence
that ܐܪܘ . . . ܐܘ function together with this meaning;
cf. Nöldeke, Grammar, pars. 258, 374-377, and Payne Smith, Dictionary, 4b ("ܐܘ"), 17a ("ܐܪ"), and 20b-21a ("ܐ"). In
any event, ܐܘ . . . ܐܘ is the more common construction, and,
in the light of #218, it is probable that the reading of ms B
in #217 is a correction to P.

WORKS CITED

Albrektson, Bertil. Studies in the Text and Theology of the Book
      of Lamentations, with a Critical Edition of the Peshitta
      Text. Studia Theologica Lundensia 21. Lund: Gleerup, 1963.

Antonelli, Nicolaus. Sancti patris nostri Iacobi, episcopi
      Nisibeni, sermones, cum praefatione, notis et disserta-
      tione de ascetis, quae omnia nunc primum in lucem pro
      deunt. Rome: Sacra Congregatio de Propaganda Fide, 1756.

Baarda, Tjitze. The Gospel Quotations of Aphrahat the Persian
      Sage. 1: Aphrahat's Text of the Fourth Gospel. Amsterdam:
      Vrije Universitet, 1975.

Barnes, W. Emery. The Peshitta Psalter According to the West-
      Syrian Text. Cambridge: Cambridge University, 1904.

_____. "A New Edition of the Pentateuch in Syriac." JTS 15
      (1913-1914) 41-44.

Baumann, Eberhard. "Die Verwendbarkeit der Pešita zum Buche Ijob
      für die Textkritik." ZAW 18 (1898) 305-338.

Baumstark, Anton. Geschichte der syrischen Literatur mit Aus-
      schluss der christlich-palästinensischen Texte. Bonn:
      Marcus & Webers, 1922.

_____. "Peschitta und palästinensisches Targum." BZ 19 (1931)
      257-270.

_____. "Das Problem der Bibelzitate in der syrischen Über-
      setzungs-Literatur." OrChr 8 (1933) 208-225.

_____. "Neue orientalistische Probleme biblischer Textge-
      schichte." ZDMG 89 (1935) 89-118.

_____. "Das Problem des christlich-palästinensischen Penta-
      teuchtextes." OrChr 10 (1935) 201-224.

_____. "Ps.-Jonathan zu Dtn 34:6 und die Pentateuchzitate
      Afrahaṭs." ZAW N.F. 18 (1942-1943) 99-111.

Bert, Georg. Aphrahat's des persischen Weisen Homilien, aus dem Syrischen übersetzt und erläutert. TU 3/3-4. Leipzig: Heinrichs, 1888.

Biblia sacra iuxta versionem simplicem quae dicitur pschitta. 2 vols. Mosul: Fratrum Praedicatorum, 1881-1887.

Bickell, Gustav. Ausgewählte Schriften der syrischen Kirchenväter Aphraates, Rabulas und Isaak von Ninive, zum ersten Male aus dem Syrischen übersetzt, Ausgewählte Abhandlungen des Bischofs Jakob Aphraates von Mar Matthäus. Bibliothek der Kirchenväter 102. Kempten: Kösel, 1874.

Black, Matthew. "The Syriac New Testament in Early Patristic Tradition." La Bible et les pères. Colloque de Strasbourg (1er-3 octobre 1969). Paris: Presses Universitaires de France, 1971, 263-278.

Blackman, Philip, ed. Mishnayoth. 7 vols. London: Mishna Press, 1951-1957.

Bloch, Joshua. "The Printed Texts of the Peshitta Old Testament." AJSL 37 (1920-1921) 136-144.

Blum, Georg C. "Afrahaṭ." TRE 1.625-635.

Bowker, John. The Targums and Rabbinic Literature, An Introduction to Jewish Interpretation of Scripture. Cambridge: Cambridge University, 1969.

Brooke, A. E.; McLean, N.; and Thackery, H. St. J., eds. The Old Testament in Greek According to the Text of Codex Vaticanus, Supplemented from Other Uncial Manuscripts, with a Critical Apparatus Containing the Variants of the Chief Ancient Authorities for the Text of the Septuagint. 1/2: Exodus and Leviticus. Cambridge: Cambridge University, 1909.

Brown, Francis; Driver, S. R.; and Briggs, Charles A., eds. A Hebrew and English Lexicon of the Old Testament. Oxford: Clarendon, 1907.

Brüll, Adolf, ed. Das samaritanische Targum zum Pentateuch. 7 parts. Franfurt am Main, 1873-1876; reprinted Hildesheim: Olms, 1971.

Burkitt, F. C. "The Syriac Psalter [Review of W. E. Barnes, ed., The Peshitta Psalter According to the West-Syrian Text (1904)]." JTS 6 (1905) 286-290.

Ceriani, Antonio Maria. Translatio syra pescitto veteris testamenti ex codice ambrosiano sec. fere VI photolithographice edita. 2 vols. London: Williams & Norgate, 1876-1883.

Connolly, R. H. "The Early Syriac Creed." ZNW 7 (1906) 202-223.

_____. "On Aphraates Hom. I sect. 19." JTS 9 (1908) 572-576.

De Boer, P. A. H., and Baars, W. General Preface, The Old Testament in Syriac According to the Peshiṭta Versions. Leiden: Brill, 1972.

Diettrich, G. Ein Apparatus Criticus zur Pešitto zum Propheten Jesaia. BZAW 8. Giessen: Topelmann, 1905.

Díez Macho, Alejandro, ed. Neophyti I. Targum palestinense MS de la bibliotheca vaticana. 6 vols. Madrid/Barcelona: Consejo Superior de Investigaciones Científicas, 1968-1979.

Dirksen, P. B. The Transmission of the Text in the Peshitta of the Book of Judges. Monographs of the Peshitta Institute 1. Leiden: Brill, 1972.

Duncan, Edward J. Baptism in the Demonstrations of Aphraates the Persian Sage. Studies in Christian Antiquity 8; Washington, D.C.: Catholic University of America, 1945.

Duplacy, Jean, and Suggs, Jack. "Les citations grecques et la critique du texte du Nouveau Testament: le passé, le présent et l'avenir." La Bible et les pères. Colloque de Strasbourg (1er-3 octobre 1969). Paris: Presses Universitaires de France, 1971, 187-262.

Elliger, K., and Rudolph, W., eds. Biblia hebraica stuttgartensia. Stuttgart: Deutsche Bibelstiftung, 1977.

Emerton, J. A. The Peshitta of the Wisdom of Solomon. SPB 2. Leiden: Brill, 1959.

Fiey, J.-M. "Notule de littérature syriaque, La démonstration XIV d'Aphraate." Muséon 81 (1968) 449-454.

Fitzmyer, Joseph A. The Dead Sea Scrolls, Major Publications and Tools for Study. SBLSBS 8. Missoula: Scholars Press, 1977.

Flusser, David. "'Do Not Commit Adultery,' 'Do Not Murder.'" Textus 4 (1964) 220-224.

271

Funk, Salomen. Die haggadischen Elemente in den Homilien des
    Aphraates, des persischen Weisen. Vienna: Knöpflmacher,
    1891.

Gall, A. F. von, ed. Der hebräische Pentateuch der Samaritaner.
    5 vols. Giessen: Topelmann, 1914-1918.

Gavin, Frank. "Aphraates and the Jews." Journal of the Society
    of Oriental Research 7 (1923) 95-166.

Ginsberger, Moses, ed. Das Fragmententhargum (Thargum Jeruschalmi
    zum Pentateuch). Berlin: Calvary, 1899.

Goshen-Gottstein, M. H. "Prolegomena to a Critical Edition of
    the Peshitta." Text and Language in Bible and Qumran.
    Jerusalem/Tel Aviv: Orient, 1960, 163-204.

_____. Review of A. Vööbus, Peschitta und Targumim des Penta-
    teuchs. JSS 6 (1961) 266-270.

Gwynn, John. "Selections Translated into English from the Hymns
    and Homilies of Ephraim the Syrian and from the Demon-
    strations of Aphrahat the Persian Sage." NPNF Second
    Series 13/2.115-433.

Haefeli, Leo. Die Peschitta des Alten Testamentes mit Rücksicht
    auf ihre textkritische Bearbeitung und Herausgabe. Alt-
    testamentliche Abhandlungen 11/1. Münster: Aschendorff,
    1927.

_____. Stilmittel bei Afrahat dem persischen Weisen. Leipziger
    Semitische Studien 4. Leipzig: Heinrichs, 1932.

Hallock, Frank H. "De caritate, Translated from the Syriac of
    Aphraates." Journal of the Society of Oriental Research
    14 (1930) 18-31.

_____. "Aphraates on Penitents." Journal of the Society of
    Oriental Research 16 (1932) 43-56.

Hidal, Sten. Interpretatio Syriaca, Die Kommentare des Heiligen
    Ephräm des Syrers zu Genesis und Exodus mit besonderer
    Berucksichtigung ihrer auslegungsgeschichtlichen Stellung.
    ConBOT 6. Lund: Gleerup, 1974.

Hospers, J. H. "The Present-day State of Research on the Pešiṭta
    (since 1948)." Verbum, Essays on Some Aspects of the
    Religious Functions of Words. Studia Theologica Rheno-
    Traiectina 6. Utrecht: Kemink, 1964, 148-157.

Kahle, Paul. The Cairo Geniza. Oxford: Blackwell, 1941; revised ed. 1959.

_____. Masoreten des Westens, II. BWAT 14. Stuttgart: Kohlhammer, 1930.

Kerschensteiner, J. "Beobachtungen zum alt-syrischen Actatext." Bib 45 (1964) 63-74.

Klein, M. L. The Fragment-Targums of the Pentateuch. AnBib 76. Rome: Pontifical Biblical Institute, in press.

Koster, M. D. The Peshiṭta of Exodus, The Development of Its Text in the Course of Fifteen Centuries. Studia Semitica Neerlandica 19. Assen/Amsterdam: Van Gorcum 1977.

_____. "The Numbering of the Ten Commandments in Some Peshitta Manuscripts." VT 30 (1980) 468-473.

Lafontaine, G., ed. La version arménienne des oeuvres d'Aphraate le Syrien. 2: Texte. CSCO 405, scriptores armeni 9. Louvain: Corpus Scriptorum Christianorum Orientalium, 1979.

Lee, Samuel, ed. Vetus testamentum syriace. London: British and Foreign Bible Society, 1823.

Le Déaut, Roger. La nuit pascale, Essai sur la signification de la Pâque juive à partir du targum d'Exode XII 42. AnBib 22. Rome: Pontifical Biblical Institute, 1963.

Le Déaut, Roger, and Robert, Jacques. Targum du Pentateuch, Traduction des deux recensions palestiniennes complètes avec introduction, parallèles, notes et index. 1: Genèse. SC 245. Paris: Cerf, 1978. 2: Exode et Lévitique. SC 256. Paris: Cerf, 1979.

Le Jay, M. G. Michel, ed. Biblia polyglotta parisiensia. Paris: Vitré, 1629-1645.

Levine, Étan. "The Aggadah in Targum Jonathan ben Uzziel and Neofiti 1 to Genesis: Parallel References." Neophyti I. Targum palestinense MS de la bibliotheca vaticana. 2: Exodo. Ed. Alejandro Díez Macho. Madrid/Barcelona: Consejo Superior de Investigaciones Científicas, 1970, 537-578.

Loretz, O. "kᶜt hyh--'wie jetzt ums Jahr' Gen 18,10." Bib 43 (1962) 75-78.

Metzger, Bruce M. The Text of the New Testament, Its Transmission, Corruption, and Restoration. New York: Oxford Univeristy, 1968.

_____. "Patristic Evidence and the Textual Criticism of the New Testament," NTS 18 (1971) 379-400.

Moss, C. "The Peshiṭta Version of Ezra." Museon 46 (1933) 55-110.

Murray, Robert. Symbols of Church and Kingdom, A Study in Early Syriac Tradition. London: Cambridge University, 1975.

_____. "Some Rhetorical Patterns in Early Syriac Literature." A Tribute to Arthur Vööbus, Studies in Early Christian Literature and Its Environment, Primarily in the Syrian East. Ed. Robert Fischer. Chicago: Lutheran School of Theology, 1977, 109-131.

_____. Review of T. Baarda, The Gospel Quotations of Aphrahat the Persian Sage. Orientalia Christiana Periodica 44 (1978) 523-526.

Neusner, Jacob. Aphrahat and Judaism, The Christian-Jewish Argument in Fourth-Century Iran. SPB 19. Leiden: Brill, 1971.

The New Testament in Syriac. London: British and Foreign Bible Society, n.d.

Nöldeke, Theodor. Review of W. Wright, The Homilies of Aphraates, the Persian Sage. Göttingische gelehrte Anzeigen 39 (1869) 1521-1532.

_____. Review of A. M. Ceriani, Translatio syra pescitto veteris testamenti ex codice ambrosiano. Literarisches Centralblatt für Deutschland 39 (1876) 1289-1292.

_____. Compendious Syriac Grammar. Tr. James Crichton. London: Williams & Norgate, 1904.

The Old Testament in Syriac According to the Peshiṭta Version. 1/1: Preface, Genesis-Exodus. Leiden: Brill, 1977.

Ortiz de Urbina, Ignatius. Patrologia syriaca. Rome: Pontificium Institutum Orientalium Studiorum, 1965.

Parisot, Ioannes. "Aphraatis sapientis persae, Demonstrationes." Patrologia syriaca. Ed. R. Graffin. 3 vols. Paris: Firmin-Didot, 1894-1907.

Pass, H. Leonard. "The Creed of Aphraates. JTS 9 (1908) 267-284.

Payne Smith, J. A Compendious Syriac Dictionary, Founded upon
the Thesaurus Syriacus of R. Payne Smith. Oxford: Clarendon, 1903.

Payne Smith, Robert. Thesaurus Syriacus. 2 vols. Oxford: Clarendon, 1879-1901.

Pinkerton, John. "The Origin and the Early History of the Syriac
Pentateuch." JTS 15 (1913-1914) 14-41.

Quispel, G. Review of J. Neusner, Aphrahat and Judaism. BO 29
(1972) 229-230.

Rieder, David, ed. Pseudo-Jonathan: Targum Jonathan ben Uziel
on the Pentateuch, Copied from the London MS. (British
Museum Add. 27031). Jerusalem: Salomon, 1974.

Roberts, Bleddyn J. The Old Testament Text and Versions, The
Hebrew Text in Transmission, and the History of the
Ancient Versions. Cardiff: University of Wales, 1951.

Running, Leona G. "An Investigation of the Syriac Version of
Isaiah." AUSS 3 (1965) 138-157; 4 (1966) 37-64, 135-148.

Sasse, Carl J. F. Prolegomena in Aphraatis sapientis persae
sermones homileticos. Leipzig: Kreysingii, 1878.

Sperber, Alexander, ed. The Bible in Aramaic. 1: The Pentateuch
According to Targum Onkelos. Leiden: Brill, 1959.

Suggs, M. J. "The Use of Patristic Evidence in the Search for
a Primitive New Testament Text." NTS 4 (1957-1958)
139-147.

Tonneau, R.-M., ed. Sancti Ephraem syri in Genesim et in Exodum
commentarii. CSCO 152, scriptores syri 71. Louvain:
Durbecq, 1955.

Van der Ploeg, J. "Recente Pešiṭta-Studies (sinds 1927)." JEOL
10 (1945-1948) 392-399.

Vetus testamentum syriace et neo-syriace. Urmia: n.p., 1852.

Vööbus, Arthur. Peschitta und Targumim des Pentateuchs, Neues
Licht zur Frage der Herkunft der Peschitta aus dem alt-
palästinischen Targum. Papers of the Estonian Theological
Society in Exile 9. Stockholm: Estonian Theological Society in Exile, 1958.

_____. "Nachträge zum Reallexikon für Antike und Christentum: 'Aphrahat.'" JAC 3 (1960) 152-155.

_____. "Methodologisches zum Studium der Anweisungen Aphrahats." OrChr 46 (1962) 25-32.

_____. "Syriac Versions." IDBSup, 848-854.

_____. "In Pursuit of Syriac Manuscripts." JNES 37 (1978) 187-193.

Walton, Brian, ed. Biblia sacra polyglotta londinensia. 6 vols. London: Roycroft, 1653-1657.

Wevers, John W., ed. Septuaginta, vetus testamentum graecum. 1: Genesis. Gottingen: Vandenhoeck & Ruprecht, 1974.

Wernberg-Møller, P. "Some Scribal and Linguistic Features of the Genesis Part of the Oldest Peshitta Manuscript (B. M. Add. 14425)." JSS 13 (1968) 136-161.

Westcott, B. F., and Hort, F. J. A. The New Testament in the Original Greek. 2 vols. London: Macmillan, 1882.

Wright, William. The Homilies of Aphraates, the Persian Sage Edited from Syriac Manuscripts of the Fifth and Sixth Centuries in the British Museum with an English Translation. 1: The Syriac Text. London: Williams & Norgate, 1869.

_____. Catalogue of Syriac Manuscripts in the British Museum, Acquired Since the Year 1838. 2 vols. London: British Museum, 1871.

_____. A Short History of Syriac Literature. London: Black, 1894.

Weber, Robert; Fischer, Boniface; Gribomont, Johanne; Sparks, H. F. D.; and Thiele, W., eds. Biblia sacra iuxta vulgatum versionem. 2 vols. Stuttgart: Wurttembergische Bibelanstalt, 1975.

Yaron, Reuben. "KA'ETH ḤAYYAH and KOH LEḤAY." VT 12 (1962) 500-501.

VITA

Robert Jessen Owens, Jr. was born on October 20, 1947, in Springfield, Illinois, where he was raised and educated in the public schools. He entered the University of Illinois at Urbana in 1965, receiving the Bachelor of Arts degree in the Teaching of English "with High Honors in the University and Distinction in the Curriculum" in 1969. All studies there were undertaken as an Edmund J. James Scholar. He was elected to Phi Beta Kappa in 1968. From 1969 to 1973 he studied at Lincoln Christian Seminary in Lincoln, Illinois, earning the Master of Divinity and the Master of Arts (Semitic Languages and Literature) degrees. In 1973 Owens began doctoral studies as a Daniel C. Gilman Fellow in the Department of Near Eastern Studies of the Johns Hopkins University. Family illness interrupted his studies from 1974 to 1976, during which time he was Assistant Professor of Old Testament at Manhattan Christian College, a private theological institute which operates in conjunction with Kansas State University in Manhattan, Kansas. He resumed studies at Johns Hopkins in 1976, completing the doctoral residency in 1979. Since 1978 he has taught part time as a member of the faculty of Sacred Scripture of the Ecumenical Institute of Theology at St. Mary's Seminary and University in Baltimore, Maryland. In 1980 he became Assistant

Professor of Old Testament at Emmanuel School of Religion in

Johnson City, Tennessee. Owens is a member of the Society of

Biblical Literature and Exegesis and an associate member of the

Catholic Biblical Association of America.